FAVORITE BRAND NAME

BEST-LOVED

RECIPES

of All Time

BARNES
&NOBLE
BOOKS
NEW YORK

Contents

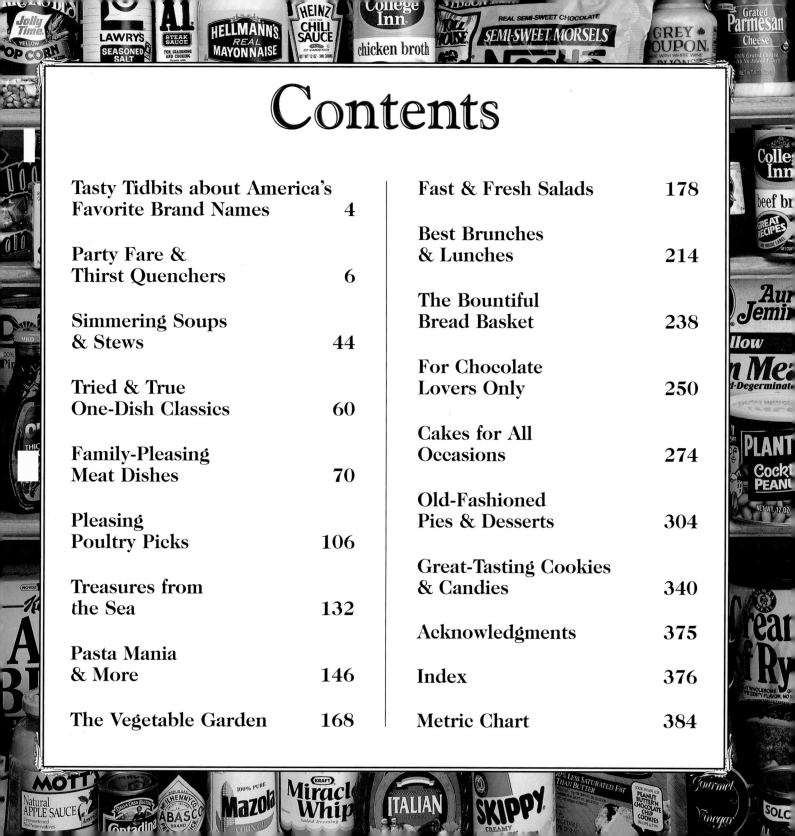

Tasty Tidbits about America's

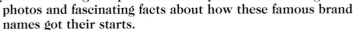

FAVORITE BRAND NAMES

At your fingertips is one of the most treasured collections of recipes from America's top brand name food companies. They've scoured their recipe files to present their true classics as well as future favorites. As you browse through these pages, you'll be taking a trip down memory lane with nostalgic photos and fascinating facts about how these famous brand names got their starts.

To entertain you, engaging tidbits of company lore are sprinkled throughout every chapter. For example, did you know Sylvester Graham, an ordained Presbyterian minister, invented the graham cracker in 1829? Or, that the Aunt Jemima trademark was inspired by a popular vaudeville routine of the late 1800s? To satisfy your curiosity, turn to page 295 to learn how the graham cracker began and page 354 for intriguing facts about Aunt Jemima.

Throughout this fabulous volume, you'll learn many captivating facts like the ones above and enjoy the many historical photos such as the three you see here. On this page we have Paul Newman and longtime friend A. E. Hotchner. Before they decided to market Paul Newman's homemade salad dressing, Paul Newman was bottling it in old wine bottles and giving it as Christmas gifts. Newman's Own® Salad Dressing was just the beginning of Newman's Own, Inc.—flip to page 186 for the rest of the story. The historical advertisement on the next page for the ever-popular Oreo® Chocolate Sandwich Cookie says it all, "I Must Have OREO SANDWICH For Dessert." This famous cookie is more than 75 years old and has been called the "King of Cookies." While Charlie the Tuna has not been around as long as Oreo cookies, he is well known in America's households as the "spokefish" and all-time purveyor of good taste for StarKist® tuna, America's best-loved and most trusted brand of tuna.

Besides fun facts, food trivia and old-time photos, this book is packed with sensational time-proven recipes. No matter what the occasion, getting together with family or friends is always a special time. Take time to reminisce over memories while beginning your meal with the wonderful creations highlighted in "Party Fare & Thirst Quenchers." You will find the perfect starters, including tasty tidbits, dips, spreads and thirst-quenching beverages. For those cozy, chilly nights by the fire, warm your guests with a heartier first course or substantial supper from "Simmering Soups & Stews."

"A family who eats together stays together," so says the old adage. But what foods will have them gathering around the table? Let five chapters of tantalizing savory entrées start you on your way. Looking for a satisfying, home-cooked meal but want easy preparation and cleanup? "Tried & True One-Dish Classics" is the perfect answer for taking the hassle out of everyday cooking. There is no end to the variety of time-tested entrées in "Family-Pleasing Meat Dishes," "Pleasing Poultry Picks," "Treasures from the Sea" and "Pasta Mania & More." The enticing aroma of these family favorites wafting through the kitchen is sure to bring them running.

Create the perfect heartwarming meal by adding a creative side dish or salad. There are dozens of terrific ideas in "The Vegetable Garden" and "Fast & Fresh Salads" to complement your carefully selected menu and bring fresh creations brimming with flavor to your table. Sure to brighten the faces of loved ones and guests, the once ordinary vegetable and tossed green salad will now become the extraordinary.

Rise and shine! Whether your morning begins with the rooster or the midday sun, jump-start your day with the welcoming cheer found in "Best Brunches & Lunches" and "The Bountiful Bread Basket." The down-home goodness of everything from eggs, waffles, coffeecakes, muffins and breads plus sandwiches and classic burgers, is the perfect addition to everyone's day.

Take time to indulge yourself. Explore a world of sinful pleasures with four chapters filled with a heavenly array of well-remembered favorites and delectable new creations to adorn the sweets table. If chocolate in any taste, shape or form is the only sweet for you, you can't go wrong with the decadent treats in "For Chocolate Lovers Only." For luscious creations featuring homemade goodness just like grandma used to bake, the recipes in "Cakes for All Occasions" and "Old-Fashioned Pies & Desserts" will help you create an irresistible showstopper. For the cookie monster in everyone, rekindle those childhood memories of scrumptious goodies with the sweet temptations in "Great-Tasting Cookies & Candies." Let any one of these sumptuous sweets create magic at your table—no one will be able to resist a taste!

When you are looking for that one special dish or a specific combination of flavors to create a cozy feeling, leaf through these pages of time-honored classics from America's most trusted brand name food companies. For old favorites, new traditions and everything in between, let *Favorite Brand Name Best-Loved Recipes of All Time* be your guide. There is no end to the memories you can create.

Party Fare & Thirst Quenchers

Create any of these dazzling appetizers and drinks for a sure-fire taste extravaganza. Impress party guests or surprise your family with a special pre-dinner treat. Discover dozens of ways to make any occasion a smashing success.

Buffalo Chicken Wings

24 chicken wings
 1 teaspoon salt
 ¼ teaspoon ground black pepper
 4 cups vegetable oil for frying
 ¼ cup butter or margarine
 ¼ cup hot pepper sauce
 1 teaspoon white wine vinegar
   Celery sticks
 1 bottle (8 ounces) blue cheese
   dressing

Cut tips off wings at first joint; discard tips. Cut remaining wings into two parts at the joint; sprinkle with salt and pepper. Heat oil in deep fryer or heavy saucepan to 375°F. Add half the wings; fry about 10 minutes or until golden brown and crisp, stirring occasionally. Remove with slotted spoon; drain on paper towels. Repeat with remaining wings.

Melt butter in small saucepan over medium heat; stir in pepper sauce and vinegar. Cook until thoroughly heated. Place wings on large platter. Pour sauce over wings. Serve warm with celery and dressing for dipping.
Makes 24 appetizers

Favorite recipe from **National Broiler Council**

Buffalo Chicken Wings

Deluxe Fajita Nachos

2½ cups shredded, cooked chicken
1 package (1.27 ounces) LAWRY'S®
    Spices & Seasonings for Fajitas
⅓ cup water
8 ounces tortilla chips
1¼ cups (5 ounces) grated Cheddar
    cheese
1 cup (4 ounces) grated Monterey Jack
    cheese
1 large tomato, chopped
1 can (2¼ ounces) sliced ripe olives,
    drained
¼ cup sliced green onions
    Salsa
    Guacamole
    Dairy sour cream

In medium skillet, combine chicken, Spices &
Seasonings and water; blend well. Bring to a
boil; reduce heat and simmer 7 minutes. In
large, shallow ovenproof platter, arrange
chips. Top with chicken and cheeses. Place
under broiler to melt cheese. Top with tomato,
olives, green onions and desired amount of
salsa.   *Makes 4 appetizer servings or*
2 main-dish servings

Presentation: Garnish with guacamole, sour
cream and salsa.

Substitution: Use 1¼ pounds cooked
ground beef in place of shredded chicken.

Hint: For spicier nachos, add sliced
jalapeños.

Chicken Saté

Chicken Kabobs (recipe follows)
1 teaspoon MAZOLA® Corn Oil
1 teaspoon dark Oriental sesame oil
¼ cup finely chopped onion
1 clove garlic, minced
½ teaspoon grated fresh ginger
¼ teaspoon crushed red pepper
    (optional)
½ cup SKIPPY® Creamy Peanut Butter
¼ cup KARO® Light or Dark Corn Syrup
1 tablespoon soy sauce
1 tablespoon cider vinegar
⅔ cup milk

Begin preparing Chicken Kabobs. Meanwhile,
in small saucepan heat oils over medium
heat; add onion, garlic, ginger and red
pepper. Stirring constantly, cook 3 to 4
minutes or until onion is translucent. Stir in
peanut butter, corn syrup, soy sauce and
vinegar until smooth. Gradually stir in milk.
Stirring constantly, bring to a boil. Remove
from heat. Cool slightly. Serve as dipping
sauce for Chicken Kabobs.
    Makes about 3 dozen appetizers

Chicken Kabobs: Soak about 36 wooden
skewers in water at least 20 minutes. In
medium bowl combine 2 tablespoons
Mazola® Corn Oil and 2 tablespoons light
teriyaki sauce. Cut 1 pound boneless skinless
chicken breasts into 1-inch pieces; stir into
teriyaki mixture. Cover and let stand at room
temperature no longer than 30 minutes or
refrigerate several hours or overnight.

Thread chicken onto skewers. Place on foil-
lined baking sheet. Broil about 6 inches from
heat, 6 to 8 minutes or until lightly browned.

Deluxe Fajita Nachos

Ham-Filled French Toast Bruschetta

- 1 package (3 ounces) cream cheese, softened
- 1 can (4 ounces) mushroom stems and pieces, drained
- 1 can (6¾ ounces) chunk ham, drained and chopped
- ½ teaspoon dried thyme
- ¼ teaspoon garlic powder
- 8 slices firm white bread
- ½ cup half-and-half or milk
- 2 eggs, beaten
- 1 can (14½ ounces) Italian-style stewed tomatoes, undrained
- ½ can (2¼ ounces) sliced ripe olives, drained
- 2 teaspoons cornstarch
  Basil or parsley sprigs

Beat cream cheese until fluffy in small bowl; mix in mushrooms, ham, thyme and garlic powder. Spread mixture on 4 bread slices; top with remaining bread slices. Combine half-and-half and eggs in shallow bowl; mix well. Soak filled bread slices in mixture, 30 seconds on each side.

Cook filled bread slices in greased skillet over medium heat until golden, 3 to 4 minutes on each side. While bread slices are cooking, mix tomatoes, olives and cornstarch in small saucepan; bring to a boil. Cook over medium heat until thickened. Serve tomato sauce over toasted bread slices. Garnish with basil.

Makes 4 servings

Favorite recipe from **Canned Food Information Council**

Canned Food Information Council

The Canned Food Information Council was established in 1984 by members of the National Food Processors Association to promote the many benefits of canned foods by educating consumers and dispelling product misconceptions. For example, canned foods offer not only great taste, variety, nutritional benefits, quality and can recyclability, but they are also convenient and adaptable to every age group.

Spicy Beef Saté

- 1 cup chopped scallions
- ½ cup A.1.® Steak Sauce
- ½ cup chunky or creamy peanut butter
- ¼ cup lemon juice
- ¼ cup firmly packed brown sugar
- ¼ cup vegetable oil
- ¼ teaspoon crushed red pepper
- 2 cloves garlic, crushed
- 2 pounds flank steak, cut crosswise into strips
  Scallion brush, for garnish

In large glass baking dish, combine scallions, steak sauce, peanut butter, lemon juice, brown sugar, oil, red pepper and garlic until well blended. Add steak strips to marinade; refrigerate at least 2 hours or overnight, stirring occasionally.

Thread steak strips onto 4-inch-long skewers. Grill or broil meat 4 inches from heat source 10 to 20 minutes or until done, turning and brushing with marinade often. Arrange on serving platter; garnish with scallion brush if desired.   *Makes 4 dozen appetizers*

Sweet 'n' Sour Meatballs

1 pound lean ground beef
1 cup soft bread crumbs
1 egg, slightly beaten
2 tablespoons minced onion
2 tablespoons milk
1 clove garlic, minced
½ teaspoon salt
⅛ teaspoon pepper
1 tablespoon vegetable oil
⅔ cup HEINZ® Chili Sauce
⅔ cup red currant or grape jelly

Combine beef, bread crumbs, egg, onion, milk, garlic, salt and pepper; form into 40 bite-size meatballs, using full teaspoon for each. Brown meatballs lightly in oil. Cover; cook over low heat 5 minutes. Drain excess fat. Combine chili sauce and jelly; pour over meatballs. Heat, stirring occasionally, until jelly is melted. Simmer 10 to 12 minutes until sauce has thickened, basting occasionally.
    Makes 40 appetizers with ¾ cup sauce

Teriyaki Scallop Roll-Ups

12 slices bacon, partially cooked,
    drained and cut in half crosswise
⅓ cup REALIME® Lime Juice from
    Concentrate
¼ cup soy sauce
¼ cup vegetable oil
1 tablespoon light brown sugar
2 cloves garlic, finely chopped
½ teaspoon pepper
½ pound sea scallops, cut in half
24 fresh pea pods
12 water chestnuts, cut in half

In small bowl, combine ReaLime® brand, soy sauce, oil, sugar, garlic and pepper; mix well. Wrap 1 scallop half, 1 pea pod and 1 water chestnut half in each bacon slice; secure with wooden pick. Place in large shallow dish; pour marinade over. Cover; marinate in refrigerator 4 hours or overnight, turning occasionally.

Preheat oven to 450°. Remove roll-ups from marinade; discard marinade. Place roll-ups on rack in aluminum foil-lined shallow baking pan; bake 6 minutes. Turn; bake 6 minutes longer or until bacon is crisp. Serve hot. Refrigerate leftovers.   *Makes 2 dozen*

Celebration Brie

1 (12- to 16-ounce) round brie cheese,
room temperature
1 teaspoon coarsely ground black
pepper
½ cup SMUCKER'S® Strawberry
Preserves
1 tablespoon balsamic vinegar
½ cup chopped BLUE RIBBON®
Calimyrna or Mission Figs
Assorted crackers

Sprinkle top of brie with pepper; press gently
into cheese. Mix preserves with vinegar. Stir
in figs. Spoon mixture over cheese. Serve
with assorted crackers.

Makes 12 servings

Cheese 'n' Rice Quesadillas

2 cups water
1 tablespoon margarine or butter
1 package LIPTON® Rice & Sauce—
Spanish
1 can (4 ounces) chopped green
chilies, drained (optional)
1 package (12½ ounces) flour tortillas
(10)
1½ cups shredded Monterey Jack cheese
(about 5 ounces)

In medium saucepan, bring water, margarine,
rice & sauce—Spanish and chilies to a boil.
Reduce heat and simmer, uncovered, stirring
occasionally, 10 minutes or until rice is tender.
Let stand 10 minutes.

Place 3 tortillas on 15½×10½×1-inch jelly-
roll pan. Spread heaping ⅓ cup rice mixture
onto each tortilla, leaving ½-inch border
around edge; top each with ¼ cup cheese,
then another tortilla. Repeat with remaining
tortillas, rice and cheese. Broil until tortillas
are lightly toasted and cheese is melted,
turning once. To serve, cut each quesadilla
into 4 wedges. Serve, if desired, with
guacamole, sour cream or chopped fresh
cilantro. *Makes 20 appetizers*

Black Bean Tortilla Pinwheels

1 (8-ounce) package cream cheese,
softened
1 cup dairy sour cream
1 cup (4 ounces) shredded Wisconsin
Monterey Jack cheese
¼ cup chopped, well-drained pimento-
stuffed green olives
¼ cup chopped red onion
½ teaspoon seasoned salt
⅛ teaspoon garlic powder
1 (15-ounce) can black beans, drained
5 (10-inch) flour tortillas
Salsa

Combine cream cheese and sour cream; mix
well. Stir in Monterey Jack cheese, olives,
onion and seasonings. Chill 2 hours.

Purée beans in food processor or blender.
Spread each tortilla with thin layer of beans.
Spread cream cheese mixture over beans.
Roll up tightly; chill. Cut into ¾-inch slices.
Serve with salsa.

Makes 12 to 16 servings

Favorite recipe from **Wisconsin Milk Marketing
Board**

Celebration Brie

Swiss Fondue

2 cups dry white wine
1 tablespoon lemon juice
1 pound Wisconsin Gruyère cheese,
**   shredded**
1 pound Wisconsin Fontina cheese,
**   shredded**
1 tablespoon arrowroot
¼ cup kirsch
**   Pinch nutmeg**
**   French bread cubes**
**   Apples, cut into wedges**
**   Pears, cut into wedges**

Bring wine and lemon juice to a boil in fondue pot. Reduce heat to low. Toss cheeses with arrowroot and gradually add to wine, stirring constantly. When cheese is melted, stir in kirsch. Sprinkle with nutmeg to serve. Serve with French bread, apples and pears.

Makes 6 servings

Favorite recipe from **Wisconsin Milk Marketing Board**

Savory Apricot Bites

4 ounces cream cheese, softened
12 fresh apricots, halved, pitted and
**   brushed with lemon juice**
½ cup pistachios, finely chopped

Stir cream cheese until smooth. Pipe or spoon cheese into pitted apricot halves. Top each half with 1 teaspoon pistachios.

Makes 2 dozen bites, 12 appetizer servings

Favorite recipe from **California Apricot Advisory Board**

Wisconsin Milk Marketing Board

The Wisconsin Milk Marketing Board (WMMB) is a non-profit, dairy farmer-funded organization designed to increase sales and consumption of Wisconsin milk and dairy products. Because of the educational and marketing efforts of the WMMB, consumers can learn not only about the 250 varieties, types and styles of Wisconsin cheeses, but can make more informed choices at the supermarket and learn how to partner cheese with pastas, grains, fruits and vegetables.

Colorado Potato Pancake Appetizers

Colorado Potato Pancake Appetizers

1 pound (2 medium) Colorado potatoes,
   peeled and shredded
1 egg
2 tablespoons all-purpose flour
1 teaspoon salt
¼ teaspoon pepper
1 cup shredded carrots
1½ cups shredded zucchini (2 small)
   Olive oil
½ cup low-fat sour cream or plain
   yogurt
2 tablespoons finely chopped basil
   plus 1 tablespoon chopped chives
   or 1½ teaspoons chili powder or
   curry powder

Heat oven to 425°F. Wrap shredded potatoes in several layers of paper towels; squeeze to wring out much of liquid. In large bowl, beat together egg, flour, salt and pepper. Add shredded potatoes, carrots and zucchini; mix well. Oil 2 nonstick baking sheets. Drop heaping tablespoonfuls of vegetable mixture, 2 inches apart, onto baking sheets; flatten to make pancakes. Bake 8 to 15 minutes, until bottoms are browned. Turn and bake 5 to 10 minutes more. Stir together sour cream and desired herbs or seasonings. Serve pancakes warm with dollop of herb cream.

Makes about 24 appetizer pancakes

*Favorite recipe from **Colorado Potato Administrative Committee***

Tortellini Kabobs

2 tablespoons olive oil
1 large clove garlic, minced
1 can (15 ounces) CONTADINA® Tomato Sauce
2 tablespoons rinsed capers
2 tablespoons chopped fresh basil leaves
1 teaspoon Italian herb seasoning
¼ teaspoon crushed red pepper flakes
6 cups of the following kabob ingredients: cooked, drained meat- or cheese-filled tortellini, cocktail franks, cooked shrimp, whole button mushrooms, bell pepper chunks, cooked broccoli, cooked cauliflowerets, onion pieces

Heat oil in medium saucepan over medium-high heat. Add garlic; cook and stir until lightly browned. Stir in tomato sauce, capers, basil, Italian seasoning and red pepper flakes. Bring to a boil. Reduce heat to low; simmer 5 to 10 minutes, stirring occasionally.

Combine kabob ingredients in medium bowl; cover with tomato sauce mixture. Marinate in refrigerator 15 minutes or longer, if desired, stirring occasionally. Place on skewers. Broil 5 inches from heat source until heated through, turning once during cooking and brushing with any remaining tomato sauce mixture.   *Makes 12 appetizer servings*

Pastry Shells with Bel Paese® and Mushrooms

8 ounces fresh mushrooms, cleaned and sliced
1 clove garlic, minced
3 to 4 tablespoons olive oil
2 teaspoons all-purpose flour
½ cup half-and-half
2 tablespoons minced fresh parsley
¼ teaspoon salt
   Dash pepper
4 ounces BEL PAESE® cheese,* cut into small pieces
8 ready-to-eat pastry shells or frozen pastry shells,** baked

*Remove wax coating and moist, white crust from cheese.

**Ready-to-eat pastry shells and frozen shells are available in bakeries, gourmet shops and speciality sections of supermarkets. These shells should not be sweet.

Preheat oven to 350°F. In small skillet, cook and stir mushrooms and garlic in olive oil over medium heat until mushrooms are tender. Stir in flour, half-and-half, parsley, salt and pepper. Remove from heat.

Arrange pastry shells on baking sheet. Line shells with half the Bel Paese® cheese. Spoon sauce over cheese. Top with remaining cheese. Bake until cheese melts, 3 to 4 minutes.   *Makes 4 to 6 servings*

Cajun-Spiced Walnuts

2 egg whites, slightly beaten
1 tablespoon garlic salt
2 teaspoons cayenne pepper
2 teaspoons mixed dried herbs
2 teaspoons paprika
4 cups (1 pound) walnut halves and
   pieces

Coat large, shallow baking pan with nonstick vegetable spray. Mix egg whites with seasonings. Stir in walnuts and coat thoroughly. Spread in prepared pan. Bake in 350°F oven 15 to 18 minutes, until dry and crisp. Cool completely before serving.

Makes 4 cups

Microwave Directions: Prepare ingredients as above. Spread prepared walnuts in microwavable dish. Microwave on HIGH in 4 or 5 batches for 2 to 3 minutes each, until dry and crisp. Cool completely.

Note: Best if made at least one day ahead. Flavors intensify overnight. Store in sealed container.

Favorite recipe from **Walnut Marketing Board**

Walnut Marketing Board

In late August, boughs of California walnut trees hang heavy with full, plump walnuts, protected by nature in thick green hulls. When these protective hulls split, the nuts are ready to be harvested. The harvest season usually continues until late November. The California walnut is America's number one consumer ingredient nut, representing over half of all supermarket sales of shelled cooking nuts. Walnuts are a good source of protein and key vitamins. They are rich in "good" polyunsaturated fat. Research at Loma Linda University showed that substituting walnuts for saturated fats in your diet can reduce your cholesterol level.

Early handling and production process of walnuts, which have become a major California crop.
Photo courtesy of Walnut Marketing Board

Indian-Spiced Walnuts

  2 egg whites, lightly beaten
  1 tablespoon ground cumin
1½ teaspoons salt
1½ teaspoons curry powder
  ½ teaspoon sugar
  4 cups walnut halves and pieces

Coat large, shallow baking pan with nonstick vegetable spray. Mix egg whites with seasonings. Stir in walnuts and coat thoroughly. Spread in prepared pan. Bake in 350°F oven 15 to 18 minutes, until dry and crisp. Cool completely before serving.

Makes 4 cups

*Favorite recipe from **Walnut Marketing Board***

Spicy Toasted Nuts

2 tablespoons vegetable oil
1 tablespoon HEINZ® Worcestershire
   Sauce
1 cup pecan or walnut halves

In bowl, combine oil and Worcestershire sauce; add nuts and toss to coat. Spread nuts in shallow baking pan; drizzle with any remaining oil mixture. Bake in 325°F oven, 15 minutes, stirring occasionally. Sprinkle with salt or garlic salt, if desired.

Makes 1 cup

Original Chex® Brand Party Mix

¼ cup margarine or butter, melted
4½ teaspoons Worcestershire sauce
1¼ teaspoons seasoned salt
8 cups of your favorite CHEX® brand cereals (Corn, Rice and/or Wheat)
1 cup mixed nuts
1 cup pretzels

1. Preheat oven to 250°F.

2. Combine margarine, Worcestershire sauce and seasoned salt; mix well. Pour cereals, nuts and pretzels into large resealable plastic food storage bag.

3. Pour margarine mixture over cereal mixture inside plastic bag. Seal top of bag securely. Shake bag until all pieces are evenly coated.

4. Pour contents of bag into open roasting pan. Bake 1 hour, stirring every 15 minutes. Spread on absorbent paper towels to cool. Store in airtight container.

Makes 10 cups

Microwave Directions:

1. Follow steps 2 and 3 above.

2. Pour contents of bag into large microwave-safe bowl. Microwave on HIGH 5 to 6 minutes, stirring thoroughly every 2 minutes. While stirring, make sure to scrape side and bottom of bowl. Cool and store as directed above.

Ralston Foods, Inc.

Through the years, Chex® cereal has changed shape and name, added several flavors and survived major wars and a depression. Today, this delicious breakfast food is also an important ingredient in many snack, dessert and main-dish recipes. According to legend, the famous Chex Party Mix, which uses Wheat, Rice and Corn Chex, first showed up at a social gathering in St. Louis in 1955. This tasty snack remains a party favorite even now.

Taco Snack Mix

4 cups SPOON SIZE® Shredded Wheat
4 cups pretzel sticks
4 cups tortilla chips
1 (1¼-ounce) package ORTEGA®
    Regular or Hot & Spicy Taco
    Seasoning Mix
¼ cup margarine, melted

In large bowl combine cereal, pretzels, tortilla chips and taco seasoning mix. Drizzle with margarine, tossing to coat well. Store in airtight container. *Makes 12 cups*

In 1906, Emilio Ortega moved to Los Angeles and founded the Ortega® Chile Company. Since the late 1800s, he had been experimenting with fire-roasting California green chilies in the kitchen of his small adobe home. His unique fire-roasting of chilies before canning or jarring became Ortega's trademark. Ortega chilies are still the only fire-roasted chilies on the market today.

Nacho Pop Corn

3 quarts popped JOLLY TIME® Pop
    Corn
2 cups corn chips
¼ cup butter or margarine
1½ teaspoons Mexican seasoning
¾ cup shredded taco cheese

Preheat oven to 300°F. Spread popped pop corn and corn chips in shallow baking pan lined with foil. Melt butter in small pan. Stir in Mexican seasoning. Pour over pop corn mixture and toss well. Sprinkle with cheese and toss to mix. Bake 5 to 7 minutes or until cheese is melted. Serve immediately.
Makes about 3½ quarts

Spicy Sweet Popcorn

¼ cup popcorn kernels
1 tablespoon granulated sugar
1 teaspoon chili powder
½ teaspoon cinnamon
¼ teaspoon salt
    Dash cayenne pepper
    Vegetable cooking spray

Pop popcorn. Mix dry ingredients in resealable plastic food storage bag. Add popcorn and spray with cooking spray. Seal bag and shake well. Repeat with cooking spray until popcorn is coated.
Makes about 6 cups

Favorite recipe from **The Sugar Association, Inc.**

Patchwork Pop Corn Party Mix

Patchwork Pop Corn Party Mix

3 quarts popped JOLLY TIME® Pop Corn
2 cups rice or wheat cereal squares
½ cup dried cranberries or dried tart cherries
1 cup coarsely chopped walnuts, toasted
3 tablespoons butter or margarine
½ teaspoon maple extract

Place popped pop corn, cereal, cranberries and walnuts in large bowl. Melt butter in small pan. Stir in maple extract. Pour over pop corn mixture; toss well.

Makes about 3½ quarts

Jolly Time® Pop Corn

Cloid H. Smith started the American Pop Corn Company in Sioux City, Iowa and established Jolly Time as the first brand name pop corn in 1914. C. H. and his son discovered a special pop corn hybrid that was crispy and tender.

Layered Taco Dip

1 pound lean ground beef
1 (4-ounce) can chopped green chilies,
  undrained
2 teaspoons WYLER'S® or STEERO®
  Beef-Flavor Instant Bouillon
1 (15- or 16-ounce) can refried beans
1 (16-ounce) container BORDEN® or
  MEADOW GOLD® Sour Cream
1 (1.7-ounce) package taco seasoning
  mix
  Guacamole (recipe follows)
  Garnishes: Shredded Cheddar or
  Monterey Jack cheese, chopped
  fresh tomatoes, sliced green
  onions, sliced ripe olives
  LAFAMOUS® Tortilla Chips

In large skillet, brown beef; pour off fat. Add
chilies and bouillon; cook and stir until
bouillon dissolves. Cool. Stir in refried beans.
In small bowl, combine sour cream and taco
seasoning; set aside. In 7- or 8-inch
springform pan or on large plate, spread beef
mixture. Top with sour cream mixture then
guacamole. Cover; chill several hours. Just
before serving, remove side of springform
pan and garnish as desired. Serve with
tortilla chips. Refrigerate leftovers.

Makes 12 to 15 servings

Guacamole: In small bowl, mash 3 ripe
avocados, pitted and peeled. Add ¾ cup
chopped fresh tomato, 2 tablespoons
REALEMON® Lemon Juice from Concentrate
or REALIME® Lime Juice from Concentrate,
½ teaspoon seasoned salt and ⅛ teaspoon
garlic salt; mix well. Makes about 2 cups.

Layered Taco Dip

Spicy Dijon Dip

1 (8-ounce) package cream cheese,
  softened
¼ cup GREY POUPON® Dijon or
  COUNTRY DIJON® Mustard
¼ cup dairy sour cream
1 tablespoon finely chopped green
  onion
1 (4¼-ounce) can tiny shrimp, drained
  or ½ cup cooked shrimp, chopped
  Sliced green onions, for garnish
  Assorted cut-up vegetables

In small bowl, with electric mixer at medium
speed, blend cream cheese, mustard, sour
cream and chopped onion; stir in shrimp.
Cover; chill at least 2 hours. Garnish with
sliced onions; serve as a dip with vegetables.

Makes 1½ cups

*The mustard business, founded by an
Englishman named Grey, flourished in
the same French community for two
centuries.*
Photo courtesy of Nabisco, Inc.

23

French Onion Dip

1 container (16 ounces) sour cream
½ cup HELLMANN'S® or BEST FOODS®
   Real or Light Mayonnaise or Low
   Fat Mayonnaise Dressing
1 package (1.9 ounces) KNORR® French
   Onion Soup and Recipe Mix

In medium bowl combine sour cream,
mayonnaise and soup mix. Cover; chill. Serve
with fresh vegetables or potato chips.
Garnish as desired.

Makes about 2½ cups

Spinach Dip

1 package (10 ounces) frozen chopped
   spinach, thawed and drained
1½ cups sour cream
1 cup HELLMANN'S® or BEST FOODS®
   Real or Light Mayonnaise or Low
   Fat Mayonnaise Dressing
1 package (1.4 ounces) KNORR®
   Vegetable Soup and Recipe Mix
1 can (8 ounces) water chestnuts,
   drained and chopped (optional)
3 green onions, chopped

In medium bowl combine spinach, sour
cream, mayonnaise, soup mix, water
chestnuts and green onions. Cover; chill.
Serve with fresh vegetables, crackers or
chips. Garnish as desired.

Makes about 3 cups

Cucumber Dill Dip

1 package (8 ounces) light cream
   cheese, softened
1 cup HELLMANN'S® or BEST FOODS®
   Real or Light Mayonnaise or Low
   Fat Mayonnaise Dressing
2 medium cucumbers, peeled, seeded
   and chopped
2 tablespoons sliced green onions
1 tablespoon lemon juice
2 teaspoons snipped fresh dill *or*
   ½ teaspoon dried dill weed
½ teaspoon hot pepper sauce

In medium bowl beat cream cheese until
smooth. Stir in mayonnaise, cucumbers,
green onions, lemon juice, dill and hot pepper
sauce. Cover; chill. Serve with fresh
vegetables, crackers or chips. Garnish as
desired.   *Makes about 2½ cups*

The Famous Lipton®
California Dip

1 envelope LIPTON® Recipe Secrets®
   Onion Soup Mix
1 container (16 ounces) sour cream

In small bowl, blend onion soup mix with sour
cream; chill.   *Makes about 2 cups dip*

California Seafood Dip: Add 1 cup finely
chopped cooked clams, crabmeat or shrimp,
¼ cup chili sauce and 1 tablespoon
horseradish.

*Left to right: French Onion Dip,
Cucumber Dill Dip and Spinach Dip*

Velveeta® Salsa Dip

Velveeta® Salsa Dip

**1 pound VELVEETA® Pasteurized
    Process Cheese Spread, cubed
1 (8-ounce) jar salsa or picante sauce
2 tablespoons chopped cilantro
    (optional)**

• Stir process cheese spread and salsa in saucepan on low heat until process cheese spread is melted. Stir in cilantro.

• Serve hot with tortilla chips or vegetable dippers.   *Makes 3 cups*

Variations:

Prepare Velveeta® Salsa Dip as directed, adding 1 (16-ounce) can refried beans.

Prepare Velveeta® Salsa Dip as directed, adding ½ pound chorizo or hot bulk pork sausage, cooked, drained.

Touch Down Taco Dip

1 (8-ounce) package cream cheese,
   softened
½ cup dairy sour cream
½ cup ORTEGA® Mild, Medium or Hot
   Thick and Smooth Taco Sauce
1 teaspoon chili powder
¼ teaspoon ground red pepper
½ cup chopped cucumber
¼ cup sliced scallions
   Shredded lettuce, chopped tomato,
   sliced black olives, for garnish
   MR. PHIPPS® Pretzel Chips

With electric mixer at medium speed, beat
cream cheese and sour cream until smooth.
Stir in taco sauce, chili powder and red
pepper. Fold in cucumber and scallions. Chill
at least 1 hour. To serve, spoon dip into
center of large round plate; top with lettuce,
tomato and olives. Arrange pretzel chips
around edge of dip. Serve with additional
pretzel chips for dipping.   *Makes 2½ cups*

Lobster Butter Log

½ pound cooked lobster, finely chopped
6 tablespoons butter, softened
1 teaspoon minced onion
½ teaspoon seasoned salt
¼ teaspoon paprika
½ cup chopped parsley

Combine all ingredients except parsley in
medium bowl. Roll mixture in plastic wrap;
roll into log shape. Refrigerate about 4 hours
or until firm. Roll log in parsley and serve with
crackers or melba toast.   *Makes 1¾ cups*

*Favorite recipe from **Florida Department of
Agriculture and Consumer Services, Bureau of
Seafood and Aquaculture***

Hot Artichoke Spread

1 cup MIRACLE WHIP® Salad Dressing
   or KRAFT® Real Mayonnaise
1 cup (4 ounces) KRAFT® 100% Grated
   Parmesan Cheese
1 (14-ounce) can artichoke hearts,
   drained, chopped

• Heat oven to 350°F.

• Mix all ingredients; spoon into 9-inch pie
plate or 2-cup casserole.

• Bake 20 minutes or until lightly browned.
Garnish as desired. Serve with tortilla chips,
crackers or party rye bread slices.

Makes about 2 cups

Wisconsin Edam and Beer Spread

1 ball (2 pounds) Wisconsin Edam Cheese*
¾ cup butter, cubed and softened
2 tablespoons snipped fresh chives
2 teaspoons Dijon mustard
½ cup amber or dark beer, at room temperature
Cocktail rye or pumpernickel bread slices

*Wisconsin Gouda can be substituted for Edam. Since Gouda is not available in ball form, this spread may be served in your favorite serving bowl.

Cut one-fifth from top of cheese to create flat surface. With butter curler or melon baller, remove cheese from center of ball leaving ½-inch-thick shell. Shred cheese removed from ball and top to measure 4 cups. Reserve remaining cheese for another use.

In large bowl, place shredded cheese, butter, chives and mustard; mix with spoon until blended. Stir in beer until blended. Spoon spread into hollowed cheese ball; reserve remaining spread for refills. Chill until serving time. Serve as spread with cocktail bread.

Makes 4 cups

Favorite recipe from **Wisconsin Milk Marketing Board**

Tabasco®

Over 125 years ago, Edmund McIlhenny developed Tabasco® pepper sauce from a special variety of red Capsicum peppers he had grown on his in-laws' sugar plantation on Avery Island, Louisiana. He mixed crushed ripe peppers with a small amount of island salt mined on the island and then aged the mixture in crockery jars for 30 days. He added fine French wine vinegar and aged the mixture for another 30 days. Originally he strained and poured it into empty cologne-type bottles and passed it out to family and friends. His sauce was so popular that he decided to market it commercially. He selected the trademark "Tabasco," a word of Central American Indian origin. McIlhenny Co. still makes Tabasco sauce in much the same way, except that today the pepper mash ages for three years in oak barrels.

Chunky Salsa

Chunky Salsa

2 tablespoons olive oil
1 cup coarsely chopped onions
1 cup coarsely diced green bell pepper
1 can (35 ounces) tomatoes, drained
  and coarsely chopped (reserve
  ½ cup juice)
1 tablespoon freshly squeezed lime
  juice
2 teaspoons TABASCO® pepper sauce
½ teaspoon salt
2 tablespoons chopped fresh cilantro
  or Italian parsley

Heat oil in large, heavy saucepan over high heat. Add onions and bell pepper; cook and stir 5 to 6 minutes, stirring frequently, until tender. Add tomatoes and juice; bring to a boil over high heat. Reduce heat to low and simmer 6 to 8 minutes, stirring occasionally, until salsa is slightly thickened. Remove from heat. Stir in lime juice, Tabasco® sauce to taste and salt. Cool to lukewarm; stir in cilantro. Spoon salsa into clean jars. Keep refrigerated for up to 5 days.

Makes 3½ cups

Kiwifruit and Tangerine Salsa

3 to 4 California kiwifruit, peeled and
   diced (1½ cups)
2 medium tangerines *or* 1 orange,
   peeled and diced
1 cup peeled and diced jicama
½ cup diced sweet yellow or red bell
   pepper
¼ cup chopped cilantro
1 tablespoon lime juice
1 tablespoon vegetable oil
½ to 1 small jalapeño pepper, seeds and
   veins removed and minced
¼ teaspoon salt

In large bowl, combine all ingredients, mixing
well. Chill briefly.   *Makes about 2½ cups*

Serving Suggestions: Serve as a dip with
tortilla chips, toasted pita bread triangles or
warm tortillas; as a sauce over grilled or
baked halibut or swordfish steaks, chicken or
roasted pork tenderloin; or serve over warm
flour tortillas filled with scrambled eggs.

*Favorite recipe from **California Kiwifruit
Commission***

California Kiwifruit Commission

*California kiwifruit
are grown on
flowering vines,
much like grapes, in
the central and northern
portions of the state. Shipped fresh
from November through May, kiwifruit
are ripe when slightly soft to the
touch. They will keep for several days
at room temperature or up to four
weeks when refrigerated. Best of all,
two medium kiwifruit contain only 90
calories and 1 gram of fat.*

Fresh Grape Salsa and Chips

Fresh Grape Salsa and Chips

¾ cup each red and green California
    seedless grapes, coarsely chopped
½ cup chopped sweet red peppers
¼ cup chopped green onions
2 tablespoons chopped cilantro or basil
1 tablespoon olive oil
1 tablespoon lime juice
2 teaspoons finely chopped jalapeño
    pepper
½ teaspoon salt
¼ teaspoon bottled hot pepper sauce
    Tortilla or bagel chips

Combine all ingredients except chips; mix well. Refrigerate for at least 1 hour to allow flavors to blend. Drain well before serving with chips.   *Makes about 1½ cups*

Serving Tip: Serve with cooked fish or chicken, on roast beef sandwiches or on salads of orange slices.

*Favorite recipe from **California Table Grape Commission***

Raspberry Mint Cooler

1 to 2 cups fresh mint leaves
5 cups DOLE® Pineapple Juice, chilled
2 cups DOLE® Fresh or Frozen
    Raspberries
1 can (6 ounces) frozen limeade
    concentrate, thawed
1 bottle (32 ounces) lemon-lime soda,
    chilled
1 lime, thinly sliced for garnish
    (optional)

• Rub mint leaves around side of punch bowl, then drop the bruised leaves in bottom of bowl.

• Combine remaining ingredients in punch bowl. *Makes 15 servings*

Kokomo Quencher

2 bottles (32 ounces each) lemon-lime
    soda, chilled
1 bottle (40 ounces) DOLE® Pure &
    Light Orchard Peach Juice, chilled
5 cups DOLE® Pineapple Juice, chilled
2 cups fresh or frozen blackberries
1 can (15 ounces) real cream of
    coconut
1 lime, thinly sliced for garnish

• Combine all ingredients in large punch bowl. *Makes 28 servings*

Sunlight Sipper

1½ cups DOLE® Pine-Passion-Banana
    Juice, chilled
1 tablespoon peach schnapps
1 tablespoon light rum
1 tablespoon orange liqueur
    Cracked ice

• Pour juice, schnapps, rum and orange liqueur in 2 glasses. Add ice. Garnish as desired. *Makes 2 servings*

Fresh out of Harvard, Jim Dole arrived in Hawaii in 1899 and two years later began growing 60 acres of pineapple. Since fresh pineapple would not withstand long ocean voyages of that day, Dole had to build a cannery to pack the fruit. By 1905, the cannery was producing an amazing 25,000 cases of canned pineapple. In 1922, Dole purchased the entire Hawaiian island of Lanai and proceeded to build roads and tap underground water sources in order to grow, harvest and transport the delectable fruit.

Clockwise from top right: Raspberry Mint Cooler, Kokomo Quencher and Sunlight Sipper

Peach-Lemon Frost

3 fresh California peaches, peeled,
  halved, pitted and quartered
1 cup 2% low fat milk
2 teaspoons grated lemon peel
½ cup fresh lemon juice
3 ice cubes, cracked
½ pint vanilla ice milk

Add peaches to food processor or blender. Process until smooth to measure 2 cups. Add low fat milk, lemon peel, lemon juice and ice cubes. Process until smooth. Continue processing at low speed; slowly add ice milk until well blended. Pour into glasses. Serve immediately.   *Makes 4 servings*

Favorite recipe from **California Tree Fruit Agreement**

Raspberry Watermelon Slush

1 cup frozen raspberries
1 cup watermelon, seeded
1 cup lemon-lime seltzer
1 tablespoon sugar

Combine all ingredients in blender or food processor. Blend thoroughly. Serve immediately.   *Makes 2 servings*

Favorite recipe from **The Sugar Association, Inc.**

Banana Pineapple Colada

½ banana
½ cup fresh or canned pineapple
½ cup pineapple juice
½ cup ice cubes
¼ teaspoon coconut extract
1 tablespoon sugar

Combine all ingredients in blender or food processor. Blend thoroughly. Pour and serve immediately.   *Makes 2 servings*

Favorite recipe from **The Sugar Association, Inc.**

Established in 1949, The Sugar Association maintains an active role informing the public about sugar, nutrition and health. By creating public education programs, the Association has worked to dispel misconceptions about sugar as well as provide opportunities for research. Recent findings have reaffirmed that when consumed in moderation, sugar can play an important role in a balanced and healthy diet.

Top to bottom: Peach-Lemon Frost and Raspberry Watermelon Slush

ReaLemonade

½ cup sugar
½ cup **REALEMON®** Lemon Juice from
    Concentrate
3¼ cups cold water
    Ice

In pitcher, dissolve sugar in ReaLemon®
brand; add water. Cover; chill. Serve over ice.
Makes about 1 quart

Variations

ReaLimeade: Substitute ReaLime® Lime
Juice from Concentrate for ReaLemon®
brand.

Sparkling: Substitute club soda for cold
water.

Slushy: Reduce water to ½ cup. In blender
container, combine ReaLemon® brand and
sugar with ½ cup water. Gradually add 4 cups
ice cubes, blending until smooth. Serve
immediately.

Pink: Stir in 1 to 2 teaspoons grenadine
syrup *or* 1 to 2 drops red food coloring.

Minted: Stir in 2 to 3 drops peppermint
extract.

Low Calorie: Omit sugar. Add 4 to 8
envelopes sugar substitute *or* 1½ teaspoons
liquid sugar substitute.

Strawberry: Increase sugar to ¾ cup. In
blender or food processor, purée 1 quart
(about 1½ pounds) fresh strawberries,
cleaned and hulled; add to lemonade. Makes
about 2 quarts.

Grape: Stir in 1 (6-ounce) can frozen grape
juice concentrate, thawed.

Honeydew Melon Shake

1 cup honeydew melon chunks, chilled
½ cup vanilla low fat yogurt
2 teaspoons sugar

Combine all ingredients in blender or food
processor. Blend thoroughly. Pour and serve.
Makes 2 servings

Variation: For strawberry melon flavor, blend
in 1 cup frozen strawberries and add another
teaspoon sugar.

*Favorite recipe from **The Sugar Association, Inc.***

Stegosaurus Milk Shakes

1 can (16 ounces) peaches in their own
    juice, drained
2 cups skim milk
1 cup low fat vanilla frozen yogurt
⅛ teaspoon ground nutmeg
    Mint sprigs

Process peaches and milk in food processor
or blender until smooth; add frozen yogurt
and nutmeg. Process until smooth. Serve
milk shakes in glasses; garnish with mint
sprigs. *Makes 4 servings*

*Favorite recipe from **Canned Food Information
Council***

*Clockwise from left: Pink Lemonade,
ReaLemonade, Sparkling Lemonade and
Slushy Lemonade*

"Lemon Float" Punch

Juice of 10 to 12 SUNKIST® Lemons
  (2 cups)
¾ cup sugar
4 cups water
1 bottle (2 liters) ginger ale, chilled
1 pint lemon sherbet or frozen vanilla
  yogurt
Lemon half-cartwheel slices and
  fresh mint leaves (optional) for
  garnish

Combine lemon juice and sugar; stir to dissolve sugar. Add water; chill. To serve, in large punch bowl, combine lemon mixture and ginger ale. Add *small* scoops of sherbet, lemon half-cartwheel slices and mint.

Makes about 15 cups
(thirty 6-ounce servings)

Oreo® Milk Shakes

18 OREO® Chocolate Sandwich Cookies
1½ pints vanilla ice cream, divided
1½ cups milk
¼ cup chocolate-flavored syrup

Coarsely chop 14 cookies. In electric blender container, blend chopped cookies, 1 pint ice cream, milk and chocolate syrup until well blended and smooth, about 1 to 2 minutes.

Pour into 4 (8-ounce) glasses; top each with scoop of remaining ice cream and cookie.

Makes 4 servings

Frozen Margaritas

1 cup confectioners' sugar
½ cup tequila
⅓ cup REALIME® Lime Juice from
  Concentrate
¼ cup triple sec or other orange-
  flavored liqueur
4 cups ice cubes

In blender container, combine all ingredients except ice; blend well. Gradually add ice, blending until smooth. Garnish as desired. Serve immediately.   *Makes about 1 quart*

Bloody Mary Mix

4 cups vegetable juice cocktail
2 tablespoons HEINZ® Worcestershire
  Sauce
1 tablespoon fresh lime or lemon juice
¼ teaspoon granulated sugar
¼ teaspoon pepper
¼ teaspoon hot pepper sauce
⅛ teaspoon garlic powder

Thoroughly mix all ingredients; cover and chill. Serve over ice. Garnish with celery stalks and lime wedges, if desired.

Makes 4 servings

Note: To prepare Bloody Mary Cocktail, add 3 or 4 parts Bloody Mary Mix to 1 part vodka.

"Lemon Float" Punch

White Sangría

¾ cup sugar
½ cup REALEMON® Lemon Juice from
     Concentrate
¼ cup REALIME® Lime Juice from
     Concentrate
1 bottle (750 mL) Rhine wine, chilled
⅓ cup orange-flavored liqueur or orange
     juice
1 (1-liter) bottle club soda, chilled
     Orange, plum or nectarine slices,
     green grapes or other fresh fruit
     Ice

In pitcher, combine sugar and juices; stir until
sugar dissolves. Cover; chill. Just before
serving, add wine, liqueur, club soda and
fruit; serve over ice.

Makes about 2 quarts

Peach Bellinis

4 fresh California peaches, peeled and
     coarsely chopped
½ cup sugar
2 tablespoons lemon juice
¾ cup water
1 bottle (750 ml) chilled sweet sparkling
     wine
     Mint sprigs (optional)

Combine fruit, sugar, lemon juice and water
in blender or food processor. Process until
smooth.* To serve, pour about ¼ cup peach
purée into 6- or 8-ounce stemmed glass.
Slowly fill glass with sparkling wine. Stir to
blend. Garnish with mint.

Makes 10 servings

*If made ahead, cover and refrigerate for up to 3
hours. When ready to serve, continue as directed.

Favorite recipe from **California Tree Fruit
Agreement**

Nectarine Sunrise

4 fresh California nectarines
1 can (6 ounces) frozen limeade
     concentrate
⅔ cup tequila
2 to 3 cups crushed ice
½ cup grenadine syrup
     Fresh mint sprigs

Slice 1 nectarine; set aside for garnish.
Coarsely chop remaining nectarines. In
blender, combine chopped nectarines,
limeade and tequila; purée until smooth.
Gradually add crushed ice, blending until
slushy and mixture measures 5 cups. Place 1
tablespoon grenadine syrup in each of 8
stemmed glasses. Add nectarine mixture. Top
each with mint sprig and nectarine slice on
side of glass. Serve immediately.

Makes 8 servings

Favorite recipe from **California Tree Fruit
Agreement**

White Sangría

40

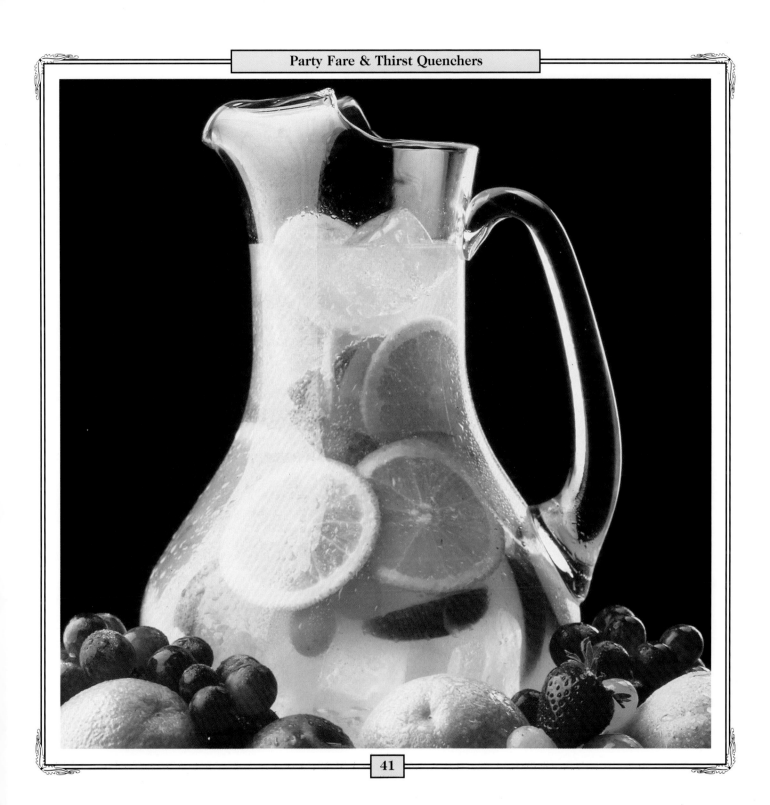

Piña Colada

1¼ cups pineapple juice, chilled
1 cup (8 ounces) light rum (optional)
⅔ cup **COCO LOPEZ®** Cream of
    Coconut
5 cups crushed ice

In large blender container, combine
ingredients; blend until smooth. Garnish as
desired. Serve immediately.

Makes about 7 cups

Iced Swiss Chocolate Peppermint

2 cups strongly brewed Swiss Dutch
    Almond coffee
2 tablespoons low fat milk
2 teaspoons sugar
½ teaspoon cocoa powder
1 drop peppermint extract

Combine all ingredients in blender or food
processor; process until smooth. Pour over
ice and serve immediately. Or refrigerate; stir
well before serving over ice.

Makes 2 servings

*Favorite recipe from **The Sugar Association, Inc.***

Iced French Roast

2 cups strongly brewed French Roast
    coffee
2 tablespoons low fat milk
2 teaspoons sugar
½ teaspoon cocoa powder
    Dash cinnamon

Combine all ingredients in blender or food
processor; process until smooth. Pour over
ice and serve immediately. Or refrigerate; stir
well before serving over ice.

Makes 2 servings

*Favorite recipe from **The Sugar Association, Inc.***

Iced Mocha

2 cups strongly brewed coffee
¾ cup skim milk
1 tablespoon brown sugar
½ teaspoon cocoa powder

Combine all ingredients in blender or food
processor; process until smooth. Pour over
ice and serve immediately. Or refrigerate; stir
well before serving over ice.

Makes 2 servings

*Favorite recipe from **The Sugar Association, Inc.***

Iced Mocha

Simmering Soups & Stews

From soups and stews to chilis and gumbos, you'll have a souper selection to choose from on those chilly days when a big bowl of hot, hearty soup hits the spot.

Veg-All® Cheesy Chowder

¼ cup butter
1 medium onion, chopped
⅓ cup all-purpose flour
2 cups milk
1 (10¾-ounce) can chicken broth
1 package (8 ounces) pasteurized
    process cheese spread, cubed
¼ teaspoon hot pepper sauce
¼ teaspoon white pepper
1 (16-ounce) can VEG-ALL® Mixed
    Vegetables, drained
2 tablespoons chopped parsley

Melt butter in large saucepan. Add onion; cook until tender. Add flour, whisking until smooth. Cook 1 minute over low heat, stirring constantly. Gradually add milk and chicken broth; cook over medium heat, stirring constantly until thickened and bubbly. Add cheese and seasonings, stirring until cheese is melted. Add Veg-All® and parsley. Reduce heat and cook until thoroughly heated. *Do not boil.* *Makes 6 servings*

Veg-All® Cheesy Chowder

Cheddar Potato Chowder

3 tablespoons margarine or butter
2 medium-size carrots, peeled and
    diced
2 medium-size celery stalks, thinly
    sliced
1 small onion, chopped
3 tablespoons all-purpose flour
¼ teaspoon dry mustard
¼ teaspoon paprika
¼ teaspoon ground pepper
2 cups milk
2 cups water
4 medium-size IDAHO® Potatoes (about
    1¾ pounds), peeled and cut into
    ½-inch cubes
2 chicken-flavor bouillon cubes or
    envelopes
1½ cups shredded Cheddar cheese
4 slices bacon, cooked and crumbled
    (optional)
Chopped chives (optional)

In 3-quart saucepan over medium heat, melt
margarine. Add carrots, celery and onion;
cook until tender, about 10 minutes, stirring
occasionally. Stir in flour, dry mustard, paprika
and pepper; cook 1 minute.

Gradually add milk, water, potatoes and
bouillon. Bring to a boil over high heat;
reduce heat to low. Cover and simmer 10
minutes or until potatoes are tender.

Remove saucepan from heat; add cheese
and stir just until melted. Top each serving
with crumbled bacon and chopped chives, if
desired.   *Makes 4 servings*

Favorite recipe from **Idaho Potato Commission**

Idaho Potato Commission

All across the country,
Idaho® Potatoes are
the potatoes of
choice for meals
ranging from trendy to
traditional. Because Idaho grows
more potatoes than any other state,
the Idaho Potato Commission is
constantly searching the nation for the
best Idaho Potato recipes.

Chicken Noodle Soup

1 (46-fluid ounce) can COLLEGE INN®
    Chicken Broth
½ pound boneless skinless chicken, cut
    into bite-size pieces
1½ cups uncooked medium egg noodles
1 cup sliced carrots
½ cup chopped onion
⅓ cup sliced celery
1 teaspoon dried dill weed
¼ teaspoon ground black pepper

In large saucepan, over medium-high heat,
heat chicken broth, chicken, noodles, carrots,
onion, celery, dill and pepper to a boil.
Reduce heat; simmer 20 minutes or until
chicken and noodles are cooked.
                            Makes 8 servings

In the 1920s, a chef named Joseph Colton saw opportunity knocking in the form of his popular recipe for chicken à la king. His delicious creation became a house specialty at the College Inn, a nightclub in the Sherman House in Chicago. Eventually, a small delicatessen was established at the hotel to handle the numerous take-home orders from patrons. Later, the Sherman House installed a cannery, and in 1923 the College Inn Food Products Corporation was born.

Seafood Bisque

½ **pound shrimp, shelled, deveined and cut in half crosswise**
½ **pound sea scallops, coarsely chopped**
1 **(16-ounce) can whole new potatoes, drained and diced**
1 **clove garlic, crushed**
¼ **cup margarine or butter**
⅔ **cup all-purpose flour**
2 **(13¾-fluid ounce) cans COLLEGE INN® Chicken Broth**
½ **teaspoon ground white pepper**
1 **cup light cream or half-and-half**

In large saucepan, over medium heat, cook shrimp, scallops, potatoes and garlic in margarine until seafood is done. Stir in flour until blended. Gradually add chicken broth and pepper. Heat to a boil, stirring constantly. Boil 1 minute. Stir in light cream; heat through. *Do not boil.*   *Makes 6 servings*

Hunt's® Hearty Manhattan Clam Chowder

2 **slices bacon, cut into ½-inch pieces**
½ **cup chopped onion**
½ **cup chopped celery**
1 **(14½-ounce) can HUNT'S® Whole Peeled Tomatoes, undrained and crushed**
1 **(14½-ounce) can HUNT'S® Whole New Potatoes, drained and cubed**
1 **(8-ounce) bottle clam juice**
1 **(6½-ounce) can chopped clams, drained and rinsed**
2 **tablespoons chopped fresh parsley**
¼ **teaspoon thyme**
⅛ **teaspoon pepper**
⅛ **teaspoon garlic powder**

In large saucepan, fry bacon until crisp. Add onion and celery; cook and stir until tender. Stir in tomatoes, potatoes, clam juice, clams, parsley, thyme, pepper and garlic powder. Simmer, uncovered, 15 minutes, stirring occasionally.   *Makes 4 servings*

Onion Soup with Bel Paese®

1 to 1½ pounds onions, sliced
   Vegetable oil for frying
1 teaspoon all-purpose flour
4 cups beef broth or beef bouillon,
   prepared
¼ teaspoon salt
⅛ teaspoon pepper
4 slices Italian bread, toasted
4 ounces BEL PAESE® Cheese,* cut
   into 4 slices
½ cup CLASSICA™ Grated Parmesan
   Cheese (about 1 ounce)

*Remove wax coating and moist, white crust from cheese.

Preheat oven to 350°F. In large saucepan, cook and stir onions in oil until golden. Sprinkle with flour and cook an additional 5 minutes. Add broth, salt and pepper. Reduce heat and simmer for 30 minutes.

In each of 4 small ovenproof crocks, place 1 slice toast. Top with 1 slice Bel Paese® Cheese and 2 tablespoons Classica™ Grated Parmesan Cheese. Ladle onion soup into crocks. Bake for 10 minutes. Serve hot.

Makes 4 servings

Cream of Broccoli and Cheddar Soup

1 pound fresh broccoli
1 can (14 ounces) reduced-sodium or
   regular chicken broth
2 tablespoons butter or margarine
2 tablespoons all-purpose flour
2 cups milk
¼ teaspoon freshly ground black
   pepper
2 cups (8 ounces) SARGENTO® Classic
   Supreme® Shredded Sharp or Mild
   Cheddar Cheese

Chop broccoli florets; thinly slice stems. Combine broccoli and broth in medium saucepan; heat to a boil. Reduce heat; cover and simmer about 7 minutes or until broccoli is fork tender.* Transfer (in thirds) to food processor or blender. Process until fairly smooth. Melt butter in same saucepan; add flour. Cook, stirring constantly, over medium heat until bubbly. Add milk and pepper; heat to a boil, stirring constantly. Reduce heat to medium; add broccoli purée. Stir in Cheddar cheese; heat just until cheese melts *(do not boil),* stirring constantly. Ladle into soup bowls.   *Makes 6 servings*

*For chunky broccoli and Cheddar soup, reserve 1 cup broccoli pieces; add to soup with purée.

Onion Soup with Bel Paese®

South-of-the-Border Chicken Soup

South-of-the-Border Chicken Soup

    3 tablespoons vegetable oil
    3 corn tortillas, cut into ½-inch strips
    ⅓ cup chopped onion
    ⅓ cup chopped green and red bell peppers
    1 clove garlic, minced
    ¼ cup all-purpose flour
    2 (13¾-ounce) cans chicken broth
    2 cups cooked chicken, cubed
    1 (16-ounce) can VEG-ALL® Mixed Vegetables, undrained
    1 teaspoon chili powder

1. Heat oil in large skillet; add tortilla strips and fry, stirring constantly, until golden. Drain on paper towel-lined plate.

2. Add onion and bell peppers to skillet; cook and stir until soft.

3. Add garlic and stir in flour; gradually stir in chicken broth.

4. Add remaining ingredients except tortilla strips; cook until thickened. Sprinkle with tortilla strips before serving.

Makes 4 to 6 servings

veg·all® *William Larsen started a produce business in 1876 in Green Bay, Wisconsin, shipping vegetables to lumber and mining camps. His four sons eventually took over the canning business that succeeded his produce operation. Veg-All® was introduced in 1926. Today the Dean Foods Vegetable Company has 18 canned and frozen vegetable production facilities in the U.S. and Mexico, shipping products to every state and several foreign countries. The company headquarters is on the site where William Larsen built the first plant in 1889.*

"Creamy" Wild Rice Soup

6 tablespoons butter
⅓ cup minced onion
½ cup all-purpose flour
3 cups chicken broth
2 cups cooked wild rice
4 ounces sliced mushrooms
½ cup finely chopped ham
½ cup finely grated carrots
3 tablespoons slivered almonds
½ teaspoon salt
1 cup half-and-half
2 tablespoons dry sherry wine
 Minced parsley or chives

Melt butter in large skillet; add onion and cook and stir until tender. Blend in flour; gradually add broth. Cook, stirring constantly, until mixture comes to a boil. Boil 1 minute. Stir in wild rice, mushrooms, ham, carrots, almonds and salt; simmer about 5 minutes. Blend in half-and-half and sherry. Garnish with minced parsley or chives.

Makes 6 servings

Favorite recipe from **Minnesota Cultivated Wild Rice Council**

Tomato Bisque

½ cup finely chopped onion
½ cup sliced celery with leaves
1 tablespoon butter or margarine
2 (16-ounce) cans FRANK'S® or
 SNOWFLOSS® Italian Style Diced
 Tomatoes
1 (14½-ounce) can beef broth
1 beef bouillon cube
1 cup water
1 teaspoon dried basil
1 bay leaf

1. Cook and stir onion and celery in butter.

2. Add tomatoes, broth, bouillon, water, basil and bay leaf; simmer 20 to 25 minutes.

3. Remove bay leaf before serving.

Makes 6 servings

Tip: May also be served cold.

Chicken Vegetable Soup

**1 pound boneless skinless chicken
   breasts, cut into 1-inch pieces**
1 cup chopped onions
2 cloves garlic, minced
**2 tablespoons FLEISCHMANN'S®
   Margarine**
**1 (10-ounce) package frozen sliced
   carrots**
**4 cups low sodium vegetable juice
   cocktail**
4 cups water
**1½ cups uncooked large bow-tie
   macaroni**
1 tablespoon Italian seasoning
**1 (10-ounce) package frozen chopped
   spinach**
60 HARVEST CRISPS® 5-Grain Crackers

In large saucepan, over medium-high heat,
cook chicken, onions and garlic in margarine
until onions are tender. Add carrots,
vegetable juice, water, macaroni and Italian
seasoning. Heat to a boil. Cover; reduce heat
to low. Simmer for 20 minutes. Stir in
spinach; cook 5 minutes more. Serve 1 cup
soup with 6 crackers.   *Makes 10 servings*

Chili con Carne Winchester

2 tablespoons vegetable oil
⅓ cup chopped onion
⅓ cup chopped green bell pepper
1 pound ground beef
2 (15-ounce) cans kidney beans
1 (16-ounce) can stewed tomatoes
1 clove garlic, minced
**1 (16-ounce) can VEG-ALL® Mixed
   Vegetables, undrained**

1. Heat oil in 3-quart saucepan. Add onion
and green pepper; cook and stir over medium
heat until soft.

2. Add ground beef, drained kidney beans,
stewed tomatoes and garlic. Bring to a boil.
Cover and reduce heat; simmer 30 minutes.

3. Stir in undrained Veg-All® and cook 10
minutes longer.   *Makes 6 servings*

Fleischmann's

*In 1942, with
butter in
increasingly
short supply
because of the
war, margarine
was added to the
Fleischmann's
product list. In
the 1950s, Fleischmann's developed
the first margarine made entirely from
corn oil. This new product was
immediately hailed by physicians and
nutritionists as a polyunsaturated
weapon against excessive serum
cholesterol.*

Brunswick Stew

1 (14½-ounce) can peeled tomatoes,
    undrained
1 (17-ounce) can green lima beans,
    undrained
1 (2½-pound) chicken, cut up
1 (13¾-fluid ounce) can COLLEGE INN®
    Chicken Broth
2 (6-ounce) cans tomato paste
2 tablespoons red wine vinegar
2 tablespoons Worcestershire sauce
¼ teaspoon ground red pepper
2 cups cubed cooked pork

Drain tomatoes and lima beans, reserving liquid; coarsely chop tomatoes. In large heavy saucepan, over medium-high heat, combine chicken, chicken broth, tomato paste, reserved tomato liquid, reserved lima bean liquid, red wine vinegar, Worcestershire sauce and pepper; heat to a boil. Reduce heat; cover and simmer 20 minutes. Add tomatoes, lima beans and pork; cover. Simmer 20 to 25 minutes more or until chicken is done. *Makes 6 servings*

Microwave Directions: In 5-quart microwaveproof casserole, combine chicken, broth, tomato paste, reserved tomato liquid, reserved bean liquid, vinegar, Worcestershire sauce and pepper as above. Cover with waxed paper. Microwave on MEDIUM (50% power) for 28 to 30 minutes, stirring twice during cooking time. Add tomatoes, lima beans and pork; cover. Microwave on LOW (30% power) for 18 to 20 minutes. Let stand, covered, 10 minutes before serving.

Hearty Chicken and Rice Soup

10 cups chicken broth
 1 medium onion, chopped
 1 cup sliced celery
 1 cup sliced carrots
 ¼ cup snipped parsley
 ½ teaspoon cracked black pepper
 ½ teaspoon dried thyme leaves
 1 bay leaf
1½ cups cubed chicken (about ¾ pound)
 2 cups cooked rice
 2 tablespoons lime juice
   Lime slices for garnish

Combine broth, onion, celery, carrots, parsley, pepper, thyme, and bay leaf in Dutch oven. Bring to a boil; stir once or twice. Reduce heat; simmer, uncovered, 10 to 15 minutes. Add chicken; simmer, uncovered, 5 to 10 minutes or until chicken is cooked. Remove and discard bay leaf. Stir in rice and lime juice just before serving. Garnish with lime slices. *Makes 8 servings*

Favorite recipe from **USA Rice Council**

Arizona Pork Chili

1½ pounds boneless pork, cut into
  ¼-inch cubes
1 tablespoon vegetable oil
1 onion, coarsely chopped
2 cloves garlic, minced
1 can (15 ounces) black, pinto or
  kidney beans, drained
1 can (14½ ounces) DEL MONTE® Chili
  Style Chunky Tomatoes
1 can (4 ounces) diced green chiles
1 teaspoon ground cumin

In large skillet, brown meat in oil over
medium-high heat. Add onion and garlic;
cook until onion is tender. Season with salt
and pepper, if desired. Add remaining
ingredients. Simmer 10 minutes, stirring
occasionally. Serve with tortillas and sour
cream, if desired.   *Makes 6 servings*

Sock-It-To-'Em Chili

1 tablespoon vegetable oil
¾ pound ground turkey or lean ground
  beef
8 ounces mushrooms, sliced
2 medium carrots, peeled and diced
1 large green bell pepper, seeded and
  diced
1 medium onion, chopped
2 cloves garlic, minced
1½ teaspoons chili powder
½ teaspoon ground cumin
1 (26-ounce) jar NEWMAN'S OWN®
  Sockarooni™ Spaghetti Sauce
2 (15- to 19-ounce) cans black beans,
  undrained
1 cup water
1 medium zucchini, diced

In 5-quart Dutch oven over medium-high
heat, heat oil. Cook meat until no longer pink,
stirring constantly. Add mushrooms, carrots,
bell pepper, onion, garlic, chili powder and
cumin; cook, stirring frequently, until onion is
tender.

Stir in Newman's Own® Sockarooni™
Spaghetti Sauce, black beans with liquid and
water. Increase heat to high and bring to a
boil. Reduce heat to low; cover and simmer
20 minutes. Add zucchini; cook, uncovered,
over medium-low heat 10 minutes or until
zucchini is just tender.   *Makes 6 servings*

Arizona Pork Chili

Gumbo

2 tablespoons WESSON® Oil
1 cup chopped onions
½ cup sliced celery
½ cup chopped green bell pepper
2 cloves garlic, minced
2 (14½-ounce) cans chicken broth
1 (15-ounce) can HUNT'S® Tomato Sauce
1 (14½-ounce) can HUNT'S® Choice-Cut Tomatoes, undrained
1½ cups cooked, chopped chicken
1 cup water
1 cup sliced fresh or frozen okra
⅓ cup uncooked rice
1 teaspoon salt
1 teaspoon hot pepper sauce
½ teaspoon thyme leaves
½ teaspoon basil leaves
½ teaspoon gumbo filé (optional)
1 bay leaf

In Dutch oven, heat oil; cook and stir onions, celery, bell pepper and garlic until tender. Stir in broth, tomato sauce, tomatoes, chicken, water, okra, rice, salt, hot pepper sauce, thyme, basil, gumbo filé and bay leaf. Bring to a boil; reduce heat and simmer 20 minutes. Remove bay leaf.   *Makes 8 cups*

Louisiana Shrimp and Chicken Gumbo

3 tablespoons vegetable oil
¼ cup all-purpose flour
2 medium onions, chopped
1 cup chopped celery
1 large green bell pepper, chopped
2 cloves garlic, minced
3 cups chicken broth
1 can (16 ounces) whole tomatoes in juice, undrained
1 package (10 ounces) frozen sliced okra
1 bay leaf
1 teaspoon TABASCO® pepper sauce
¾ pound shredded cooked chicken
½ pound raw shrimp, peeled, deveined
Hot cooked rice

In large saucepan or Dutch oven heat oil. Add flour and cook over low heat until mixture turns dark brown and develops a nutty aroma; stir frequently. Add onions, celery, bell pepper and garlic; cook 5 minutes or until vegetables are tender. Gradually add broth. Stir in tomatoes, okra, bay leaf and Tabasco® sauce; bring to a boil. Add chicken and shrimp; cook 3 to 5 minutes or until shrimp turn pink. Remove bay leaf. Serve with rice.   *Makes 6 servings*

Hearty Chorizo and Bean Soup

1 tablespoon crushed dried chiles
1 pound CORTE'S® SPECIALS,* sliced
   or crumbled
1 large onion, chopped
3 carrots, diced
1 cup chopped celery
2 cups cooked kidney beans, cooking
   water reserved (1 cup)
2 tomatoes, peeled and diced
3 cups water or stock
1 teaspoon Worcestershire sauce
1 teaspoon distilled white vinegar
   Sour cream

*The Mexican sausage, chorizo, is available in the meat section of the supermarket.

Cook and stir chiles and chorizo over medium heat in Dutch oven or large saucepan. Pour off excess fat. Add onion, carrots and celery; cook and stir 2 to 3 minutes.

Add beans, 1 cup cooking water from beans, tomatoes, water, Worcestershire sauce and vinegar; simmer for 30 minutes.

Serve soup in individual bowls garnished with dollop of sour cream.

Makes 4 to 6 servings

Sausage, Bean and Barley Soup

1 package (16 ounces) LOUIS RICH®
   Turkey Smoked Sausage or Turkey
   Polska Kielbasa
5 cups water
1 can (15½ ounces) Great Northern
   beans, drained
1 can (14½ ounces) stewed tomatoes
1 medium onion, chopped
2 stalks celery, sliced (about ½ cup)
2 carrots, coarsely chopped (about
   ½ cup)
½ cup quick-cooking barley
2 teaspoons Worcestershire sauce
½ teaspoon dried basil leaves

• Cut turkey smoked sausage into ¼-inch slices.

• Place sausage slices and remaining ingredients in 5-quart Dutch oven or saucepan; bring to a boil.

• Cover. Reduce heat; simmer 15 minutes or until vegetables are tender. Season to taste with hot pepper sauce, if desired.

Makes 6 (2-cup) servings

White Bean Stew

2½ quarts chicken stock *or* 5 cans
    (14½ ounces each) chicken broth
    plus ½ cup water
1 pound dried white beans
½ cup chopped onion
3 cloves garlic, minced
1 teaspoon LAWRY'S® Seasoned Salt
½ teaspoon LAWRY'S® Pinch of Herbs
½ teaspoon LAWRY'S® Lemon Pepper
5 boneless, skinless chicken breast
    halves (about 1 pound), cooked and
    diced
1 can (4 ounces) diced green chiles
2 teaspoons ground cumin
2 teaspoons dried oregano
2 teaspoons chopped cilantro
1 cup (4 ounces) shredded Cheddar
    cheese for garnish
¼ cup chopped green onions for
    garnish

In Dutch oven or large saucepan, combine
2 quarts chicken stock, beans, onion, garlic,
Seasoned Salt, Pinch of Herbs and Lemon
Pepper. Bring to a boil; reduce heat. Cover
and simmer until beans are tender, about
1½ hours. (If bean mixture becomes too
thick, add additional chicken stock to thin.)
When beans are tender, add remaining
ingredients except cheese and green onions;
cover and simmer 20 minutes, stirring
occasionally. Garnish as desired.

Makes 6 servings

Presentation: Serve stew in individual bowls.
Sprinkle with cheese and green onions.

Irish Stew in Bread

1½ pounds lean, boned American lamb
    shoulder, cut into 1-inch cubes
¼ cup all-purpose flour
2 tablespoons vegetable oil
2 cloves garlic, crushed
2 cups water
¼ cup Burgundy wine
5 medium carrots, chopped
3 medium potatoes, peeled and sliced
2 large onions, peeled and chopped
2 celery ribs, sliced
¾ teaspoon black pepper
1 beef bouillon cube, crushed
1 cup frozen peas
¼ pound fresh sliced mushrooms
    Round bread, unsliced*

*Stew may be served individually or in one large
loaf. Slice bread crosswise near top to form lid.
Hollow larger piece, leaving 1-inch border. Fill
"bowl" with hot stew; cover with "lid." Serve
immediately.

Coat lamb with flour while heating oil over
low heat in Dutch oven. Add lamb and garlic;
cook and stir until brown. Add water, wine,
carrots, potatoes, onions, celery, pepper and
bouillon. Cover; simmer 30 to 35 minutes.

Add peas and mushrooms. Cover; simmer 10
minutes. Bring to a boil; correct seasonings, if
necessary. Serve in bread.

Makes 6 to 8 servings

Favorite recipe from **American Lamb Council**

White Bean Stew

Tried & True One-Dish Classics

With these one-dish creations, preparing dinner will be lickety-split. Your family and friends will thank you and keep coming back for more.

Coq au Vin

4 thin slices bacon, cut into ½-inch pieces
6 chicken thighs, skinned
¾ teaspoon dried thyme, crushed
1 large onion, coarsely chopped
4 cloves garlic, minced
½ pound small red potatoes, quartered
10 mushrooms, quartered
1 can (14½ ounces) DEL MONTE® Italian Recipe Stewed Tomatoes
1½ cups dry red wine

In 4-quart heavy saucepan, cook bacon until just starting to brown. Sprinkle chicken with thyme; season with salt and pepper, if desired. Add chicken to pan; brown over medium-high heat. Add onion and garlic.

Cook 2 minutes; drain. Add potatoes, mushrooms, tomatoes and wine. Cook, uncovered, over medium-high heat about 25 minutes or until potatoes are tender and sauce thickens, stirring occasionally. Garnish with chopped parsley, if desired.

Makes 4 to 6 servings

Coq au Vin

Classic Arroz con Pollo

2 tablespoons olive oil
1 cut-up chicken
2 cups uncooked rice*
1 cup chopped onions
1 medium-size red bell pepper,
    chopped
1 medium-size green bell pepper,
    chopped
1 clove garlic, minced
1½ teaspoons salt, divided
1½ teaspoons dried basil
4 cups chicken broth
1 tablespoon lime juice
⅛ teaspoon ground saffron *or*
    ½ teaspoon ground turmeric
1 bay leaf
2 cups chopped tomatoes
½ teaspoon ground black pepper
1 cup fresh or frozen green peas
    Fresh basil for garnish

*Recipe based on regular-milled long grain white rice.

Heat oil in large Dutch oven over medium-high heat until hot. Add chicken; cook 10 minutes or until brown, turning occasionally. Remove chicken; keep warm. Add rice, onions, bell peppers, garlic, ¾ teaspoon salt and dried basil to pan; cook and stir 5 minutes or until vegetables are tender and rice is browned. Add broth, lime juice, saffron and bay leaf. Bring to a boil; stir in tomatoes. Arrange chicken on top and sprinkle with remaining ¾ teaspoon salt and black pepper. Cover; reduce heat to low. Cook 20 minutes

more. Stir in peas; cover and cook 10 minutes more or until fork can be inserted into chicken with ease and juices run clear, not pink. Remove bay leaf. Garnish with fresh basil. Serve immediately.

Makes 8 servings

*Favorite recipe from **National Broiler Council***

Easy Chicken Pot Pie

1¼ cups hot water
3 tablespoons PARKAY® Spread Sticks,
    cut into pieces
3 cups STOVE TOP® Stuffing Mix for
    Chicken in the Canister
1 can (10¾ ounces) condensed cream
    of chicken soup
1 cup milk
3 cups cooked chicken or turkey cubes
1 package (10 ounces) frozen mixed
    vegetables, thawed
1 can (4 ounces) sliced mushrooms,
    drained
¼ teaspoon dried thyme leaves

• Heat oven to 350°F.

• Mix hot water and spread in large bowl until margarine is melted. Stir in stuffing mix just to moisten; set aside.

• Mix soup and milk in another large bowl until smooth. Stir in chicken, vegetables, mushrooms and thyme. Pour into 12×8-inch glass baking dish. Spoon stuffing evenly over top.

• Bake 35 minutes or until heated through.

Makes 4 to 6 servings

Classic Arroz con Pollo

Sweet & Sour Chicken Stir-Fry

1 package (8 ounces) BANQUET®
   Breast Tenders
4 cups frozen stir-fry vegetables
1 cup sweet & sour sauce
4 cups hot cooked rice

Prepare tenders as directed on package. Spray large nonstick skillet with nonstick cooking spray; cook and stir vegetables until crisp-tender. Stir in sauce; heat thoroughly. Pour vegetable mixture over hot rice; top with hot tenders. *Makes 4 servings*

Veg-All® Chicken Pot Pie

2 (10¾-ounce) cans cream of potato
   soup
1 (16-ounce) can VEG-ALL® Mixed
   Vegetables, drained
2 cups diced cooked chicken
½ cup milk
½ teaspoon thyme
½ teaspoon black pepper
2 (9-inch) frozen pie crusts, thawed
1 egg, slightly beaten (optional)

Combine soup, Veg-All®, chicken, milk, thyme and pepper. Spoon into 1 thawed pie crust. Cover with top crust; crimp edges to seal. Slit top crust and brush with egg, if desired. Bake at 375°F, 40 minutes. Cool 10 minutes.
Makes 6 servings

RICE A RONI®

The founder of Rice-A-Roni®, Domenic DeDomenico, traveled to America from Italy in 1890. He made his way to San Francisco, California, and started a pasta company called Golden Grain. In 1958, his sons developed a product based on seasoned rice and macaroni and named it Rice-A-Roni®. Through the years, Rice-A-Roni's "The San Francisco Treat®" jingle and cable car symbol have become part of America's heritage.

Beef & Broccoli Pepper Steak

Beef & Broccoli Pepper Steak

1 tablespoon margarine or butter
1 pound well-trimmed top round steak,
cut into thin strips
1 package (6.8 ounces) RICE-A-RONI®
Beef Flavor
2 cups broccoli flowerets
½ cup red or green bell pepper strips
1 small onion, thinly sliced

1. In large skillet, melt margarine over medium heat. Add meat; sauté just until browned.

2. Remove from skillet; set aside. Keep warm.

3. In same skillet, prepare Rice-A-Roni® Mix as package directs; simmer 10 minutes. Add meat and remaining ingredients; simmer additional 10 minutes or until most of liquid is absorbed and vegetables are crisp-tender.

Makes 4 servings

Mexican Lasagna

1½ pounds lean ground beef
1 teaspoon LAWRY'S® Seasoned Salt
1 package (1.25 ounces) LAWRY'S®
   Taco Spices & Seasonings
1 cup diced tomatoes, fresh or canned
2 cans (8 ounces each) tomato sauce
1 can (4 ounces) diced green chiles
8 ounces ricotta cheese
2 eggs, beaten
9 corn tortillas
2½ cups (10 ounces) shredded Monterey
   Jack cheese

In large skillet, brown ground beef until crumbly; drain fat. Add Seasoned Salt, Taco Spices & Seasonings, tomatoes, tomato sauce and chiles; blend well. Bring to a boil; reduce heat and simmer, uncovered, 10 minutes. In small bowl, combine ricotta cheese and eggs.

In bottom of 13×9×2-inch baking dish, spread half of meat mixture. Top with half of tortillas. Spread half of ricotta-egg mixture over tortillas; top with half of Jack cheese. Repeat once more, ending with shredded cheese. Bake, uncovered, in 350°F oven 20 to 30 minutes. Let stand 10 minutes before cutting into squares. *Makes 8 servings*

Quick Chili Bake

1 can (15 to 16 ounces) chili
1 jar (12 ounces) chunky salsa
1 can (12 ounces) corn, drained
7 ounces MUELLER'S® Twists, cooked
   5 minutes and drained
½ cup (2 ounces) shredded Cheddar
   cheese

In large bowl, combine chili, salsa and corn. Add pasta; toss to coat. Spoon into 2-quart casserole; top with cheese. Bake in 400°F oven 30 minutes or until heated. If desired, serve with corn chips. *Makes 6 servings*

Cheesy Chicken Nugget Casserole

1 package (7¼ ounces) macaroni and
   cheese dinner
1 package (10 ounces) frozen broccoli
   cuts, thawed
1 package (10 ounces) BANQUET®
   Chicken Nuggets

Prepare macaroni and cheese as directed on package. Add to 2-quart casserole with broccoli and mix; top with nuggets. Bake at 350°F, 30 to 35 minutes. *Makes 6 servings*

Chicken Enchiladas

4 cups finely chopped cooked chicken
1 cup chopped onions
¼ cup margarine or butter
¼ cup unsifted flour
2½ cups hot water
1 tablespoon WYLER'S® or STEERO®
   Chicken-Flavor Instant Bouillon *or*
   3 Chicken-Flavor Bouillon Cubes
1 (8-ounce) container BORDEN® or
   MEADOW GOLD® Sour Cream
2 cups (8 ounces) shredded Cheddar
   cheese
1 (4-ounce) can chopped green chilies,
   drained
1 teaspoon ground cumin
10 (8-inch) flour tortillas

Preheat oven to 350°. In medium saucepan, cook and stir onions in margarine until tender. Stir in flour, then water and bouillon; cook and stir until thickened and bouillon is dissolved. Remove from heat; add sour cream.

In large bowl, combine *2 cups* sauce, chicken, *1 cup* cheese, chilies and cumin. Soften tortillas according to package directions. Place equal portions of chicken mixture on tortillas; roll up. Arrange, seam side down, in greased 13×9-inch baking dish. Top with remaining sauce and *1 cup* cheese. Cover; bake 25 minutes or until hot. Garnish as desired. Refrigerate leftovers.

Makes 6 to 8 servings

Spicy Tuna and Linguine with Garlic and Pine Nuts

2 tablespoons olive oil
4 cloves garlic, minced
2 cups sliced mushrooms
½ cup chopped onion
½ teaspoon crushed red pepper
2½ cups chopped plum tomatoes
1 can (14½ ounces) chicken broth plus water to equal 2 cups
½ teaspoon salt
¼ teaspoon coarsely ground black pepper
1 package (9 ounces) uncooked fresh linguine
1 can (12 ounces) STARKIST® Solid White Tuna, drained and chunked
⅓ cup chopped fresh cilantro
⅓ cup toasted pine nuts or almonds

In 12-inch skillet, heat olive oil over medium-high heat; sauté garlic, mushrooms, onion and red pepper until golden brown. Add tomatoes, chicken broth mixture, salt and black pepper; bring to a boil.

Separate uncooked linguine into strands; place in skillet and spoon sauce over. Reduce heat to simmer; cook, covered, 4 more minutes or until cooked through. Toss gently; add tuna and cilantro and toss again. Sprinkle with pine nuts.

Makes 4 to 6 servings

Almond-Chicken Casserole

1 cup fresh bread cubes
1 tablespoon PARKAY® Margarine, melted
3 cups chopped cooked chicken
1½ cups diagonally cut celery slices
1 cup MIRACLE WHIP® Salad Dressing
1 cup (4 ounces) shredded 100% Natural KRAFT® Swiss Cheese
½ cup (1½-inch-long) red or green pepper strips
¼ cup slivered almonds, toasted
¼ cup chopped onion

• Combine bread cubes and margarine; toss lightly. Set aside. Combine remaining ingredients; mix lightly. Spoon into 10×6-inch baking dish. Top with bread cubes. Bake at 350°, 30 minutes or until lightly browned. Garnish as desired.   *Makes 6 servings*

Tuna Mac and Cheese

1 package (7¼ ounces) macaroni and cheese dinner
1 can (12 ounces) STARKIST® Solid White or Chunk Light Tuna, drained and chunked
1 cup frozen peas
½ cup shredded Cheddar cheese
½ cup milk
1 teaspoon Italian herb seasoning
¼ teaspoon garlic powder (optional)
1 tablespoon grated Parmesan cheese

Microwave Directions: Prepare macaroni and cheese dinner according to package directions. Add remaining ingredients except Parmesan cheese. Pour into 1½-quart microwavable serving dish. Cover with vented plastic wrap; microwave on HIGH 2 minutes. Stir; continue heating on HIGH 2½ to 3½ more minutes or until cheese is melted and mixture is heated through. Sprinkle with Parmesan cheese.   *Makes 5 to 6 servings*

Classic Macaroni and Cheese

2 cups elbow macaroni
3 tablespoons butter or margarine
¼ cup chopped onion (optional)
2 tablespoons all-purpose flour
½ teaspoon salt
⅛ teaspoon pepper
2 cups milk
2 cups (8 ounces) SARGENTO® Classic Supreme® or Fancy Supreme® Shredded Mild Cheddar Cheese, divided

Cook macaroni according to package directions; drain. In medium saucepan, melt butter and cook onion about 5 minutes or until tender. Stir in flour, salt and pepper. Gradually add milk and cook, stirring occasionally, until thickened. Remove from heat. Add 1½ cups Cheddar cheese and stir until cheese melts. Combine cheese sauce with cooked macaroni. Place in 1½-quart casserole; top with remaining ½ cup Cheddar cheese. Bake at 350°F, 30 minutes or until bubbly and cheese is golden brown.
Makes 6 servings

Almond-Chicken Casserole

Family-Pleasing Meat Dishes

When it comes to the meat lovers in your household, look to this selection to give them a long list of meaty family favorites.

Beef with Dry Spice Rub

3 tablespoons firmly packed brown sugar
1 tablespoon black peppercorns
1 tablespoon yellow mustard seeds
1 tablespoon whole coriander seeds
4 cloves garlic
1½ to 2 pounds beef top round steak or London Broil (about 1½ inches thick)
Vegetable or olive oil
Salt

Place sugar, peppercorns, seeds and garlic in blender or food processor; process until seeds and garlic are crushed. Rub beef with oil, then pat on spice mixture. Season with salt. Oil hot grid to help prevent sticking. Grill beef, on covered grill, over medium-low KINGSFORD® briquets, 16 to 20 minutes for medium doneness, turning once. Let stand 5 minutes before slicing. Cut across grain into thin, diagonal slices.   *Makes 6 servings*

Grilled Mushrooms: Thread mushrooms on metal or bamboo* skewers. Brush lightly with oil; season with salt and pepper. Grill 7 to 12 minutes, turning occasionally.

Grilled New Potatoes: Cook or microwave small new potatoes until barely tender. Thread on metal or bamboo* skewers. Brush lightly with oil; season with salt and pepper. Grill 10 to 15 minutes, turning occasionally.

*Bamboo skewers should be soaked in water at least 20 minutes to keep them from burning.

Top to bottom: Grilled New Potatoes, Grilled Mushrooms and Beef with Dry Spice Rub

Pronto Spicy Beef and Black Bean Salsa

1 beef tri-tip (bottom sirloin) roast or top sirloin steak, cut 1½ inches thick
1 can (15 ounces) black beans, rinsed, drained
1 medium tomato, chopped
1 small red onion, finely chopped
3 tablespoons coarsely chopped fresh cilantro
Fresh cilantro sprigs (optional)

Seasoning

1 tablespoon chili powder
1 teaspoon ground cumin
1 teaspoon salt
½ teaspoon ground red pepper

1. Combine seasoning ingredients; reserve 2 teaspoons for salsa. Trim fat from beef roast. Press remaining seasoning mixture evenly into surface of roast.

2. Place tri-tip on grid over medium coals (medium-low coals for top sirloin). Grill tri-tip 30 to 35 minutes (top sirloin 22 to 30 minutes) for rare to medium doneness, turning occasionally. Let stand 10 minutes before carving.

3. Meanwhile, in medium bowl, combine beans, tomato, onion, chopped cilantro and reserved seasoning mixture; mix until blended.

4. Carve roast across the grain into slices. Arrange beef and bean salsa on serving platter; garnish with cilantro sprigs, if desired.
Makes 6 servings

Favorite recipe from **National Live Stock & Meat Board**

Country-Style Pot Roast

1 boneless pot roast (3 to 3½ pounds), rump, chuck or round
1 envelope LIPTON® Recipe Secrets® Onion-Mushroom Soup Mix
2½ cups water, divided
4 potatoes, cut into 1-inch pieces
4 carrots, thinly sliced
2 to 4 tablespoons all-purpose flour

In 5-quart Dutch oven or heavy saucepan, brown roast over medium-high heat. Add onion-mushroom soup mix blended with 2 cups water. Reduce heat to low and simmer covered, turning occasionally, 2 hours. Add vegetables and cook additional 30 minutes or until vegetables and roast are tender; remove roast and vegetables. Blend remaining ½ cup water with flour; stir into Dutch oven. Bring to a boil over high heat. Reduce heat to low and simmer, stirring constantly, until thickened, about 5 minutes.
Makes about 6 servings

Note: Also terrific with Lipton® Recipe Secrets® Onion, Beefy Onion or Italian Herb with Tomato Soup Mix.

Menu Suggestion: Serve with warm rolls and apple pie for dessert.

Pronto Spicy Beef and Black Bean Salsa

Spiced Beef Roast

Spiced Beef Roast

¼ **cup margarine**
2 **pounds beef stew meat, cubed**
¼ **cup all-purpose flour**
½ **cup onion, thinly sliced**
½ **teaspoon garlic, minced**
1 **teaspoon dried thyme**
1 **bay leaf**
½ **teaspoon salt**
¼ **teaspoon pepper**
1 **tablespoon brown sugar**
1 **cup beer or water**
1 **(12-ounce) can beef broth**
1 **(16-ounce) can VEG-ALL® Mixed
   Vegetables, drained**

1. Melt margarine over medium heat in large skillet; brown beef.

2. Add flour; mix well.

3. Add onion, garlic, thyme, bay leaf, salt, pepper, sugar, beer and broth; mix well. Transfer to large casserole.

4. Place casserole in 350°F oven; bake 1½ hours or until meat is tender, adding Veg-All® 15 minutes before done.

5. Remove and discard bay leaf; serve.
Makes 6 servings

Prime Ribs of Beef à la Lawry's®

1 (8-pound) prime rib roast
LAWRY'S® Seasoned Salt
Rock salt

Preheat oven to 500°F.

Score fat on meat and rub generously with Seasoned Salt. Cover bottom of roasting pan with rock salt 1 inch deep. Place roast directly on rock salt and bake, uncovered, 8 minutes per pound for rare.

Makes 8 servings

 *The USA Rice Council is the nonprofit, nonbranded market development association for the United States' rice industry. It is funded by rice farmers and mills. The Rice Council's mission is to promote the use of U.S. grown rice in domestic and international markets and to unite all segments of the industry for its common good.*

Sherried Beef

¾ pound boneless beef top round steak
1 cup water
¼ cup dry sherry
3 tablespoons soy sauce
2 large carrots, cut into diagonal slices
1 large green pepper, cut into strips
1 medium onion, cut into chunks
2 tablespoons vegetable oil, divided
1 tablespoon cornstarch
2 cups hot cooked rice

Partially freeze steak; slice across grain into ⅛-inch strips. Combine water, sherry, and soy sauce. Pour over beef in dish; marinate 1 hour. Stir-fry vegetables in 1 tablespoon oil in large skillet over medium-high heat. Remove from skillet; set aside. Drain beef; reserve marinade. Brown beef in remaining 1 tablespoon oil. Combine cornstarch with marinade in bowl. Add vegetables and marinade to beef. Cook, stirring, until sauce is thickened; cook 1 minute longer. Serve over rice.

Makes 4 servings

Favorite recipe from **USA Rice Council**

Beef Storage Tip

If meat will be cooked within 6 hours of purchase, leave in package.

Otherwise, remove packaging and store unwrapped in refrigerator's meat compartment up to 2 days for ground beef and 3 days for other cuts.

Szechuan Beef & Snow Peas

½ pound boneless tender beef steak
    (sirloin, rib eye or top loin)
2 tablespoons cornstarch, divided
3 tablespoons KIKKOMAN® Soy Sauce,
    divided
1 tablespoon dry sherry
1 clove garlic, minced
¾ cup water
¼ to ½ teaspoon crushed red pepper
2 tablespoons vegetable oil, divided
6 ounces fresh snow peas, trimmed
1 medium onion, chunked
    Salt
1 medium tomato, chunked
    Hot cooked rice

Slice beef across grain into thin strips.
Combine 1 tablespoon *each* cornstarch and
soy sauce with sherry and garlic in small
bowl; stir in beef. Let stand 15 minutes.
Meanwhile, combine water, remaining 1
tablespoon cornstarch, 2 tablespoons soy
sauce and red pepper; set aside. Heat 1
tablespoon oil in hot wok or large skillet over
high heat. Add beef and stir-fry 1 minute;
remove. Heat remaining 1 tablespoon oil in
same pan. Add snow peas and onion; lightly
sprinkle with salt and stir-fry 3 minutes. Add
beef, soy sauce mixture and tomato. Cook
and stir until sauce boils and thickens and
tomato is heated through. Serve immediately
with rice.   *Makes 2 to 3 servings*

Fantastic Stir-Fried Beef Fajitas

1 pound beef top round or boneless
    chuck shoulder steaks, cut ½ inch
    thick
1 green or red bell pepper, cut
    lengthwise into thin strips
1 medium onion, cut lengthwise into
    thin wedges
8 flour tortillas (8 inches), warmed
1 cup shredded Co-Jack cheese
1 cup prepared picante sauce
2 avocados, peeled, seeded, cut
    lengthwise into thin slices

Marinade

2 tablespoons orange juice
2 tablespoons white vinegar
1 teaspoon finely chopped garlic *or*
    1 large clove garlic, crushed
½ teaspoon ground cumin
½ teaspoon ground oregano
⅛ teaspoon salt
⅛ teaspoon pepper

1. Combine marinade ingredients. Trim fat
from beef steak. Cut steak lengthwise in half
and then crosswise into ⅛-inch-thick strips.
Place beef and half of marinade in
resealable plastic food storage bag, turning
to coat. Close bag securely and marinate in
refrigerator 6 to 8 hours or overnight, if
desired, turning occasionally.

2. Place bell pepper, onion and remaining
marinade in separate resealable plastic food
storage bag, turning to coat. Close bag
securely and marinate in refrigerator while
marinating beef.

Fantastic Stir-Fried Beef Fajitas

3. Heat large nonstick skillet over medium-high heat until hot. Remove vegetables from marinade. Add vegetables to skillet and stir-fry 3 minutes or until crisp-tender. Remove from skillet.

4. Heat same skillet until hot. Remove beef from marinade; discard marinade. Add beef to skillet and stir-fry (½ at a time) 1 to 2 minutes or until outside surface is no longer pink. *Do not overcook.* Return vegetables to skillet; toss to combine.

5. Serve beef and vegetable mixture in tortillas; serve with cheese, picante sauce and avocados.   *Makes 4 servings*

*Favorite recipe from **National Live Stock & Meat Board***

Gazpacho Steak Roll

1 (2-pound) beef flank steak, butterflied
⅔ cup A.1.® Steak Sauce
1 cup (4 ounces) shredded Monterey
    Jack cheese
½ cup chopped tomato
⅓ cup chopped cucumber
¼ cup chopped green pepper
2 tablespoons sliced green onion

Open butterflied steak like a book on smooth surface and flatten slightly. Spread ⅓ cup steak sauce over surface. Layer remaining ingredients over sauce. Roll up steak from short edge; secure with wooden toothpicks or tie with string if necessary.

Grill steak roll over medium heat for 30 to 40 minutes or until done, turning and brushing often with remaining steak sauce during last 10 minutes of cooking. Remove toothpicks; slice and serve garnished as desired.

Makes 8 servings

Spicy Teriyaki Glazed Beef Short Ribs

½ cup KIKKOMAN® Teriyaki Baste &
    Glaze
2 tablespoons minced green onions
    and tops
2 cloves garlic, pressed
1 teaspoon crushed red pepper
½ teaspoon vegetable oil
2 pounds beef short ribs, trimmed of
    excess fat and cut crosswise into
    ½-inch-thick slices

Combine teriyaki baste & glaze, green onions, garlic, red pepper and oil. Place ribs on grill 4 to 5 inches from hot coals; brush with baste & glaze mixture. Cook 5 minutes, turning over and brushing frequently with remaining baste & glaze mixture. (Or, place ribs on rack of broiler pan; brush with baste & glaze mixture. Broil 3 minutes; turn over. Brush with remaining baste & glaze mixture. Broil 3 minutes longer.) *Makes 4 servings*

In 1820, King George IV of England asked his royal chef for something outstanding in the way of a steak sauce. The chef experimented with dozens of ingredients and formulations and eventually delivered his masterpiece. The moment King George tasted it, the sauce acquired a name. "This is A-One," the King is said to have proclaimed. And A.1. is the name it has borne ever since. The sauce came to the U.S. in 1906 after being produced and marketed in Great Britain for many years. In 1936, the formula was changed slightly to appeal to more American tastes.

Gazpacho Steak Roll

Greco-American Beef Kabobs

4 large pattypan squash (about
    1 pound), quartered
½ cup water
1½ pounds boneless tender beef steak,
    1½ inches thick
1 large red bell pepper
½ cup KIKKOMAN® Teriyaki Marinade
    & Sauce
2 tablespoons olive oil
4 teaspoons white wine vinegar
2 large bay leaves, each broken into
    4 pieces
1 large clove garlic, pressed
¾ teaspoon dried oregano leaves,
    crumbled

Arrange squash in single layer in microwave-safe dish; add water. Cover. Microwave on HIGH 7 minutes, rotating dish after 4 minutes. Drain squash; cool. Meanwhile, cut beef into 1-inch-square pieces; cut bell pepper into 18 square pieces. Place beef and bell pepper with squash in large plastic food storage bag. Combine teriyaki sauce, oil, vinegar, bay leaves, garlic and oregano; pour over beef and vegetables. Press air out of bag; close top securely. Turn bag over several times to coat all pieces well. Marinate 30 minutes, turning bag over frequently. Thread each of 6 (12-inch) metal or bamboo* skewers alternately with beef and vegetables. Place kabobs 5 inches from hot coals. Cook 3 minutes on each side (for rare), or to desired doneness. (Or, place kabobs on rack of broiler pan. Broil 5 inches from heat 3 minutes on each side [for rare], or to desired doneness.) *Makes 4 to 6 servings*

*Soak bamboo skewers in water 30 minutes to prevent burning.

Teriyaki Glazed Beef Kabobs

1¼ to 1½ pounds beef top or bottom
    sirloin, cut into 1-inch cubes
½ cup bottled teriyaki glaze
1 teaspoon Oriental sesame oil
    (optional)
1 clove garlic, minced
8 to 12 green onions
1 or 2 plum tomatoes, cut into slices
    (optional)

Thread beef cubes on metal or bamboo skewers. (Soak bamboo skewers in water for at least 20 minutes to keep them from burning.) Combine teriyaki glaze, sesame oil and garlic in small bowl. Brush beef and onions with part of glaze, saving some for grilling; let stand 15 to 30 minutes.

Oil hot grid to help prevent sticking. Grill beef, on covered grill, over medium KINGSFORD® briquets, 6 to 9 minutes for medium doneness, turning several times and brushing with glaze. Add onions and tomatoes, if desired, to grid 3 to 4 minutes after beef; grill until onions and tomatoes are tender. Remove from grill; brush skewers, onions and tomatoes with remaining glaze.

Makes 4 servings

Hunt's®

From rather modest beginnings, Hunt-Wesson has grown steadily to become one of the largest and most successful food companies in the nation. Brothers Joseph and William Hunt established their company as the Hunt Brothers Food Packing Company in 1890. In 1960, they merged with Wesson Oil and Snowdrift Company and became Hunt-Wesson Foods. Some of their widely recognized brand name products include Hunt's tomato products, Wesson oil, Peter Pan peanut butter and Orville Redenbacher's popping corn.

Hunt's® Marvelous Meatloaf

1½ **pounds ground beef**
12 **ounces pork sausage, casings removed**
1 **(8-ounce) can HUNT'S® Tomato Sauce, divided**
1 **cup finely chopped onions**
¾ **cup fine, dry bread crumbs**
½ **cup finely chopped celery**
1 **egg**
1 **teaspoon garlic salt**
½ **teaspoon rubbed sage**
½ **cup HUNT'S® Tomato Ketchup**

In large bowl, combine ground beef, sausage, ½ cup tomato sauce, onions, bread crumbs, celery, egg, garlic salt and sage until well blended. Place mixture in shallow baking pan; form into loaf. Bake, uncovered, at 375°F for 1 hour 15 minutes; drain. Meanwhile, in small bowl, combine remaining tomato sauce and ketchup. Spoon over loaf, coating well. Bake 15 minutes longer.

Makes 8 servings

Potato Topped Meat Loaf

1 **jar (12 ounces) HEINZ® HomeStyle Mushroom or Brown Gravy**
1½ **pounds lean ground beef**
1 **cup soft bread crumbs**
¼ **cup finely chopped onion**
1 **egg, slightly beaten**
½ **teaspoon salt**
  Dash pepper
2½ **cups hot mashed potatoes**
1 **tablespoon melted butter or margarine**
  Paprika

Measure ¼ cup gravy from jar; combine with beef, bread crumbs, onion, egg, salt and pepper. Shape into 8×4×1½-inch loaf in shallow baking pan. Bake in 350°F oven 1 hour. Remove from oven and carefully drain fat. Spread potatoes over top and sides of meat loaf. Drizzle melted butter over potatoes; garnish with paprika. Return meat loaf to oven; bake additional 20 minutes. Let stand 5 minutes. Heat remaining gravy and serve with meat loaf slices.

Makes 6 servings

Grilled Meat Loaf and Potatoes

1 pound ground beef
½ cup A.1.® Steak Sauce
½ cup plain dry bread crumbs
1 egg
¼ cup finely chopped green bell pepper
¼ cup finely chopped onion
2 tablespoons margarine, melted
4 (6-ounce) red skin potatoes, parboiled and sliced into ¼-inch-thick rounds
Grated Parmesan cheese

In large bowl, combine ground beef, ¼ cup steak sauce, bread crumbs, egg, pepper and onion. Divide mixture and shape into 4 (4-inch) oval loaves. In small bowl, combine remaining ¼ cup steak sauce and margarine; set aside.

Over medium heat, grill meat loaves for 20 to 25 minutes and potato slices for 10 to 12 minutes, turning and brushing both occasionally with steak sauce mixture. Sprinkle potatoes with Parmesan cheese; serve immediately. *Makes 4 servings*

Souperior Meat Loaf

1 envelope LIPTON® Recipe Secrets® Onion Soup Mix
2 pounds ground beef
1½ cups fresh bread crumbs
2 eggs
¾ cup water
⅓ cup ketchup

Grilled Meat Loaf and Potatoes

Preheat oven to 350°F. In large bowl, combine all ingredients. In 13×9-inch baking or roasting pan, shape into loaf. Bake 1 hour or until done. Let stand 10 minutes before serving. *Makes about 8 servings*

The first sauce!
The finest sauce!
The best sauce of all!

BRAND'S A.I. *THE ORIGINAL THICK SAUCE*
A fine digestive & an excellent relish
BRAND & CO LTD. MAYFAIR WORKS, VAUXHALL

A.1. Steak Sauce got its name when King George IV of England tasted it and proclaimed, "This is A-One."

Chef Paul Prudhomme

Chef Paul Prudhomme is well-known not only for his celebrated New Orleans restaurant, K-Paul's Louisiana Kitchen, but also for his warmth, knowledge and personality. Due to the popularity of his famous eatery, Chef Paul's Magic Seasoning Blends® became available nationally. The seasoning blends allow you to recreate the wonderful fresh tasting foods of Louisiana by combining an array of seasonings in just the right combination to build on and improve food's taste. The seven original spice blends plus a number of new products can be used as cooking ingredients or sprinkled on as condiments at the table.

Wonderful Meat Loaf

4 tablespoons unsalted butter
¾ cup finely chopped onion
½ cup finely chopped celery
½ cup finely chopped green bell pepper
¼ cup finely chopped green onions
2 tablespoons plus ½ teaspoon Chef Paul Prudhomme's MEAT MAGIC®
1 tablespoon Worcestershire sauce
2 teaspoons minced garlic
2 bay leaves
½ cup evaporated milk
½ cup ketchup
1½ pounds ground beef
½ pound ground pork
2 eggs, lightly beaten
1 cup very fine dry bread crumbs

Preheat oven to 350°F. Melt butter in 1-quart saucepan over medium heat. Add onion, celery, bell pepper, green onions, Meat Magic®, Worcestershire sauce, garlic and bay leaves. Cook and stir until mixture starts sticking excessively, about 6 minutes, stirring occasionally and scraping pan bottom well. Stir in milk and ketchup. Cook about 2 minutes, stirring occasionally. Cool to room temperature. Discard bay leaves.

Place ground beef and pork in ungreased 13×9-inch baking pan. Add eggs, cooked vegetable mixture and bread crumbs. Mix by hand until thoroughly combined. In center of pan, shape mixture into 12×6×1½-inch loaf. Bake, uncovered, 25 minutes. Increase heat to 400°F; bake until no longer pink in center, about 35 minutes longer. Serve immediately.

Makes 6 servings

Cheeseburger Pie

Cheeseburger Pie

1 (9-inch) unbaked pastry shell
8 slices BORDEN® Process American
    Cheese Food
1 pound lean ground beef
½ cup tomato sauce
⅓ cup chopped green bell pepper
⅓ cup chopped onion
1 teaspoon WYLER'S® or STEERO®
    Beef-Flavor Instant Bouillon *or*
    1 Beef-Flavor Bouillon Cube
3 eggs, beaten
2 tablespoons flour
    Chopped tomato and shredded
    lettuce (optional)

Preheat oven to 425°. Bake pastry shell 8 minutes. Remove from oven. *Reduce oven temperature to 350°.* Meanwhile, cut *6 slices* cheese food into pieces. In large skillet, brown meat; pour off fat. Add tomato sauce, green pepper, onion and bouillon; cook and stir until bouillon dissolves. Remove from heat; stir in eggs, flour and cheese food pieces. Turn into prepared pastry shell. Bake 20 to 25 minutes or until hot. Arrange remaining *2 slices* cheese food on top. Return to oven 3 minutes or until cheese food begins to melt. Garnish with tomato and lettuce if desired. Refrigerate leftovers.

Makes one 9-inch pie

Deep Dish All-American Pizza

Sauce

1 pound lean ground beef
½ cup chopped onion
½ cup chopped green pepper
1 cup ketchup
1 tablespoon Worcestershire sauce
1 teaspoon dry mustard
1 teaspoon garlic salt
¼ teaspoon black pepper

Crust

3 to 3½ cups all-purpose flour, divided
1 package RED STAR® Active Dry Yeast
    or QUICK•RISE™ Yeast
1½ teaspoons salt
1 cup warm water
3 tablespoons oil

Toppings

2 medium firm, ripe tomatoes, sliced
1 cup sliced fresh mushrooms
2 cups (8 ounces) shredded Cheddar
    cheese

Preheat oven to 425°F.

Cook and stir beef, onion and green pepper in skillet until meat is lightly browned; drain if necessary. Add ketchup, Worcestershire sauce, mustard, garlic salt and black pepper. Simmer 15 minutes.

In large mixer bowl, combine 1½ cups flour, yeast and salt; mix well. Add very warm water (120° to 130°F) and oil to flour mixture. Blend at low speed until moistened; beat 3 minutes at medium speed. Gradually stir in enough remaining flour to make a firm dough.

Knead 3 to 5 minutes on floured surface. Lightly flour surface and roll dough into 16-inch circle or 15×11-inch rectangle. Place in greased 14-inch-round deep-dish pizza pan or 13×9-inch baking pan, pushing dough halfway up sides of pan. Cover; let rise in warm place about 15 minutes.

Spread sauce over dough. Arrange tomatoes on sauce. Sprinkle mushrooms on top. Sprinkle with cheese. Bake 20 to 25 minutes until edge is crisp and golden brown and cheese is melted. Serve immediately.

*Makes one 14-inch-round or
13×9-inch deep-dish pizza*

Tip: Pizza may also be baked in lasagna pan.

Universal Foods Corporation incorporated in Wisconsin in 1882 as Meadow Springs Distilling Company. Because of prohibition, the name was changed in 1919 to Red Star Yeast & Products. The company was instrumental in the development of active dry yeast and produced it for the Army during World War II. The company is now the largest manufacturer of yeast in the United States.

Chex® Mexican Pie

Chex® Mexican Pie

1 pound lean ground beef
1 can (10¾ ounces) condensed tomato
   soup
1 egg, beaten
1 package (1.25 ounces) taco
   seasoning mix, dry
4 cups CORN CHEX® brand cereal,
   crushed to 2 cups, divided
½ cup (2 ounces) shredded Cheddar or
   Monterey Jack cheese
1 large tomato, chopped
¼ cup chopped green onions
¼ cup sliced stuffed green olives
2 tablespoons chopped parsley

Preheat oven to 375°F. Combine ground beef, soup, egg and taco seasoning until well blended; stir in 1½ cups cereal. Press meat mixture evenly onto bottom and side of 10-inch quiche dish or pie plate, forming 1-inch-wide rim. Sprinkle remaining ½ cup cereal on top of rim; press gently. Bake 30 to 35 minutes or until brown. Sprinkle cheese over center of pie. Top with tomato, onions, olives and parsley; let stand 5 minutes before serving. *Makes 8 servings*

National Live Stock & Meat Board

The Meat Board has affected the lives and diets of Americans. In 1973, 315 cuts of meat carried 1,000 different names. By developing a list of standardized names, consumers could get the same cut of meat in Kansas City as they did in Los Angeles. The Meat Board also initiated a new series of studies on meat composition proving that modern, leaner livestock did indeed make leaner meat.

Osso Buco

4 pounds veal cross cut shanks, cut 1½ inches thick
2 tablespoons olive oil
1 teaspoon salt
1 cup chopped onions
½ cup finely chopped carrot
3 cloves garlic, crushed
1 can (14½ to 16 ounces) Italian-style diced tomatoes, undrained
1 cup dry white wine
1 teaspoon dried basil leaves
Gremolata (recipe follows)

1. In Dutch oven, heat ½ the oil over medium heat until hot. Add veal shanks (⅓ at a time) and brown evenly, stirring occasionally; add remaining oil as necessary. Remove from pan; season with salt.

2. In same pan, add onions, carrot and garlic; cook 6 to 8 minutes or until vegetables are tender, stirring occasionally.

3. Add tomatoes, wine and basil. Bring to a boil over high heat, stirring to dissolve any brown bits attached to pan. Return veal to pan. Reduce heat; cover tightly and simmer 1½ hours or until veal is tender.

4. Meanwhile, prepare Gremolata; set aside.

5. Remove veal to warm platter. Skim off fat from cooking liquid. Return cooking liquid to pan; bring to a boil. Cook until slightly thickened, stirring occasionally. Spoon about ¾ cup sauce over shanks; sprinkle with reserved Gremolata. Serve with remaining sauce.   *Makes 6 servings*

Gremolata: Combine 1 tablespoon chopped fresh parsley, 2 teaspoons shredded lemon peel and ½ teaspoon finely chopped garlic.

Cook's Tips: To retain shape, veal cross cut shanks may be tied with string before cooking. Remove string before serving.

To prepare in oven, use covered, ovenproof Dutch oven or roasting pan. After veal is added to tomato mixture, cook in preheated 325°F oven; cooking time remains the same.

*Favorite recipe from **National Live Stock & Meat Board***

Carolina Barbecue

1 (5-pound) Boston butt roast
2 teaspoons vegetable oil
1½ cups water
1 can (8 ounces) tomato sauce
¼ cup packed brown sugar
¼ cup cider vinegar
¼ cup Worcestershire sauce
    Salt and pepper, to taste
1 teaspoon celery seeds
1 teaspoon chili powder
    Dash hot pepper sauce

Randomly pierce roast with sharp knife. In Dutch oven, brown roast on all sides in hot oil. In mixing bowl, combine remaining ingredients; mix well. Pour sauce over roast and bring to a boil. Reduce heat; cover and simmer 2 hours or until pork is fork-tender. Baste roast with sauce during cooking time. Slice or chop to serve.

Makes 20 servings

*Favorite recipe from **National Pork Producers Council***

Honey Sesame Tenderloin

1 pound pork tenderloin
½ cup soy sauce
2 cloves garlic, minced
1 tablespoon grated fresh ginger *or*
    1 teaspoon dry ginger
1 tablespoon sesame oil
¼ cup honey
2 tablespoons brown sugar
4 tablespoons sesame seeds

Combine soy sauce, garlic, ginger and sesame oil. Place tenderloin in resealable plastic food storage bag; pour soy mixture over to coat. Let marinate 2 hours at room temperature or overnight in refrigerator. Remove pork from marinade; pat dry. Mix together honey and brown sugar in shallow plate. Place sesame seeds on separate shallow plate. Roll pork in honey mixture, coating well; roll in sesame seeds. Roast in shallow pan at 400°F for 20 to 30 minutes, until meat thermometer inserted registers 160°F. Remove to serving platter; slice thinly to serve.

Makes 4 servings

*Favorite recipe from **National Pork Producers Council***

National Pork Producers Council

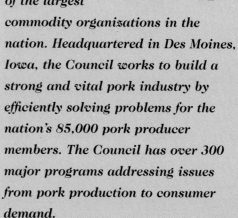

The National Pork Producers Council is one of the largest commodity organizations in the nation. Headquartered in Des Moines, Iowa, the Council works to build a strong and vital pork industry by efficiently solving problems for the nation's 85,000 pork producer members. The Council has over 300 major programs addressing issues from pork production to consumer demand.

Micro-Grilled Pork Ribs

1 tablespoon firmly packed brown
   sugar
2 teaspoons ground cumin
1 teaspoon salt
½ teaspoon black pepper
   Dash ground red pepper (optional)
3 pounds pork back ribs
⅓ cup water
½ cup K.C. MASTERPIECE® Barbecue
   Sauce
   Grilled Sweet Potatoes (recipe
   follows)

Combine brown sugar, cumin, salt and
peppers in small bowl. Rub onto ribs.
Arrange ribs in single layer in 13×9-inch
microwave-safe baking dish. Pour water over
ribs; cover loosely with plastic wrap.
Microwave on MEDIUM-HIGH (70% power)
15 minutes, rearranging ribs and rotating dish
halfway through cooking time.

Arrange medium-hot KINGSFORD® briquets
on one side of grill. Place ribs on grid area
opposite briquets. Barbecue ribs, on covered
grill, 15 to 20 minutes, turning every 5
minutes and basting with sauce the last 10
minutes. Ribs should be browned and cooked
through. Serve with Grilled Sweet Potatoes.
Makes 4 servings

**Grilled Sweet Potatoes or Baking
Potatoes:** Slice potatoes into ¼-inch-thick
rounds, allowing about ⅓ pound potatoes per
serving. Brush both sides of slices lightly with
oil. Place on grid around edges of medium-
hot Kingsford® briquets. Cook potatoes, on
covered grill, 10 to 12 minutes until golden
brown and tender, turning once.

In the early 1900s, Henry Ford operated a northern Michigan sawmill that made wooden framing for his Model Ts. As piles of wood scraps grew, he searched for a way to make them useful. He soon learned how to chip the wood and convert it into the now familiar pillow-shaped briquets. These convenient briquets, originally sold through Ford automobile agencies, marked the beginning of the all-American tradition of barbecuing. Ford charcoal, later named Kingsford® charcoal briquets, is the original and still the number one brand sold in the nation today.

*Top to bottom: Micro-Grilled Pork Ribs and
Grilled Sweet Potatoes*

Spareribs with Zesty Honey Sauce

1 cup chili sauce
½ to ¾ cup honey
¼ cup minced onion
2 tablespoons dry red wine (optional)
1 tablespoon Worcestershire sauce
1 teaspoon Dijon-style mustard
3 pounds pork spareribs
Salt and pepper

Combine chili sauce, honey, onion, wine, if desired, Worcestershire sauce and mustard in small saucepan. Cook and stir over medium heat until mixture comes to a boil. Reduce heat to low and simmer, uncovered, 5 minutes.

Sprinkle spareribs with salt and pepper. Place on rack in roasting pan; cover with foil. Roast at 375°F 35 to 45 minutes. Uncover and brush generously with sauce. Roast 45 minutes, brushing with sauce every 15 minutes, until spareribs are fully cooked and tender. Cut spareribs into serving portions and serve with remaining sauce.

Makes 4 servings

Favorite recipe from **National Honey Board**

Stuffed Pork Chops

4 rib pork chops, cut 1¼ inches thick,
    slit for stuffing
1½ cups prepared stuffing
1 tablespoon vegetable oil
Salt and pepper
1 bottle (12 ounces) HEINZ® Chili Sauce

Trim excess fat from chops. Place stuffing in pockets of chops; secure with toothpicks. Brown chops in oil; season with salt and pepper. Place chops in 2-quart oblong baking dish. Pour chili sauce over chops. Cover dish with foil; bake in 350°F oven, 30 minutes. Stir sauce to blend; turn and baste chops. Cover; bake additional 30 to 40 minutes or until chops are tender. Remove toothpicks from chops. Skim excess fat from sauce.

Makes 4 servings

National Honey Board

The honey bee is the only insect that produces food eaten by man. Bees have been producing honey for 15 million years; man has harvested honey for three million years. Honey is also the only natural sweetener that needs no additional refining or processing to be utilized. Honey bees must tap two million flowers, flying over 55,000 miles, to make one pound of honey.

® © NHB

Spareribs with Zesty Honey Sauce

Chorizos with Onions à la Gonzalez

1 or 2 large Spanish onions sliced
    wafer thin to cover bottom of
    roasting pan
2 or 3 pounds CORTE'S® CHORIZOS*
1 or 2 bay leaves
½ cup dry white wine or wine and
    chicken broth combined to equal
    ½ cup

*Mexican sausage is available in the meat section of the supermarket.

Place onions in roasting pan. Cut chorizos diagonally into ⅜-inch pieces. Place over onions. Add bay leaves and wine. Bake at 375°F for 40 minutes or until crisp, turning once. Remove and discard bay leaves before serving. *Makes 8 servings*

Honey Glazed Ham

¼ cup honey
3 tablespoons water
1½ teaspoons dry mustard
½ teaspoon ground ginger
¼ teaspoon ground cloves
1 fully cooked ham steak (about 12 to
    16 ounces)
    Fresh sage leaves for garnish
    (optional)

Combine honey, water and spices in small bowl. On top rack of preheated oven broiler, broil ham steak on both sides until lightly browned and thoroughly heated. Or, pan-fry ham steak on both sides in nonstick skillet over medium-high heat.

Place ham on heated serving dish; set aside. Add honey mixture to pan drippings and bring to a boil. Simmer 1 to 2 minutes, stirring. Brush sauce over ham; serve remaining sauce separately. Garnish with fresh sage leaves, if desired. *Makes 4 servings*

Favorite recipe from **National Honey Board**

Corte & Co.

Established in 1922, Corte & Co. manufactures Spanish and Portuguese sausages. Their chorizo sausages were developed for use in the kitchens of the Spanish Pavilion at the 1965 World's Fair in New York. Spicy or spicy hot, these smoked sausages have universal appeal for adding some zest to your favorite dish.

Herb Crusted Racks of Lamb

Herb Crusted Racks of Lamb

**2 racks of American lamb (8 ribs each),
let stand at room temperature for
20 minutes***
1 cup finely chopped parsley
1 medium onion, finely chopped
**1 tablespoon fresh dill weed, chopped,
or 1 teaspoon dried dill weed**
¼ cup fine dry bread crumbs
**2 teaspoons fresh oregano leaves,
chopped, *or* ½ teaspoon dried
oregano**
1 teaspoon salt
⅛ teaspoon ground pepper

*If lamb is roasted at refrigerator temperature, add
10 minutes to cooking time.

Preheat oven to 425°F. Combine all
ingredients, except lamb; mix well. Pat
mixture on outside of lamb.

Place on broiler rack in shallow roasting pan.
Roast 30 minutes for medium rare.
Makes 4 servings

Note: Have butcher remove chine bone (back
bone) and all excess fat.

*Favorite recipe from **American Lamb Council***

Homestyle Ground Lamb Gyros

1 pound ground American lamb
2 tablespoons snipped parsley
1 large clove garlic, pressed
2 teaspoons lemon juice
½ teaspoon dried basil leaves
½ teaspoon dried thyme leaves
½ teaspoon rosemary
½ teaspoon pepper
¼ teaspoon ground marjoram
¼ teaspoon salt
6 pita pockets
2 tomatoes, chopped
2 onions, chopped

Sauce

2 cups sour cream
1 medium cucumber, processed in
    blender and strained to remove
    liquid
2 cloves garlic, pressed
¼ teaspoon salt
2 tablespoons sugar

Combine lamb, parsley, 1 clove garlic, lemon juice, basil, thyme, rosemary, pepper, ¼ teaspoon salt and marjoram in large mixing bowl; blend well.

Place mixture in large skillet; cook over medium heat, stirring constantly until meat is browned. Drain off excess drippings. Combine sour cream, cucumber, 2 cloves garlic, ¼ teaspoon salt and sugar in bowl; blend well.

Cut pita pockets in half; spoon in meat mixture. Top with tomatoes and onions. Spoon sauce over each sandwich and serve immediately.   *Makes 6 servings*

*Favorite recipe from **American Lamb Council***

Stir-Fry Lamb with Flower Buns

Flower Buns (recipe follows)
¾ pound boneless lamb leg or shoulder
4 tablespoons KIKKOMAN® Soy Sauce,
    divided
2 tablespoons cornstarch, divided
1 clove garlic, minced
¼ cup water
3 tablespoons vegetable oil, divided
1 teaspoon minced fresh gingerroot
½ pound fresh bean sprouts
¼ pound fresh snow peas, trimmed and
    cut into julienne strips
2 medium carrots, cut into julienne
    strips

Prepare Flower Buns. Cut lamb into thin strips. Combine 1 tablespoon *each* soy sauce and cornstarch with garlic in medium bowl; stir in lamb. Let stand 10 minutes. Meanwhile, combine remaining 3 tablespoons soy sauce, 1 tablespoon cornstarch and water; set aside. Heat 1 tablespoon oil in hot wok or large skillet over high heat. Add lamb and stir-fry 1 minute; remove. Heat remaining 2 tablespoons oil in same pan. Add ginger; stir-fry 30 seconds. Add bean sprouts, snow peas and carrots; stir-fry 2 minutes. Add lamb and soy sauce mixture. Cook and stir until sauce boils and thickens. Serve immediately with Flower Buns.   *Makes 4 to 6 servings*

Flower Buns

2 cups quick biscuit mix
2 tablespoons chopped green onion
    and tops
1 tablespoon sugar
⅓ cup plus 1 tablespoon water
All-purpose flour
Vegetable oil

Combine quick biscuit mix, green onion and sugar. Add water all at once; stir to form soft dough. Turn out onto lightly floured surface; knead gently 30 seconds. Divide dough in half; roll out half of dough to 9-inch square. Brush lightly with vegetable oil, leaving 1-inch border at top edge. Starting at bottom edge, roll up dough, jelly-roll fashion; seal edge. Cut roll crosswise into 6 equal slices. Firmly press center of each slice, parallel to cut edges, with chopstick. Place on greased steamer rack; set wire rack in large saucepan or wok of boiling water. *(Do not allow water level to reach buns.)* Cover and steam 12 minutes. Remove to rack placed over cake pan and keep warm in 200°F oven. Repeat procedure with remaining dough.

Makes 12 buns

In Los Angeles in 1938, Frank Lawrence opened a restaurant like one he heard of in London, where prime rib was carved and served at the table. He wanted to call it Larry's but decided Lawry's sounded more English. From salad greens tossed tableside to valet parking, the successful eatery brought many firsts to the U.S. restaurant scene. Lawrence also turned his home kitchen into a lab to create the world's largest selling spice blend, Lawry's® Seasoned Salt.

Lemon Lamb Lawry's®

2 teaspoons LAWRY'S® Lemon Pepper
1 cup water
2 pounds boneless lamb, cut into
**   1-inch cubes**
2 tablespoons vegetable oil
1 large onion, sliced
1 tablespoon olive oil
½ cup lemon juice
1 teaspoon LAWRY'S® Seasoned Salt
1½ pounds fresh green beans, cut into
**   1-inch pieces**
1 teaspoon dried oregano

In small bowl, combine Lemon Pepper and water; let stand while browning lamb. In large skillet or Dutch oven, brown lamb well in vegetable oil; add onion and sauté. Add olive oil and toss with lamb and onion to coat. Add water mixture, lemon juice, Seasoned Salt, green beans and oregano. Bring to a boil; reduce heat. Cover and simmer 1 hour, stirring occasionally. Add additional ¼ cup water during cooking if necessary.

Makes 6 servings

Presentation: Serve with tossed green salad and crusty bread.

Grecian Lamb Kabobs

1 cup dry white wine
¼ cup olive oil
24 bay leaves
12 strips lemon peel, about 3 inches
2 medium onions, peeled, cut into
    9 wedges and wedges cut in half
½ teaspoon salt
¼ teaspoon black pepper
2 pounds boneless leg of American
    lamb, cut into 1-inch cubes
2 green peppers, cut into 1-inch pieces
12 cherry tomatoes
    Minted Orzo (recipe follows)

Combine wine, olive oil, bay leaves, lemon peel, onions, salt and black pepper in large bowl. Pour into large resealable plastic bag. Add lamb. Marinate overnight; turn lamb once. Alternate lamb, bay leaves and lemon peel on skewers. On separate skewers, alternate peppers and onions; brush kabobs with marinade. Boil remaining marinade 1 minute. Broil kabobs 5 to 7 minutes each side. Add tomato to end of each lamb kabob during last 3 minutes. Baste with marinade throughout cooking. Serve with Minted Orzo.

Makes 6 servings

Minted Orzo

1 package (12 ounces) orzo pasta
2 tablespoons chopped fresh mint
2 teaspoons grated lemon peel
    Salt and pepper to taste

Cook orzo in boiling water about 5 minutes. Drain and toss with remaining ingredients.

*Favorite recipe from **American Lamb Council***

Grilled Lamb Chops with Rosemary Plum Sauce

4 well-trimmed lamb shoulder arm or
    blade chops, cut ¾ inch thick

Marinade

½ cup plum preserves
2 tablespoons white wine vinegar
2 tablespoons Worcestershire sauce
1 tablespoon fresh rosemary, snipped,
    or 1 teaspoon dried rosemary
    leaves, crushed
2 cloves garlic, crushed
1 teaspoon pepper
½ teaspoon salt

1. Combine marinade ingredients. Cover and refrigerate ⅓ cup marinade for brushing on lamb chops during grilling. Place chops in plastic bag; add remaining marinade, turning to coat. Close bag securely and marinate in refrigerator 6 to 8 hours (or overnight, if desired), turning occasionally.

2. Remove chops from marinade; discard marinade. Place chops on grid over medium coals. Grill 12 to 14 minutes for rare to medium doneness, turning once. Brush both sides of chops with reserved marinade during last 5 minutes of grilling.

Makes 4 servings

*Favorite recipe from **National Live Stock & Meat Board***

Grecian Lamb Kabobs

Maple Cherry Sauce

⅓ cup cherry juice blend or water
2 tablespoons cornstarch
1 cup frozen unsweetened tart cherries, thawed and well drained
1 teaspoon grated orange peel
¾ cup maple-flavored syrup
½ cup chopped walnuts

In medium saucepan, combine cherry juice blend and cornstarch; mix well. Cook over medium heat until thickened. Add cherries, orange peel, syrup and walnuts; mix well. Cook, stirring frequently, over low heat until all ingredients are hot. Serve warm over roasted or grilled meats. *Makes 1½ cups*

*Favorite recipe from **Cherry Marketing Institute, Inc.***

Pimiento Sauce

1 can (10¾ ounces) cream of celery soup
1 can (4 ounces) pimiento pieces, drained
¼ cup sour cream
1 teaspoon Italian seasoning
3 to 4 drops hot pepper sauce

Add soup, pimiento and sour cream to blender or food processor. Process until smooth. Add to large saucepan. Stir in seasonings; heat through and serve with meat, fish or hot, cooked spaghetti squash. *Makes 2 cups*

*Favorite recipe from **Canned Food Information Council***

Golden Mushroom Sauce

2 tablespoons butter or margarine
2 tablespoons chopped shallots
1 can (10¾ ounces) condensed golden mushroom soup
⅓ cup water
¼ cup dry red wine
1 tablespoon chopped fresh parsley

In 2-quart saucepan over medium heat, cook butter until hot. Add shallots; cook until tender, stirring occasionally. Stir in soup, water, wine and parsley; heat until boiling, stirring frequently. Serve over beef, lamb or meat loaf. *Makes 2 cups*

*Favorite recipe from **Canned Food Information Council***

Orient Express Stir-Fry Sauce

2½ cups chicken broth
½ cup ARGO® or KINGSFORD'S® Corn Starch
½ cup soy sauce
½ cup KARO® Light Corn Syrup
½ cup dry sherry
¼ cup cider vinegar
2 cloves garlic, minced or pressed
2 teaspoons grated fresh ginger
¼ teaspoon ground red pepper

Combine all ingredients in 1½-quart jar with tight-fitting lid. Shake well. Store in refrigerator up to 3 weeks. Shake well before using. *Makes about 4 cups*

Maple Cherry Sauce

Smucker's® Orange Chili Barbecue Sauce

**1 cup SMUCKER'S® Sweet Orange
      Marmalade**
**1 cup tomato sauce or crushed
      tomatoes packed in tomato purée**
2 tablespoons chili powder
2 tablespoons red wine vinegar
1 teaspoon ground cumin
1 teaspoon fresh chopped garlic
½ teaspoon salt
**¼ teaspoon cayenne pepper or hot
      pepper sauce (for spicier sauce)**

Combine all ingredients in small saucepan;
mix well. Bring sauce to a boil, stirring
constantly. Reduce heat; simmer 1 minute.

Use sauce immediately as a marinade and
baste for baked or grilled chicken, ribs, beef
or pork. Or, cool and store in refrigerator for
future use.   *Makes 6 servings*

Microwave Directions: Combine all
ingredients in microwavable bowl. Cover with
plastic wrap; microwave at HIGH for 2
minutes. Stir; recover and heat again for 1
minute.

Sweet 'n Spicy Onion Glaze

**1 envelope LIPTON® Recipe Secrets®
      Onion Soup Mix**
1 jar (20 ounces) apricot preserves
**1 cup WISH-BONE® Sweet 'n Spicy
      French Dressing**

In small bowl, blend all ingredients. Use as
glaze for chicken, spareribs, kabobs,
hamburgers or frankfurters. Brush on during
last half of cooking. Glaze can be stored
covered in refrigerator up to 2 weeks.
                              Makes 2½ cups glaze

Note: Recipe can be doubled.

• Also terrific with Wish-Bone® Lite Sweet 'n
Spicy French, Russian or Lite Russian
Dressing.

Honey 'n' Spice Glaze

½ cup HEINZ® 57 Sauce
¼ cup honey

Combine 57 Sauce and honey. Spoon over
sliced ham, ham loaf or pork chops or use as
a glaze for:

Ham: Score ham and stud with whole cloves.
Brush with glaze during last 30 minutes of
baking time.

Chicken: Broil or grill chicken pieces 25 to
30 minutes, turning once. Brush with glaze.
Grill additional 10 to 15 minutes or until
chicken is no longer pink, turning and
brushing with glaze.

Ribs: Broil or grill ribs until tender, turning
and brushing with glaze during last 10 to 15
minutes of cooking time.

Chicken Kabobs: Thread chunks of chicken,
pineapple and green pepper on skewers.
Brush with melted butter, then glaze. Grill or
broil 15 minutes or until chicken is no longer
pink, turning and brushing with glaze.

Ham Glaze

Ham Glaze

1 cup KARO® Light or Dark Corn Syrup
½ cup packed brown sugar
3 tablespoons prepared mustard
½ teaspoon ground ginger
 Dash ground cloves

In medium saucepan, combine corn syrup, brown sugar, mustard, ginger and cloves. Bring to a boil over medium heat; boil 5 minutes, stirring constantly. Brush on ham frequently during last 30 minutes of baking.

Makes about 1 cup

Wish-Bone® Marinade Italiano

½ cup WISH-BONE® Italian Dressing*
2½ to 3 pounds chicken pieces**

*Also terrific with Wish-Bone® Robusto Italian, Lite Italian or Honey Dijon Dressing.

**Variations: Use 1 (2- to 2½-pound) T-bone, boneless sirloin or top loin steak *or* 4 boneless skinless chicken breast halves (about 1 pound) or 2½ pounds center cut pork chops (about 1 inch thick).

In large shallow baking dish or plastic food storage bag, pour Italian dressing over chicken. Cover, or close bag, and marinate in refrigerator, turning occasionally, 3 hours or overnight. Remove chicken, reserving marinade.

Grill or broil chicken, turning and basting frequently with reserved marinade, until chicken is done. Do not brush with marinade last 5 minutes of cooking.

Makes about 4 servings

Balsamic Marinade

2 pounds beef, pork, lamb or veal
½ cup FILIPPO BERIO® Olive Oil
½ cup balsamic vinegar
2 cloves garlic, slivered
1 teaspoon dried oregano leaves
½ teaspoon salt
½ teaspoon dried marjoram leaves
¼ teaspoon freshly ground pepper

Place meat in shallow glass dish. In small bowl, whisk together olive oil, vinegar, garlic, oregano, salt, marjoram and pepper. Pour marinade over meat, using about ½ cup for each pound of meat. Turn to coat both sides. Cover; marinate several hours or overnight, turning meat occasionally. Remove meat; boil marinade 1 minute. Grill meat, brushing frequently with marinade.

Makes 1 cup marinade

Mediterranean Marinade

1 envelope GOOD SEASONS® Italian Salad Dressing Mix
⅓ cup each cider vinegar and olive oil
2 tablespoons lemon juice
1 teaspoon each dried oregano leaves and grated lemon peel (optional)

MIX all ingredients in cruet or medium bowl. Reserve ¼ cup marinade for basting; refrigerate.

POUR remaining marinade over 1 to 1½ pounds meat, poultry, seafood or vegetables; cover and refrigerate as directed on chart on page 105 to marinate. Drain and discard marinade.

BROIL or grill as directed on chart, turning and brushing frequently with reserved marinade. Discard any remaining marinade.

Makes 1 cup

Grilling

U.S. barbecue history began with early Native Americans who were cooking meat over an outdoor fire long before Columbus' arrival. Learning the technique from local Native Americans, the first settlers of Virginia also added a social dimension to the barbecue by holding community gatherings around the outdoor pit. In the mid-1800s, barbecuing hit the U.S. culinary mainstream and was gaining notoriety in the Midwest and South. Today, Kansas City is recognized as the barbecue capital of the world with over 60 barbecue restaurants and its own Barbecue Society.

Italian Marinade

1 envelope GOOD SEASONS® Italian, Zesty Italian or Garlic & Herb Salad Dressing Mix
⅓ cup oil
⅓ cup dry white wine or water
2 tablespoons lemon juice

MIX salad dressing mix, oil, wine and juice in cruet or medium bowl until well blended. Reserve ¼ cup marinade for basting. Refrigerate.

POUR remaining marinade over 1½ to 2 pounds meat, poultry or seafood. Toss to coat well; cover. Refrigerate as directed below to marinate. Drain and discard marinade before grilling.

BROIL or grill as directed below, turning and brushing frequently with reserved marinade. Discard any remaining marinade.

Makes ⅔ cup

MEAT	MARINATING TIME	GRILL/BROIL TIME
Boneless skinless chicken breast halves	1 to 4 hours	10 to 12 minutes
Bone-in chicken pieces	4 hours to overnight	40 to 45 minutes
Beef flank steak	4 hours to overnight	12 to 14 minutes
One-inch beef cubes for kabobs	1 to 4 hours	8 to 10 minutes
Pork chops (¾ inch thick)	4 hours to overnight	10 to 12 minutes
Fish fillets (¾ inch thick)	30 minutes to 1 hour	6 to 8 minutes
Shrimp	30 minutes to 1 hour	3 to 5 minutes
Scallops	30 minutes to 1 hour	5 to 7 minutes
Vegetables	30 minutes to 1 hour	10 to 12 minutes

Pleasing Poultry Picks

Savor the exciting flavors of these chicken and turkey favorites. Fast, easy and versatile, these poultry selections are sure to spice up your dinner menus.

Chicken Morocco

1 cup uncooked bulgur wheat
4 chicken thighs, skinned
½ medium onion, chopped
1 tablespoon olive oil
1 can (14½ ounces) DEL MONTE®
   Original Recipe Stewed Tomatoes
   (No Salt Added)
½ cup DEL MONTE® Prune Juice
6 DEL MONTE® Pitted Prunes, diced
¼ teaspoon ground allspice

In large saucepan, bring 1½ cups water to boil; add bulgur. Cover and cook over low heat 20 minutes or until tender. Meanwhile, season chicken with salt-free herb seasoning, if desired. In large skillet, brown chicken with onion in oil over medium-high heat; drain. Stir in tomatoes, prune juice, prunes and allspice. Cover and cook 10 minutes over medium heat.

Remove cover; cook over medium-high heat 10 to 12 minutes or until sauce thickens and chicken is no longer pink, turning chicken and stirring sauce occasionally. Serve chicken and sauce over bulgur. Garnish with chopped parsley, if desired.   *Makes 4 servings*

Chicken Morocco

Stuffed Chicken with Apple Glaze

1 broiler-fryer chicken (3½ to 4 pounds)
½ teaspoon salt
¼ teaspoon pepper
2 tablespoons vegetable oil
1 package (6 ounces) chicken-flavored stuffing mix plus ingredients to prepare mix
1 cup chopped apple
¼ cup chopped walnuts
¼ cup raisins
¼ cup thinly sliced celery
½ teaspoon grated lemon peel
½ cup apple jelly
1 tablespoon lemon juice
½ teaspoon ground cinnamon

Preheat oven to 350°F. Sprinkle inside of chicken with salt and pepper; rub outside with oil. Prepare stuffing mix in large bowl according to package directions. Add apple, walnuts, raisins, celery and lemon peel; mix thoroughly. Stuff body cavity loosely with stuffing.* Place chicken in baking pan. Cover loosely with aluminum foil; roast 1 hour. Meanwhile, combine jelly, lemon juice and cinnamon in small saucepan. Simmer over low heat 3 minutes or until blended. Remove foil from chicken; brush with glaze. Roast chicken, uncovered, brushing frequently with glaze, 30 minutes or until meat thermometer inserted into thickest part of thigh registers 185°F and juices run clear. Let chicken stand 15 minutes before carving.

Makes 4 servings

*Bake any leftover stuffing in covered casserole alongside chicken until heated through.

*Favorite recipe from **Delmarva Poultry Industry, Inc.***

Oven Tender Chicken™

1 broiler-fryer chicken, cut up (3 to 3½ pounds)
1 (18-ounce) bottle KRAFT® Original Barbecue Sauce

• Heat oven to 350°F.

• Place chicken in 13×9-inch baking dish. Pour barbecue sauce over chicken. Bake, uncovered, 1 hour or until cooked through.

Makes 4 servings

Double-Coated Chicken

7 cups KELLOGG'S® CORN FLAKES® cereal, crushed to 1¾ cups
1 egg
1 cup skim milk
1 cup all-purpose flour
½ teaspoon salt
¼ teaspoon black pepper
3 pounds broiler chicken pieces, washed and patted dry
3 tablespoons margarine, melted

1. Measure crushed Kellogg's® Corn Flakes® cereal into shallow dish or pan. Set aside.

2. In small mixing bowl, beat egg and milk until combined. Add flour, salt and pepper. Mix until smooth. Dip chicken in batter. Coat with cereal. Place in single layer, skin side up, in foil-lined shallow baking pan. Drizzle with margarine.

3. Bake at 350°F about 1 hour or until chicken is tender. *Do not cover pan or turn chicken while baking.*   *Makes 8 servings*

Stuffed Chicken with Apple Glaze

Magically Moist Chicken

1 chicken (2½ to 3½ pounds), cut into pieces
½ cup HELLMANN'S® or BEST FOODS® Real or Light Mayonnaise or Low Fat Mayonnaise Dressing
1¼ cups Italian seasoned bread crumbs

Brush chicken on all sides with mayonnaise. Place bread crumbs in large plastic food storage bag. Add chicken 1 piece at a time; shake to coat well. Arrange on rack in broiler pan. Bake in 425°F oven about 40 minutes or until golden brown and tender.

Makes 4 servings

Creole Chicken Thighs

8 skinless broiler-fryer chicken thighs
2 tablespoons butter or margarine
½ pound mushrooms, sliced
1 medium onion, chopped
½ cup chopped green bell pepper
½ cup thinly sliced celery
2 cloves garlic, minced
1 can (16 ounces) tomatoes, cut up
½ teaspoon salt
½ teaspoon sugar
½ teaspoon dried thyme leaves, crumbled
½ teaspoon hot pepper sauce
2 bay leaves
2 cups hot cooked rice

In skillet, melt butter over medium-high heat. Add mushrooms, onion, bell pepper, celery and garlic. Cook, stirring constantly, about 3 minutes or until onion is translucent, but not brown. Stir in tomatoes, salt, sugar, thyme, pepper sauce and bay leaves. Add chicken, spooning sauce over chicken. Cook, covered, over medium heat 35 minutes or until chicken is tender and juices run clear. Remove and discard bay leaves. Serve chicken and sauce over rice.

Makes 4 servings

*Favorite recipe from **Delmarva Poultry Industry, Inc.***

Lemon Herbed Chicken

½ cup butter or margarine
½ cup vegetable oil
⅓ cup lemon juice
2 tablespoons finely chopped parsley
2 tablespoons garlic salt
1 teaspoon dried rosemary, crushed
1 teaspoon dried summer savory, crushed
½ teaspoon dried thyme, crushed
¼ teaspoon coarsely cracked black pepper
6 chicken quarters (breast-wing or thigh-drumstick combinations)

Combine butter, oil, lemon juice, parsley, garlic salt, rosemary, summer savory, thyme and pepper in small saucepan. Heat until butter melts. Place chicken in shallow glass dish. Brush with some of sauce. Let stand 10 to 15 minutes. Oil hot grid to help prevent sticking. Place dark meat pieces on grill 10 minutes before white meat pieces (dark meat takes longer to cook). Grill chicken, on uncovered grill, over medium-hot KINGSFORD® briquets, 30 to 45 minutes for breast quarters or 50 to 60 minutes for leg quarters. Chicken is done when meat is no longer pink by bone. Turn quarters over and baste with sauce every 10 minutes.

Makes 6 servings

For homes that want the best in cooking — CRISCO

stays sweet!

CRISCO
For Frying For Shortening
for Cake Making

for FRYING *for* SHORTENING *for* CAKE-MAKING

In 1911, Procter & Gamble began producing Crisco®. Following the introduction, home economists traveled the country touting Crisco® as the latest invention for the modern homemaker.

Classic Fried Chicken

¾ **cup all-purpose flour**
 1 **teaspoon salt**
¼ **teaspoon pepper**
 1 **frying chicken (2½ to 3 pounds), cut up or chicken pieces**
½ **cup CRISCO® all-vegetable shortening** *or* ½ **CRISCO® Stick**

1. **Combine** flour, salt and pepper in paper or plastic bag. **Add** a few pieces of chicken at a time. **Shake** to coat.

2. **Heat** shortening to 365°F in electric skillet or on medium-high heat in large heavy skillet. **Fry** chicken 30 to 40 minutes without lowering heat. **Turn** once for even browning. **Drain** on paper towels.   *Makes 4 servings*

All-American Fried Chicken

½ **cup all-purpose flour**
1 to 2 teaspoons LAWRY'S® Seasoned
  Salt
1 to 2 teaspoons LAWRY'S® Seasoned
  Pepper
2½ **to 3 pounds chicken pieces**
  Vegetable oil, for frying

In paper or plastic bag, combine flour,
Seasoned Salt and Seasoned Pepper. Wash
chicken; pat dry and place in flour mixture to
coat. Coat only a few pieces at a time.

In large skillet, pour oil to coat pan. When
hot, brown chicken, a few pieces at a time,
and remove as browned. Repeat as needed.
When all chicken is browned, drain fat and
return chicken to skillet. Reduce heat; cover
and simmer about 25 minutes or until chicken
is tender. Uncover during last 10 minutes to
crisp skin.   *Makes 4 servings*

Hot, Spicy, Tangy, Sticky Chicken

1 chicken (3½ to 4 pounds), cut up
1 cup cider vinegar
1 tablespoon Worcestershire sauce
1 tablespoon chili powder
1 teaspoon salt
1 teaspoon black pepper
1 teaspoon hot pepper sauce
¾ **cup K.C. MASTERPIECE® Barbecue**
  Sauce (about)

Place chicken in shallow glass dish or large
heavy plastic bag. Combine vinegar,
Worcestershire sauce, chili powder, salt,
pepper and hot pepper sauce in small bowl;
pour over chicken pieces. Cover dish or close
bag. Marinate in refrigerator at least 4 hours,
turning several times.

Oil hot grid to help prevent sticking. Place
dark meat pieces on grill 10 minutes before
white meat pieces (dark meat takes longer to
cook). Grill chicken, on covered grill, over
medium KINGSFORD® briquets, 30 to 45
minutes, turning once or twice. Turn and
baste with K.C. Masterpiece® Barbecue
Sauce last 10 minutes of cooking. Remove
chicken from grill; baste with sauce. Chicken
is done when meat is no longer pink by bone.
                        Makes 4 servings

Herb Garlic Grilled Chicken

¼ **cup chopped parsley**
1½ **tablespoons minced garlic**
4 teaspoons grated lemon peel
1 tablespoon chopped fresh mint
1 chicken (2½ to 3 pounds), quartered

Combine parsley, garlic, lemon peel and mint.
Loosen skin from breast and thigh portions of
chicken quarters by running fingers between
skin and meat. Rub some of seasoning
mixture evenly over meat under skin, then
replace skin and rub remaining seasonings
over outside of chicken to cover evenly.
Arrange medium-hot KINGSFORD® briquets
on one side of covered grill. Place chicken on
grid opposite coals. Cover grill and cook
chicken 45 to 55 minutes, turning once or
twice. Chicken is done when juices run clear.
                        Makes 4 servings

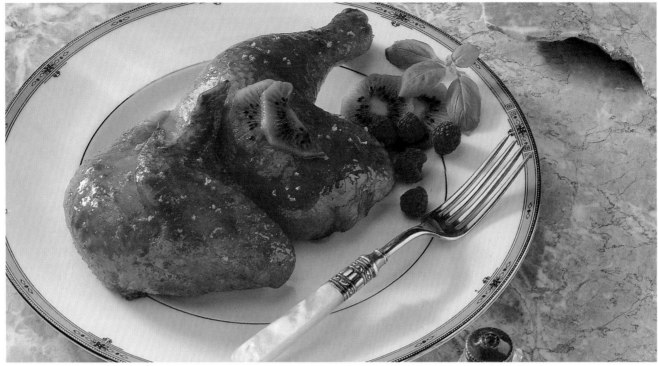

Roast Chicken & Kiwifruit with Raspberry Glaze

Roast Chicken & Kiwifruit with Raspberry Glaze

2 broiler-fryer chickens, halved (3½ to 4 pounds each)
1 teaspoon salt
¼ teaspoon pepper
¼ cup butter or margarine, melted
Raspberry Glaze (recipe follows)
2 kiwifruit, peeled and sliced

Preheat oven to 400°F. Sprinkle chicken with salt and pepper. Place, skin side up, in single layer in large, shallow pan; brush with butter. Roast, basting frequently with butter, about 45 minutes or until chicken is tender and juices run clear; drain fat. While chicken is roasting, prepare Raspberry Glaze. Spoon glaze over chicken; top with kiwifruit slices. Spoon glaze from bottom of pan over chicken and kiwifruit. Bake 3 minutes or until kiwifruit and chicken are well glazed.

Makes 4 servings

Raspberry Glaze: Combine 1 cup seedless raspberry preserves, ½ cup white port wine and grated peel of 1 lemon in small saucepan. Cook over low heat about 5 minutes or until slightly thickened.

*Favorite recipe from **Delmarva Poultry Industry, Inc.***

113

Country Herb Roasted Chicken

1 chicken (2½ to 3 pounds), cut into serving pieces (with or without skin) or 1½ pounds boneless skinless chicken breast halves
1 envelope LIPTON® Recipe Secrets® Savory Herb with Garlic or Golden Herb with Lemon Soup Mix
2 tablespoons water
1 tablespoon olive or vegetable oil

Preheat oven to 375°F.

In 13×9-inch baking or roasting pan, arrange chicken. In small bowl, combine remaining ingredients; brush on chicken.

For *chicken pieces,* bake uncovered 45 minutes or until chicken is no longer pink. For *chicken breast halves,* bake uncovered 20 minutes or until chicken is no longer pink.
Makes about 4 servings

Baked Chicken with Red-Peppered Onions

1 broiler-fryer chicken, quartered
2 teaspoons lemon pepper seasoning
1 teaspoon olive oil
4 cups thinly sliced sweet onions
4 tablespoons red hot pepper jelly
1 small sweet red pepper, cut into rings
Cilantro

On oiled rack of large broiler pan, place chicken. Sprinkle chicken with lemon pepper seasoning. Bake in 400°F oven, skin side up, 50 minutes or until chicken is fork-tender.

Meanwhile, add olive oil to large nonstick skillet; heat to medium temperature. Add onions; cook until barely wilted, about 5 minutes. Add jelly and stir gently until melted. Spoon half of onion mixture on large platter. Arrange chicken over onions; top with remaining onions. Garnish with pepper rings and cilantro.   *Makes 4 servings*

*Favorite recipe from **Delmarva Poultry Industry, Inc.***

Hunter-Style Chicken

4 slices bacon, cut into 1-inch pieces
1 medium onion, sliced
1 tablespoon vegetable oil
2 to 2½ pounds broiler-fryer pieces
1 can (16 ounces) tomatoes, cut into bite-size pieces
⅓ cup HEINZ® 57 Sauce
⅛ teaspoon pepper
Hot cooked rice or noodles

In large skillet, cook and stir bacon until crisp. Remove bacon; drain fat. Cook and stir onion in oil until tender; remove. In same skillet, brown chicken adding more oil if necessary. Drain excess fat. Combine bacon, onion, tomatoes, 57 Sauce and pepper; pour over chicken. Cover; simmer 20 to 25 minutes or until chicken is tender, basting occasionally. Remove chicken. Skim excess fat from sauce. If thicker sauce is desired, gradually stir in mixture of equal parts flour and water, simmering until thickened. Serve chicken and sauce with rice or noodles.
Makes 4 to 5 servings

Country Herb Roasted Chicken

Tarragon Chicken with Asparagus

¼ cup instant minced onion
1 tablespoon vegetable oil
1 pound fresh asparagus, cut into
   1-inch pieces (about 3 cups)
1¼ cups diced red bell pepper
12 ounces boneless skinless chicken
   breasts, cut into 1-inch pieces
1¼ cups orange juice, divided
1 teaspoon cornstarch
1 teaspoon dried tarragon leaves,
   crushed
¼ teaspoon salt
⅛ teaspoon ground black pepper
   Hot cooked fettuccine

In small cup combine onion and ¼ cup water; set aside for 10 minutes to soften. In large nonstick skillet over medium-high heat, heat oil until hot. Add asparagus and red pepper; cook, stirring constantly, until nearly crisp-tender, about 3 minutes.

Add chicken and reserved onion mixture; cook, stirring constantly, until chicken is opaque, about 2 minutes. In small bowl combine ¼ cup orange juice and cornstarch; mix until smooth. Stir orange juice mixture into skillet along with remaining 1 cup orange juice, tarragon, salt and black pepper; cook, stirring constantly, until mixture thickens and boils, 2 to 3 minutes. Boil, stirring constantly, 1 minute longer.

Serve over hot cooked fettuccine and garnish with orange slices, if desired.

Makes 4 servings

Favorite recipe from **American Spice Trade Association**

Chicken Breasts Diavolo

6 chicken breast halves, boned,
   skinned and slightly flattened
½ cup finely minced fresh parsley
1 teaspoon lemon pepper seasoning
   Dash salt
   Dash garlic powder
3 tablespoons olive oil
3 (6-ounce) jars marinated artichoke
   hearts
1 tablespoon fresh lemon juice
1 (26-ounce) jar NEWMAN'S OWN®
   Diavolo Sauce
½ cup red wine (preferably Chianti)
1½ cups shredded mozzarella cheese
1½ cups onion-garlic flavor croutons
   (tossed with 1 tablespoon olive oil)
6 cups hot cooked pasta or rice

Preheat oven to 350°F. Sprinkle chicken breasts with parsley, lemon pepper seasoning, salt and garlic powder. Roll each breast, seasoned side in; secure with wooden toothpicks. Cook and stir in olive oil in large skillet until golden brown. Remove from pan with tongs and place in 13×9-inch baking dish. Carefully remove toothpicks.

Drain artichoke hearts; sprinkle with lemon juice and distribute among rolled chicken breasts.

Combine Newman's Own® Diavolo Sauce with wine; pour over chicken and artichokes. Sprinkle cheese evenly over top. Sprinkle with crouton mixture. Bake 30 to 40 minutes until golden brown and bubbly.

Spoon chicken over pasta or rice. Serve with crusty Italian bread or rolls, a green salad and remaining red wine.

Makes 6 servings

Chicken Marsala

4 boneless, skinless chicken breasts
  Salt and pepper to taste
¼ cup all-purpose flour
2 tablespoons WESSON® Oil
3 cups sliced mushrooms
1 cup sliced onions
1 teaspoon minced garlic
1 (15-ounce) can HUNT'S® Ready
  Tomato Sauces Chunky Special
⅓ cup Marsala wine
½ teaspoon salt
¼ teaspoon sugar

Season chicken with salt and pepper; coat lightly with flour. In large skillet, in hot oil, lightly brown chicken on both sides; remove and set aside. Add mushrooms, onions and garlic to skillet; cook and stir until tender. Stir in remaining ingredients. Return chicken to skillet; spoon sauce over to coat. Simmer, covered, 15 minutes. *Makes 4 servings*

Simple Marinated Chicken Breasts

2 teaspoons Dijon mustard
1 clove garlic, minced
½ teaspoon salt
½ teaspoon ground black pepper
⅛ teaspoon dried savory
⅛ teaspoon dried tarragon
2 tablespoons olive oil, divided
¼ cup dry white wine
4 boneless, skinless chicken breast
  halves (about 1½ pounds)
½ cup warm water
  Fresh thyme for garnish

Combine mustard, garlic, salt, pepper, savory, tarragon, 1 tablespoon oil and wine in small bowl. Place chicken in shallow dish; pour mixture over chicken, turning to coat. Cover; marinate in refrigerator overnight.

Heat remaining 1 tablespoon oil in large skillet over medium heat until hot. Add chicken, reserving marinade; cook 15 minutes or until brown and no longer pink in center, turning occasionally. Remove to warm platter. Place marinade and warm water in skillet. Bring to a boil; cook and stir about 3 minutes. Pour over chicken. Garnish with thyme. Serve immediately.

Makes 4 servings

Favorite recipe from **National Broiler Council**

NBC
National Broiler Council

The National Broiler Council is the nonprofit trade organization for the broiler chicken industry. Membership includes broiler producers and processors, firms that supply goods and services to the broiler industry and other companies involved in the industry. Members produce, process and market over 90% of all U.S. broilers. The Council is located in Washington, D.C., and is the primary source of information concerning the production, marketing and use of chicken.

Glazed Citrus Chicken

2 large, whole chicken breasts, halved,
 boned and skinned
2 oranges, sliced in half
2 lemons, sliced in half
2 limes, sliced in half
1 tablespoon LAWRY'S® Seasoned Salt
1 tablespoon LAWRY'S® Seasoned
 Pepper
1 can (12 ounces) apricot halves,
 drained
2 tablespoons brown sugar
1 tablespoon butter or margarine
 Dash of ground nutmeg
 Mint leaves (garnish)

In 13×9×2-inch glass baking dish, place chicken. Squeeze juice from one half of each orange, lemon and lime over chicken. Thinly slice and set aside remaining citrus fruit halves for garnish. Sprinkle Seasoned Salt and Seasoned Pepper evenly over chicken. Cover and bake in 400°F oven 30 minutes.

While chicken is baking, prepare glaze. In blender, process apricot halves. In small saucepan, combine processed apricots, brown sugar, butter and nutmeg. Heat until bubbles appear. Reduce heat; cover and simmer 5 minutes, stirring once or twice. Pour glaze over chicken breasts and bake, uncovered, an additional 10 minutes.

Makes 4 servings

Presentation: Top with citrus slices and mint leaves. Perfect with sautéed bell peppers, black beans and rice.

Chicken Fajitas

¼ cup orange juice
2 tablespoons lime juice
2 tablespoons lemon juice
1 clove garlic, minced
4 boneless, skinless chicken breast
 halves (about 1½ pounds)
1 teaspoon chili powder
½ teaspoon salt
1 tablespoon vegetable oil
1 red bell pepper, cut into strips
1 green bell pepper, cut into strips
1 yellow bell pepper, cut into strips
1 medium onion, sliced
10 flour tortillas, warmed
1 cup sour cream
1 cup salsa
1 can (2¼ ounces) sliced black olives,
 drained

Combine juices and garlic in large nonmetal bowl. Season chicken with chili powder and salt; add to juice mixture, turning to coat. Cover; marinate in refrigerator 30 minutes. Remove chicken. Place marinade in small saucepan. Bring to a boil over medium-high heat; keep warm. Place chicken on broiler rack or grill about 6 inches from heat. Broil or grill, turning and basting with marinade, 10 minutes or until no longer pink in center. Heat oil in large skillet over medium-high heat until hot. Add peppers and onion; cook and stir about 5 minutes or until onion is tender. Slice chicken into strips; add to pepper-onion mixture. Divide chicken-pepper mixture evenly in centers of tortillas. Roll up tortillas; top each with dollop of sour cream, salsa and olives. *Makes 5 servings*

Favorite recipe from **National Broiler Council**

Glazed Citrus Chicken

Parmesan Chicken Breasts

½ cup (2 ounces) KRAFT® 100% Grated
    Parmesan Cheese
¼ cup dry bread crumbs
1 teaspoon dried oregano leaves
1 teaspoon parsley flakes
¼ teaspoon paprika
¼ teaspoon salt
¼ teaspoon black pepper
6 boneless skinless chicken breast
    halves (about 2 pounds)
2 tablespoons PARKAY® Spread Sticks,
    melted

• Heat oven to 400°F. Spray 15×10×1-inch
baking pan with nonstick cooking spray.

• Mix cheese, crumbs and seasonings. Dip
chicken in melted spread; coat with crumb
mixture. Place in prepared pan.

• Bake 20 to 25 minutes or until cooked
through.   *Makes 6 servings*

Variation:
Spicy Parmesan Chicken Breasts:
Substitute ⅛ to ¼ teaspoon ground red
pepper for black pepper.

Dijon Chicken Elegant

4 whole boneless chicken breasts, split
⅓ cup GREY POUPON® Dijon or
    Country Dijon Mustard
1 teaspoon dried dill weed *or*
    1 tablespoon chopped fresh dill
¼ pound Swiss cheese slices
2 frozen puff pastry sheets, thawed
1 egg white
1 tablespoon cold water

Pound chicken breasts to ½-inch thickness.
Blend mustard and dill; spread on chicken
breasts. Top each breast with cheese slice;
roll up.

Roll each pastry sheet to 12-inch square; cut
each into 4 (6-inch) squares. Beat egg white
and water; brush edges of each square with
egg mixture. Place 1 chicken roll diagonally
on each square. Join 4 points of pastry over
chicken; seal seams. Place on ungreased
baking sheets. Brush with remaining egg
mixture. Bake at 375°F for 30 minutes or until
chicken is done. Serve immediately.
          Makes 8 servings

National Sunflower Association

*Many of us still
marvel at a swaying
field of sunflowers
turning to the sun.
But the real beauty
is the economic diversity the crop
provides. The National Sunflower
Association nurtures and promotes
that diversity while raising the status
of producers and the industry.
Incorporated in 1981 with
headquarters in Bismarck, North
Dakota, the organization works in
areas of market development,
education, production and legislative
matters.*

Sunflower Chicken

Sunflower Chicken

½ cup cornflake crumbs
½ cup chopped sunflower kernels
2 tablespoons whole sunflower kernels
2 teaspoons paprika
½ teaspoon salt
½ teaspoon ground ginger
⅛ teaspoon pepper
1 egg, beaten
2 tablespoons honey
1 tablespoon lemon juice
2 to 3 chicken breast halves (about
    1¼ pounds), skins removed
1 teaspoon sunflower oil

Microwave Directions: In medium bowl, combine cornflake crumbs, sunflower kernels, paprika, salt, ginger and pepper; mix well. In separate medium bowl, combine egg, honey and lemon juice; mix well. Dip chicken in egg mixture then crumb mixture. Place in microwave-safe dish; drizzle with oil. Cover with waxed paper.

Microwave at HIGH 3 minutes; turn one-quarter turn. Microwave 3 to 4 minutes longer or until juices run clear and chicken is no longer pink. Let stand 5 minutes before serving.   *Makes 2 to 3 servings*

*Favorite recipe from **National Sunflower Association***

Fleischmann's

In 1955, the leading margarines were made with a combination of cottonseed and soybean oils. Standard Brands had just purchased a ground corn processing company, but there was little demand for corn oil, one of the company's products. Using available margarine technology, Standard Brands launched Fleischmann's margarine, the first margarine made from 100% corn oil. In 1959, medical research showed that of all liquid oils available, corn oil was the most beneficial in reducing the amount of cholesterol the body manufactures. Sales increased greatly when consumers realized the health benefits of corn oil.

Lightly Lemon Chicken

¾ cup fine dry bread crumbs
1 tablespoon chopped parsley
2 whole boneless chicken breasts, split and pounded (about 1 pound)
¼ cup **EGG BEATERS**® Real Egg Product
1 clove garlic, crushed
3 tablespoons **FLEISCHMANN'S**® Margarine
1 lemon
¼ cup low-sodium chicken broth

Mix bread crumbs and parsley. Dip chicken pieces into egg product, then coat with bread crumb mixture.

In skillet, over medium-high heat, cook garlic in margarine for 1 minute. Add chicken and brown on both sides. Cut half the lemon into thin slices; arrange over chicken. Squeeze juice from remaining lemon half into chicken broth; pour into skillet. Heat to boil; reduce heat. Cover and simmer 10 minutes or until chicken is tender.   *Makes 4 servings*

Sesame Chicken Nuggets

4 tablespoons sesame seeds
2 tablespoons Worcestershire sauce
2 tablespoons water
2 teaspoons granulated sugar
2 teaspoons chili powder
½ teaspoon garlic powder
2 pounds chicken breasts, skinned and cut into 1-inch cubes
Barbecue Sauce (recipe follows)

In large bowl, combine all ingredients except chicken and Barbecue Sauce; mix well. Add chicken and coat evenly. Spread on broiler pan. Broil 10 minutes or until lightly browned, turning once. Serve with Barbecue Sauce or stuff into pita pockets with lettuce and tomato. *Makes 4 servings*

Barbecue Sauce

1 (8-ounce) can tomato sauce
1 teaspoon red wine vinegar
1 teaspoon granulated sugar
½ teaspoon Worcestershire sauce
½ teaspoon chili powder
¼ teaspoon garlic powder

In medium saucepan, combine all ingredients; simmer 15 minutes, stirring occasionally. Use as dipping sauce for chicken nuggets. *Makes 1 cup*

Favorite recipe from **The Sugar Association, Inc.**

Ninety-nine percent of the commercial walnut crop in the U.S. is grown in California.
Photo courtesy of Walnut Marketing Board

Classic Chicken Curry with Winter Fruit and Walnuts

4 tablespoons butter
2 cloves garlic, minced
1 tablespoon curry powder
1 teaspoon paprika
¼ teaspoon ground cayenne pepper (optional)
1 tablespoon cornstarch
1 cup chicken broth
6 chicken breast halves, skinned and boned
2 pears, cored and thickly sliced
¾ cup chopped walnuts
½ cup chopped green onions
¼ cup cranberries or currants

Microwave Directions: Microwave butter in uncovered 3-quart glass casserole dish 2 minutes at HIGH. Stir in garlic and spices; microwave at HIGH 3 minutes. Mix cornstarch with broth; add to garlic mixture and stir. Arrange chicken breasts in single layer in sauce. Cover and microwave at HIGH 6 to 8 minutes, stirring every 2 minutes. Stir in pears, walnuts, green onions and cranberries. Cover and cook at HIGH additional 6 to 8 minutes, until chicken is cooked through. Arrange chicken and pears on serving platter. Pour remaining sauce over chicken and serve with rice or couscous, if desired. *Makes 4 to 6 servings*

Favorite recipe from **Walnut Marketing Board**

Chicken Breasts Stuffed with Tomato and Mozzarella

2 COOKIN' GOOD® Boneless, Skinless Chicken Breasts
2 plum tomatoes
2 ounces mozzarella cheese, shredded (½ cup)
3 tablespoons thinly sliced fresh basil leaves
⅛ teaspoon salt
⅛ teaspoon pepper
1 tablespoon olive oil
1 clove garlic, sliced
2 tablespoons dry Marsala wine
½ cup chicken broth

1. Slice one tomato; dice remaining tomato. Set aside. In small bowl, combine mozzarella and basil.

2. With sharp knife, make shallow cut lengthwise down center of chicken breast. Gently inserting knife in opening, cut pocket into one side of breast, cutting through top and bottom of breast to form open flap. Repeat with remaining side. Repeat procedure with other breast. Arrange tomato slices and mozzarella mixture in center of each breast. Fold left and right sides of chicken over stuffing. From short side, roll stuffed chicken breast jelly-roll style; fasten edges with toothpicks. Sprinkle each breast with salt and pepper.

3. In 10-inch skillet heat olive oil. Cook chicken and garlic over medium heat, turning frequently, 10 to 12 minutes or until chicken is lightly browned and cooked through. Remove chicken rolls to plate; pour off fat from skillet.

Chicken Breasts Stuffed with Tomato and Mozzarella

4. Add wine to skillet; bring to a boil for 1 minute, scraping up any browned bits from bottom of skillet. Add chicken broth and diced tomato. Return chicken to skillet. Bring to a boil over high heat. Reduce heat to low; cover and simmer 5 minutes.

Makes 2 to 4 servings

Cookin' Good® Chicken Scallopini

2 COOKIN' GOOD® Chicken Breasts, boned and split
1 egg, beaten with 1 tablespoon water
½ cup Italian seasoned bread crumbs
¼ cup olive or vegetable oil
1 clove garlic
½ teaspoon dried basil
¼ cup sherry
1 lemon, thinly sliced
2 teaspoons capers (optional)

Pound chicken breasts very thin between 2 sheets of waxed paper. Place egg mixture in small bowl. Dip chicken breasts into egg mixture, then into seasoned bread crumbs. In medium skillet, heat oil with garlic; remove garlic and brown chicken 3 minutes on each side over medium heat. Add basil and sherry; top with lemon slices and capers. Simmer 5 to 6 minutes or until tender.

Makes 4 servings

Chicken Ribbons Satay

½ cup creamy peanut butter
½ cup water
¼ cup soy sauce
4 cloves garlic, pressed
3 tablespoons lemon juice
2 tablespoons firmly packed brown sugar
¾ teaspoon ground ginger
½ teaspoon crushed red pepper flakes
4 boneless skinless chicken breast halves
Sliced green onion tops for garnish

Combine peanut butter, water, soy sauce, garlic, lemon juice, brown sugar, ginger and red pepper flakes in small saucepan. Cook over medium heat 1 minute or until smooth; cool. Remove garlic from sauce; discard. Reserve half of sauce for dipping. Cut chicken lengthwise into 1-inch-wide strips. Thread onto 8 metal or bamboo skewers. (Soak bamboo skewers in water at least 20 minutes to keep them from burning.)

Oil hot grid to help prevent sticking. Grill chicken, on covered grill, over medium-hot KINGSFORD® briquets, 6 to 8 minutes until chicken is cooked through, turning once. Baste with sauce once or twice during cooking. Serve with reserved sauce garnished with sliced green onion tops.

Makes 4 servings

Curried Chicken with Pears

2 (4- to 6-ounce) boneless, skinless chicken breast halves
1 teaspoon oil
Salt and pepper to taste
1 tablespoon all-purpose flour
½ teaspoon paprika
¼ teaspoon curry powder
¼ teaspoon ground ginger
3 tablespoons lime juice
2 tablespoons honey
1 USA Bartlett pear, pared, cored and halved
6 to 8 cooked small new potatoes
Chives

Microwave Directions: Brush chicken with oil and sprinkle with salt and pepper. Combine flour, paprika, curry powder and ginger; rub onto all surfaces of chicken. Combine lime juice and honey; mix well. Coat pear halves with lime mixture. Arrange chicken and pears in microwave-safe dish with thickest portion of pear and chicken facing outer edge. Cover with waxed paper; microwave at HIGH 4 to 6 minutes or until chicken is no longer pink. Rearrange food halfway through cooking time. Let stand 5 minutes. Slice pear halves to within ½ inch of stem end. Fan pears onto edge of chicken. Serve with boiled new potatoes; garnish with chives. *Makes 2 servings*

*Favorite recipe from **Canned Fruit Promotion Service, Inc.***

Chicken Ribbons Satay

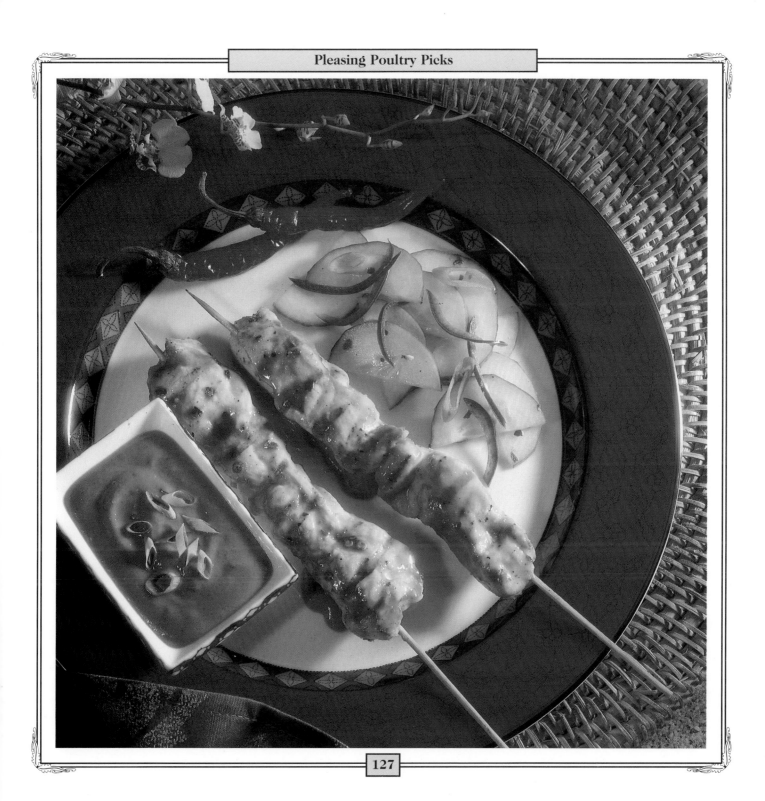

Skillet Chicken Vesuvio

1 package (6.9 ounces) RICE-A-RONI® Chicken Flavor
12 unpeeled garlic cloves
3 tablespoons olive oil or vegetable oil
1½ teaspoons dried oregano leaves
½ teaspoon salt (optional)
½ teaspoon freshly ground black pepper
¼ teaspoon dried rosemary leaves (optional)
4 skinless, boneless chicken breast halves
1 medium tomato, chopped
4 lemon wedges (optional)

1. Prepare Rice-A-Roni® Mix as package directs.

2. While Rice-A-Roni® is simmering, combine garlic cloves and oil in second large skillet. Cover; cook over medium heat 5 minutes.

3. Combine seasonings; sprinkle over chicken.

4. Push garlic to edge of skillet. Add chicken; cook about 5 minutes on each side or until chicken is no longer pink inside. Remove garlic with slotted spoon. Squeeze softened garlic over chicken; discard garlic peels.

5. Stir tomato into rice. Serve rice topped with chicken, juices and lemon wedges.

Makes 4 servings

Stuffed Turkey Breasts

2 skinned and boned turkey breast halves* (about ¾ pound each)
¼ cup dry bread crumbs
1 tablespoon dried basil, crushed, *or* 3 tablespoons chopped fresh basil
1 teaspoon seasoned salt, divided Pepper to taste
1 can (16 ounces) USA Bartlett pear halves or slices
1 can (4 ounces) whole pimiento
1 tablespoon olive oil
½ cup dry white wine
1 teaspoon lemon juice

*One large turkey breast (about 1½ pounds) may be used.

Spread turkey breasts on cutting board. If necessary, pound with meat tenderizer to even thickness. Combine bread crumbs, basil, ½ teaspoon seasoned salt and pepper. Drain pears reserving ¼ cup pear liquid. If using pear halves, slice each into thirds. Layer pimiento, pears and crumb mixture on turkey. Roll up and tie or fasten with skewers or wooden picks. Place in oiled baking dish; brush with oil and sprinkle with remaining ½ teaspoon seasoned salt. Bake at 375°F, 30 minutes or until juices run clear. Transfer drippings to small saucepan; add wine and reserved pear liquid. Boil mixture until reduced by half. Add lemon juice and adjust seasonings. Slice turkey; spoon sauce over slices. *Makes 4 servings*

Favorite recipe from **Canned Fruit Promotion Service, Inc.**

Skillet Chicken Vesuvio

Curried Turkey with Pear Chutney

¼ cup chutney
⅓ cup chopped pear (about ½ pear)
2 teaspoons cider vinegar or wine vinegar
1 teaspoon canola oil or walnut oil
¼ cup (1 ounce) chopped California walnuts
5 to 6 teaspoons curry powder, divided
1 tablespoon unsalted butter
1 tablespoon canola oil
1 onion, sliced
¼ cup all-purpose flour
2 cups no-salt-added chicken broth
1 cup nonfat milk
  Salt and pepper (optional)
1 pound cooked turkey breast meat, cut into 1-inch cubes
2 cups cooked rice

Combine chutney, pear and vinegar; cover and chill until serving.

Heat 1 teaspoon oil in medium skillet. Add nuts; toss 3 to 4 minutes until lightly toasted. Sprinkle with 1 teaspoon curry powder; toss to combine. Set aside to cool.

Heat butter and 1 tablespoon oil in large saucepan. Add remaining 4 to 5 teaspoons curry powder; cook 1 minute. Add onion; cook about 5 minutes. Add flour and cook, stirring constantly, 2 minutes longer. Add chicken broth and milk; whisk until smooth. Bring to a boil; season with salt and pepper, if desired. Add turkey; simmer until heated through. Serve over rice, with sides of chutney and curried walnuts.

Makes about 4 servings

Favorite recipe from **Walnut Marketing Board**

Busy Day Turkey Loaf

1 cup KELLOGG'S® CROUTETTES® Stuffing Mix
½ cup skim milk
2 egg whites
2 teaspoons Worcestershire sauce
¼ cup finely chopped onion
½ teaspoon salt
1 pound lean ground turkey
¼ cup ketchup
1 teaspoon prepared mustard
2 teaspoons brown sugar

1. Combine Kellogg's® Croutettes® Stuffing Mix and milk in large mixing bowl. Let stand 5 minutes or until Croutettes are softened.

2. Add egg whites, Worcestershire sauce, onion and salt. Beat well. Add ground turkey. Mix until well combined.

3. Shape into loaf. Place in foil-lined shallow baking pan. Score loaf by making several diagonal grooves across top.

4. Stir together ketchup, mustard and sugar. Fill grooves with ketchup mixture.

5. Bake at 350°F about 45 minutes or until browned. *Makes 6 servings*

Curried Turkey with Pear Chutney

Treasures from the Sea

Enjoy the wonders of the sea with these time-tested treasures. This spectacular collection of fish and shellfish recipes is sure to delight the entire crew.

Albacore Stir-Fry

3 tablespoons vegetable oil
½ cup sliced onion
1 clove garlic, minced or pressed
1 bag (16 ounces) frozen Oriental vegetables, thawed and drained*
1 can (12 ounces) STARKIST® Solid White Tuna, drained and chunked
3 tablespoons soy sauce
1 tablespoon lemon juice
1 tablespoon water
1 teaspoon sugar
2 cups hot cooked rice

*May use 4 cups fresh vegetables, such as carrots, peapods, broccoli, bell peppers, mushrooms, celery and bean sprouts.

In wok or large skillet, heat oil over medium-high heat; sauté onion and garlic until onion is soft. Add vegetables; cook about 3 to 4 minutes or until vegetables are crisp-tender. Add tuna, soy sauce, lemon juice, water and sugar. Cook 1 more minute; serve over rice.

Makes 4 servings

Albacore Stir-Fry

Company's Coming Fish Roll-Ups

1 tablespoon margarine
2 tablespoons flour
¼ teaspoon paprika
⅛ teaspoon salt
1¼ cups lowfat milk
¾ cup shredded reduced fat Cheddar cheese, divided
6 cups (10-ounce package or 1-pound bunch) fresh spinach leaves, coarsely chopped, cooked and well drained
2 tablespoons thinly sliced green onion
6 sole, haddock or flounder fillets (about 1½ pounds)
   Grated peel and juice of ½ SUNKIST® Lemon
3 cups hot cooked rice
   Lemon cartwheel twists or wedges

For cheese sauce, in small saucepan, melt margarine; remove from heat. Stir in flour, paprika and salt; gradually stir in milk. Cook over medium heat, stirring until thickened; remove from heat. Stir in ½ cup cheese. Add ⅓ cup cheese sauce to spinach and green onion; blend well. Sprinkle both sides of fish fillets with lemon juice. Divide spinach mixture on fillets; roll up. Place seam side down in 9-inch baking dish. Sprinkle roll-ups with lemon peel. Spoon remaining cheese sauce over fish roll-ups. Bake in preheated 350°F 30 to 35 minutes or until fish flakes easily with fork. Sprinkle with remaining ¼ cup cheese; bake until cheese melts. Garnish with additional sliced green onion, if desired. Serve each roll-up with ½ cup hot rice. Stir remaining sauce; serve over fish and rice. Garnish with lemon cartwheel twists or wedges.
Makes 6 servings

Festive Baked Stuffed Fish

4 tablespoons butter or margarine
2 teaspoons DILIJAN® Liquid Spice Dill
1½ teaspoons DILIJAN® Liquid Spice Garlic
½ cup chopped celery
½ cup chopped red bell pepper
¼ cup chopped shallots
¼ pound shiitake mushrooms, sliced
6 slices KAVLI® Hearty Thick Crispbread, crumbled
1 cup diced JARLSBERG LITE™ Cheese
1 tablespoon chopped parsley
8 flounder fillets (about 1 pound)
8 salmon fillets (about 1 pound)
   Salt and pepper to taste
   Additional chopped parsley

Melt butter in medium skillet. Add Liquid Dill and Garlic. Add celery, bell pepper, shallots and mushrooms; cook 8 to 10 minutes or until tender but not browned. Stir in crispbread crumbs, cheese and 1 tablespoon parsley. Spoon into 11×8×1½-inch ovenproof shallow baking dish.

Preheat oven to 350°F. Season fillets with salt and pepper. Fold fillets in half or thirds and arrange over cheese stuffing in baking dish, alternating for braid effect. Cover loosely with foil. Bake 20 to 25 minutes or until fish flakes easily when tested with fork and cheese is melted. Sprinkle with additional parsley.
Makes 8 servings

Company's Coming Fish Roll-Ups

Blackened Fish Fillets

1½ cups (3 sticks) unsalted butter, melted
6 (½- to ¾-inch-thick) redfish or other firm-fleshed fish fillets* (8 to 10 ounces each)
3 tablespoons Chef Paul Prudhomme's BLACKENED REDFISH MAGIC®

*Redfish and pompano are ideal for this method of cooking. If tilefish is used, you may have to split the fillets in half horizontally to have the proper thickness. If you can't get any of these fish, red snapper, wall-eyed pike or sac-a-lait fillets or salmon or tuna steaks can be substituted. In any case, the fillets or steaks must not be more than ¾ inch thick.

Heat outdoor grill, if using. Heat large, cast-iron skillet on stove over very high heat until it is beyond the smoking stage and you see white ash in skillet bottom, at least 10 minutes.

Meanwhile, pour 2 tablespoons melted butter in each of 6 small ramekins; set aside and keep warm. Reserve remaining butter. Heat 6 serving plates in 250°F oven.

Dip each fillet into reserved melted butter, coating both sides; sprinkle Blackened Redfish Magic® generously and evenly on both sides of fillets. Carefully place skillet on hot outdoor grill or butane cooker. Place 1 or 2 fillets in skillet. Cook, uncovered, over very high heat until underside becomes deep-brown, almost black (but not burned), about 2 minutes. (Time will vary according to the fillet's thickness and heat of skillet.) Turn fish over and pour 1 teaspoon butter on top of each fillet. Cook until fish flakes easily when tested with fork, about 2 minutes more. Repeat with remaining fillets. Serve piping hot.

To serve, place one fillet and ramekin of melted butter on each plate.

Makes 6 servings

An Alaskan wilderness contractor in 1950, looking for something delicious and healthful to serve his workers, developed a buttermilk-based salad dressing. It was so popular that when he opened a guest ranch in California a few years later, he continued to serve it. He later started a small mail order business to satisfy the demand for Hidden Valley Ranch® Recipe. The business became part of the Clorox Company in 1972, who captured the great taste of this salad dressing in a dry mix form and in a ready-to-use bottle. The Original Ranch flavor is now the most successful selling item among bottled dressings.

Savory Salmon

Savory Salmon

6 small salmon steaks (6 ounces each)
¾ cup prepared HIDDEN VALLEY
    RANCH® Original Ranch® Salad
    Dressing
2 teaspoons chopped fresh dill *or*
    ¼ teaspoon dried dill weed
1 teaspoon chopped parsley
    Lemon wedges
    Fresh dill sprigs (optional)

Preheat oven to 375°F. Arrange salmon in 13×9×2-inch buttered baking dish; spread 2 tablespoons salad dressing over each steak. Sprinkle with dill and parsley. Bake until fish flakes easily when tested with fork, 10 to 15 minutes. Place under broiler 45 to 60 seconds to brown. Serve with lemon wedges and garnish with dill sprigs, if desired. *Makes 6 servings*

Seafood Kabobs

Seafood Kabobs

1 medium avocado
⅓ cup pineapple juice
⅓ cup **REALEMON®** Lemon Juice from
    Concentrate or **REALIME®** Lime
    Juice from Concentrate
2 tablespoons vegetable oil
1 to 2 tablespoons brown sugar
1 teaspoon grated orange rind
¼ teaspoon ground cinnamon
¾ pound large raw shrimp, peeled and
    deveined
½ pound sea scallops
1 cup melon chunks or balls

Peel and seed avocado; cut into chunks. In large shallow dish or plastic bag, combine juices, oil, sugar, orange rind and cinnamon; mix well. Add seafood and melon. Cover; marinate in refrigerator 4 hours or overnight. Remove seafood and melon from marinade; heat marinade thoroughly. Alternately thread shrimp, scallops, melon and avocado on skewers. Grill or broil 3 to 6 minutes or until shrimp are pink and scallops are opaque, basting frequently with marinade. Refrigerate leftovers. *Makes 4 servings*

Blue Diamond Growers

During World War II, the demand for almonds increased greatly in order to supply the Armed Forces with the popular chocolate and almond candy bars.

Trout Almondine

    2 tablespoons flour
 1½ teaspoons salt, divided
  ¼ teaspoon pepper
    2 pounds trout or fish fillets
    6 tablespoons butter or margarine,
      divided
  ¼ cup BLUE DIAMOND® Blanched
      Slivered Almonds
    3 tablespoons lemon juice*
    1 tablespoon chopped parsley

*If desired, reduce lemon juice to 1 teaspoon and add ¼ cup sherry or sauterne wine.

Mix flour, 1 teaspoon salt and pepper; sprinkle on fish. In skillet, over medium heat, fry fish in 4 tablespoons butter about 6 minutes or until lightly browned. Arrange fish on warmed platter. Add remaining butter to skillet and brown almonds lightly, stirring as needed. Stir in remaining salt, lemon juice and parsley; pour over fish. Serve immediately.   *Makes 4 to 6 servings*

Shrimp Curry

    2 pounds raw medium or large shrimp,
      peeled and deveined
    1 cup chopped onions
  ¼ cup margarine or butter
  ¼ cup unsifted flour
 2½ cups BORDEN® or MEADOW GOLD®
      Milk or Half-and-Half
  ¾ cup COCO LOPEZ® Cream of
      Coconut
    1 tablespoon curry powder
    1 teaspoon salt
  ½ teaspoon ground ginger
  ¼ cup REALEMON® Lemon Juice from
      Concentrate or REALIME® Lime
      Juice from Concentrate
    Hot cooked rice

In large skillet, cook and stir onions in margarine until tender; stir in flour. Gradually add milk; stir until smooth. Add cream of coconut, curry, salt and ginger. Over medium heat, cook and stir until thickened. Add ReaLemon® brand. Reduce heat; simmer uncovered 20 minutes, stirring occasionally. Add shrimp. Over medium heat, cook 5 to 10 minutes, stirring occasionally, until shrimp are opaque. Serve over rice with condiments. Refrigerate leftovers.

Makes 6 to 8 servings

Condiments: Toasted coconut, sunflower meats, chopped peanuts, sliced green onion, chopped hard-cooked eggs, chutney, crumbled bacon or raisins.

Garlic Shrimp with Noodles

4 tablespoons butter, divided
¼ cup finely chopped onion
2 cups water
1 package LIPTON® Noodles & Sauce—
  Butter & Herb
2 tablespoons olive oil
1 tablespoon finely chopped garlic
1 pound uncooked medium shrimp,
  cleaned
1 can (14 ounces) artichoke hearts,
  drained and halved
¼ cup finely chopped fresh parsley
  Pepper to taste

In medium saucepan, melt 2 tablespoons butter; cook onion until tender. Add water; bring to a boil. Stir in noodles & sauce—butter & herb and continue boiling over medium heat, stirring occasionally, 8 minutes or until noodles are tender.

Meanwhile, in large skillet, heat remaining 2 tablespoons butter with olive oil. Add garlic; cook over medium-high heat 30 seconds. Add shrimp and artichokes; cook, stirring occasionally, 3 minutes or until shrimp turn pink. Stir in parsley and pepper. To serve, combine shrimp mixture with hot noodles. Garnish, if desired, with watercress.

Makes about 4 servings

Devilishly Stuffed Soft-Shell Crab

8 soft-shell crabs, cleaned, fresh or
  frozen
¼ cup chopped onion
¼ cup chopped celery
2 tablespoons chopped green bell
  pepper
1 clove garlic, minced
¼ cup margarine or butter, melted
1 cup buttery cracker crumbs
2 tablespoons milk
1 egg, beaten
1 tablespoon chopped parsley
½ teaspoon dry mustard
½ teaspoon Worcestershire sauce
¼ teaspoon salt
⅛ teaspoon cayenne pepper
¼ cup margarine or butter, melted

Thaw crabs if frozen. Wash crabs thoroughly; drain well. Cook onion, celery, green pepper and garlic in margarine until tender. In medium bowl, combine mixture with cracker crumbs, milk, egg, parsley, mustard, Worcestershire sauce, salt and cayenne pepper. Place crabs in shallow, well-greased baking pan. Remove top shell from crabs and fill each cavity with 1 tablespoon stuffing mixture. Replace top shell. Brush crabs with melted margarine. Bake in preheated 400°F oven 15 minutes or until shells turn red and crabs brown slightly.   *Makes 4 servings*

*Favorite recipe from **Florida Department of Agriculture and Consumer Services, Bureau of Seafood and Aquaculture***

Garlic Shrimp with Noodles

Crystal Shrimp with Sweet & Sour Sauce

½ cup **KIKKOMAN®** Sweet & Sour Sauce
1 tablespoon water
2 teaspoons cornstarch
½ pound medium-size raw shrimp,
    peeled and deveined
1 egg white, beaten
2 tablespoons vegetable oil, divided
1 clove garlic, minced
2 carrots, cut diagonally into thin slices
1 medium-size green bell pepper,
    chunked
1 medium onion, chunked
1 tablespoon sesame seed, toasted

Blend sweet & sour sauce and water; set aside. Measure cornstarch into large plastic food storage bag. Coat shrimp with egg white; drain off excess egg. Add shrimp to cornstarch in bag; shake bag to coat shrimp. Heat 1 tablespoon oil in hot wok or large skillet over medium-high heat. Add garlic; stir-fry 10 seconds, or until fragrant. Add shrimp and stir-fry 2 minutes, or until pink; remove. Heat remaining 1 tablespoon oil in same pan over high heat. Add carrots, green pepper and onion; stir-fry 4 minutes. Add shrimp and sweet & sour sauce mixture. Cook and stir until shrimp and vegetables are coated with sauce. Remove from heat; stir in sesame seed. Serve immediately.

Makes 4 servings

Steamed Bucket of Clams

18 to 24 hard-shell clams
 1 gallon cold water
⅓ cup cornmeal
⅓ cup salt
    Juice of 1 SUNKIST® Lemon
 2 tablespoons olive or vegetable oil
    Grated peel of ½ SUNKIST® Lemon
 2 tablespoons chopped parsley
    Lemon wedges

Scrub clams well. To purge clams, combine water, cornmeal and salt. Add clams and soak for 2 hours. Rinse well. In 10-inch skillet, arrange clams in single layer and drizzle with lemon juice and oil. Bring liquid to a boil over medium-high heat; cover tightly and cook 5 minutes. Do not lift lid of skillet during this cooking time. (If most clams have not opened, cook, covered, 1 to 2 minutes longer.) Remove clams to serving bowl; discard any unopened clams. Stir lemon peel and parsley into clam juice in skillet. Pour over clams. Serve with lemon wedges.

Makes 2 to 4 servings

The Florida Department of Agriculture and Consumer Services' *Bureau of Seafood and Aquaculture was formed to promote the wise utilization and consumption of the vast array of seafood. A primary goal is to increase public knowledge and awareness of Florida seafood.*

Shrimp Miami

Shrimp Miami

2 pounds shrimp, fresh or frozen
¼ cup olive or vegetable oil
2 teaspoons salt
½ teaspoon white pepper
¼ cup extra dry vermouth
2 tablespoons lemon juice

Thaw frozen shrimp. Peel shrimp, leaving last section of shell on. Remove sand veins and wash. Preheat electric frying pan to 320°F. Add oil, salt, pepper and shrimp. Cook 8 to 10 minutes or until shrimp are pink and tender, stirring constantly. Increase temperature to 420°F. Add vermouth and lemon juice. Cook 1 minute longer, stirring constantly. Drain. Serve hot or cold as an appetizer or entrée.   *Makes 6 servings*

*Favorite recipe from **Florida Department of Agriculture and Consumer Services, Bureau of Seafood and Aquaculture***

New West Crab Cakes

1 pound crabmeat
2 egg whites
1 egg yolk
¾ pound Idaho potatoes, mashed (or
1 cup instant mashed potatoes)
⅓ cup chopped red onion or chives
½ cup chopped California Walnuts,
divided
1 cup bread crumbs, divided
Pinch of salt

Combine crabmeat, egg whites, egg yolk, potatoes, onion, ¼ cup chopped walnuts, ½ cup bread crumbs and salt in medium bowl. Form into 8 flat patties. Mix together remaining ½ cup bread crumbs and ¼ cup finely chopped walnuts. Coat crab patties with bread crumb mixture. Cook over medium heat in skillet brushed with oil.

Serve with lemon wedges, fresh tomato relish or prepared salsa. *Makes 4 servings*

Favorite recipe from **Walnut Marketing Board**

Hot Crab Melt

1 (6-ounce) can HARRIS® or ORLEANS®
Crab Meat, drained
¼ cup BENNETT'S® Cocktail or Tartar
Sauce
2 tablespoons finely chopped celery
2 tablespoons finely chopped green
bell pepper
2 English muffins, split and toasted
4 slices BORDEN® Process American
Cheese Food

Preheat oven to 350°F. In small bowl, combine crab meat, sauce, celery and green pepper; spread equal amounts on muffin halves. Bake 5 minutes. Top each with cheese food slice; bake 5 minutes longer or until melted. Serve immediately. Refrigerate leftovers. *Makes 4 servings*

White Clam Sauce

2 cloves garlic, finely chopped
¼ cup olive oil
2 (6½-ounce) cans DOXSEE® or
SNOW'S® Minced or Chopped
Clams, drained, reserving liquid
1 (8-ounce) bottle DOXSEE® or
SNOW'S® Clam Juice
1 tablespoon chopped parsley
¼ teaspoon basil leaves
Dash pepper

In medium saucepan, cook garlic in oil until tender. Add reserved clam liquid, clam juice, parsley, basil and pepper. Bring to a boil. Reduce heat; simmer 5 minutes. Add clams; heat through. Serve over hot cooked CREAMETTE® Linguine topped with grated Parmesan cheese. Refrigerate leftovers. *Makes about 2½ cups*

Heinz® factory workers hand peeling tomatoes in 1910.

Seafood Cocktail Sauce

1 cup HEINZ® Chili Sauce
1 tablespoon prepared horseradish
1 teaspoon lemon juice*
  Hot pepper sauce to taste

*One teaspoon Heinz® Vinegar may be substituted.

Combine all ingredients. Serve with chilled shrimp, seafood, broiled fish or fish sticks.

Makes about 1 cup

Pasta
Mania &
More

Not just spaghetti anymore!
The versatility of pasta is apparent
with these taste-tempting sensations
for all occasions.

Rigatoni with Creamy Tomato Sauce

8 ounces dry pasta (rigatoni or penne), cooked, drained and kept warm
1 tablespoon olive oil
½ cup diced onion
2 tablespoons dry vermouth or white wine
1¾ cups (14.5-ounce can) CONTADINA® Pasta Ready™ Chunky Tomatoes, Primavera
½ cup heavy cream
1 cup California Ripe Olives, halved
½ cup grated Parmesan cheese
¼ cup sliced green onions

In large skillet, heat oil; add onion and sauté 4 to 5 minutes. Add vermouth; cook 1 minute. Stir in tomatoes and juice, cream, pasta, olives and Parmesan cheese; toss well. Sprinkle with green onions.

Makes 4 servings

Rigatoni with Creamy Tomato Sauce

Tomato Caper Sauce

Tomato Caper Sauce

3 tablespoons olive oil
2 cloves garlic, crushed
2 cans (14½ ounces) CONTADINA®
  Recipe Ready Diced Tomatoes,
  undrained
½ cup rinsed capers
¼ cup chopped fresh cilantro
1 tablespoon chopped fresh basil
1 tablespoon chopped fresh thyme
  Dash pepper
1 pound rigatoni, cooked and drained

Heat oil in medium saucepan over medium-high heat. Add garlic; cook and stir 1 to 2 minutes or until lightly browned. Add tomatoes and capers. Reduce heat to low; simmer, uncovered, 15 to 20 minutes. Stir in cilantro, basil, thyme and pepper; simmer an additional 5 minutes. Serve over hot pasta.

Makes 8 servings

Hunt's® Spaghetti Sauce

½ pound ground beef
¼ cup chopped onion
2 (8-ounce) cans HUNT'S® Tomato
    Sauce
¾ teaspoon sugar
½ teaspoon dried basil
¼ teaspoon dried oregano
¼ teaspoon garlic powder

Brown beef with onion in medium saucepan over medium-high heat until no longer pink; drain. Stir in tomato sauce, sugar, basil, oregano and garlic powder. Simmer, covered, 10 minutes; stir occasionally.

Makes 2 cups

Spinach Tortellini with Bel Paese®

2 tablespoons butter
4 ounces BEL PAESE® Cheese,* cut
    into small chunks
¾ cup half-and-half
3 ounces chopped GALBANI®
    Prosciutto di Parma
Pepper
8 ounces spinach tortellini

*Remove wax coating and moist, white crust from cheese.

In small saucepan, melt butter over low heat. Add Bel Paese® cheese and half-and-half; cook until smooth, stirring constantly. Stir in Galbani® Prosciutto di Parma; sprinkle with pepper to taste. Remove from heat; set aside.

In large saucepan of boiling water, cook tortellini until "al dente" (tender but still firm); drain. Place in serving bowl. Pour sauce over pasta; toss to coat. Serve immediately.

Bel Paese®

Wisconsin, well-known as the heart of America's dairyland, is also home for the main plant of Cucina Classica Italiana, Inc., a major producer of specialty Italian cheeses. Their most famous cheese is the world-renowned semi-soft table cheese, Bel Paese®. In addition to the delicious original, new varieties have been created, including Bel Paese with Sun-Dried Tomatoes and Basil, and Bel Paese Primavera, made with fresh carrots, green peppers, onions and celery.

Hunt's® Linguine with Red Clam Sauce

1 tablespoon olive oil
¾ cup finely chopped onion
½ teaspoon fresh minced garlic
1 (15-ounce) can HUNT'S® Tomato
    Sauce
1 (10-ounce) can whole baby clams,
    reserve ¼ cup clam juice
1 tablespoon chopped fresh parsley
1 teaspoon crushed basil
½ teaspoon crushed oregano
⅛ teaspoon pepper
¾ pound linguine, cooked and drained
    Grated Parmesan cheese

In large saucepan, heat oil; sauté onion and garlic until tender. Stir in tomato sauce, clams, clam juice, parsley, basil, oregano and pepper. Simmer, uncovered, for 10 to 15 minutes; stir occasionally. Serve over linguine and top with Parmesan cheese.

Makes 4 servings

Four-Pepper Penne

1 medium onion, sliced
1 small red bell pepper, thinly sliced
1 small green bell pepper, thinly sliced
1 small yellow bell pepper, thinly sliced
1½ teaspoons minced garlic
1 tablespoon vegetable oil
1 (26-ounce) jar HEALTHY CHOICE®
    Traditional Pasta Sauce
1 teaspoon dried basil
½ teaspoon dried savory
¼ teaspoon black pepper
½ pound penne, cooked and drained

In Dutch oven or large nonstick saucepan, cook and stir onion, bell peppers and garlic in hot oil until vegetables are tender-crisp. Add pasta sauce, basil, savory and black pepper. Heat through over medium heat. Serve over penne.

Makes 6 servings

HEALTHY CHOICE

Healthy Choice® introduced its first products, frozen dinners, in 1988. Today, Healthy Choice offers consumers more than 300 products that are found in nearly every section of the grocery store. Products include frozen meals, cold cuts, franks, smoked sausages, service deli meats, pasta sauces, fat-free cheese, ready-to-serve soup, premium low-fat ice cream and multigrain cereal. All Healthy Choice® products contain less than 30 percent of calories from total fat and less than 10 percent of calories from saturated fat.

Angel Hair al Fresco

Angel Hair al Fresco

¾ cup skim milk
1 tablespoon margarine or butter
1 package (4.8 ounces) PASTA RONI™
    Angel Hair Pasta with Herbs
1 can (6⅛ ounces) white tuna in water,
    drained, flaked *or* 1½ cups chopped
    cooked chicken
2 medium tomatoes, chopped
⅓ cup sliced green onions
¼ cup dry white wine or water
¼ cup slivered almonds, toasted
    (optional)
1 tablespoon chopped fresh basil *or*
    1 teaspoon dried basil

1. In 3-quart saucepan, combine 1⅓ cups water, skim milk and margarine. Bring just to a boil.

2. Stir in pasta, contents of seasoning packet, tuna, tomatoes, onions, wine, almonds and basil. Return to a boil; reduce heat to medium.

3. Boil, uncovered, stirring frequently, 6 to 8 minutes. Sauce will be thin, but will thicken upon standing.

4. Let stand 3 minutes or until desired consistency. Stir before serving.

Makes 4 servings

Roasted Vegetables Provençal

8 ounces medium or large mushrooms, halved
1 large zucchini, cut into 1-inch pieces, halved
1 large yellow squash or additional zucchini, cut into 1-inch pieces, quartered
1 large red or green bell pepper, cut into 1-inch pieces
1 small red onion, cut into ¼-inch slices, separated into rings
3 tablespoons olive oil
2 cloves garlic, minced
1 teaspoon dried basil
1 teaspoon dried thyme leaves
½ teaspoon salt (optional)
¼ teaspoon freshly ground black pepper
4 large plum tomatoes, quartered
⅔ cup milk
2 tablespoons margarine or butter
1 package (5.1 ounces) PASTA RONI™ Angel Hair Pasta with Parmesan Cheese

1. Heat oven to 425°F. In 15×10-inch jelly-roll pan combine first 5 vegetables; add combined oil, garlic, basil, thyme, salt and pepper. Toss to coat. Bake 15 minutes; stir in tomatoes. Continue baking 5 to 10 minutes or until vegetables are tender.

2. While vegetables are roasting, combine 1⅓ cups water, milk and margarine in medium saucepan; bring just to a boil. Gradually add pasta while stirring. Stir in contents of seasoning packet. Reduce heat to medium.

3. Boil, uncovered, stirring frequently, 4 minutes. Sauce will be very thin, but will thicken upon standing. Remove from heat.

4. Let stand 3 minutes or until desired consistency. Stir before serving. Serve pasta topped with vegetables.

Makes 4 servings

Stroganoff Noodles & Meatballs

½ pound ground beef or turkey
¼ cup Italian-style dry bread crumbs
1 tablespoon water
1 tablespoon vegetable or olive oil
1½ cups water
½ cup milk
1 package LIPTON® Noodles & Sauce— Stroganoff
1 jar (4.5 ounces) sliced mushrooms, drained
1 teaspoon chopped fresh parsley

In medium bowl, combine ground beef, bread crumbs and 1 tablespoon water. Shape into sixteen 1-inch meatballs. In 10-inch skillet, heat oil and cook meatballs over medium heat 5 minutes or until done; set aside.

In medium saucepan, bring 1½ cups water and milk to the boiling point. Stir in noodles & sauce—stroganoff and continue boiling over medium heat, stirring occasionally, 7 minutes. Stir in mushrooms, parsley and meatballs and continue cooking, stirring frequently, 3 minutes or until noodles are tender.

Makes 2 (2-cup) servings

Roasted Vegetables Provençal

Flash Primavera

1 pound mostaccioli, ziti or other
    medium pasta shape, uncooked
1 head broccoli or cauliflower, cut into
    small florets
1 tablespoon cornstarch
3 cloves garlic, minced
1 (15½-ounce) can low-sodium chicken
    broth
1 (10-ounce) package frozen mixed
    vegetables
1 (10-ounce) package frozen chopped
    spinach, thawed
  Salt and pepper to taste
1 cup grated Parmesan cheese

Prepare pasta according to package directions. Three minutes before pasta is done, stir in broccoli or cauliflower. Drain pasta and vegetables; transfer to large bowl.

In small bowl, dissolve cornstarch in ¼ cup of water. Combine garlic and chicken broth in large saucepan. Simmer over medium heat 3 minutes. Whisk in cornstarch mixture. Stir in mixed vegetables and spinach; cook about 5 minutes or until heated through. Toss sauce and vegetable mixture with pasta. Season with salt and pepper and sprinkle with Parmesan cheese; serve.

Makes 6 servings

*Favorite recipe from **National Pasta Association***

National Pasta Association

The National Pasta Association is the trade association for the U.S. pasta industry. Founded in 1904, the member companies provide a variety of pasta products. Currently, there are about 30 companies producing a record volume of pasta for the insatiable appetites of U.S. consumers.

Pennini with Vegetable Sauce "Springtime"

12 ounces (3 cups) uncooked
    mostaccioli
1 red bell pepper
2 small zucchini
⅔ cup fresh Oriental pea pods *or*
    10 ounces frozen pea pods
3 green onions
4 tablespoons olive oil
2 carrots, cut into julienne strips
1½ cups diced fresh tomatoes
2 tablespoons chopped chives
2 tablespoons fresh chopped dill *or*
    ½ teaspoon dried dill
  Salt and fresh ground pepper
¼ cup toasted sunflower kernels

Cook pasta according to package directions; drain well. Cut red pepper and zucchini into small slices. Cut pea pods in half or thirds and slice green onions. While pasta is cooking, heat oil in large nonstick saucepan over medium heat. Add red pepper and carrots; cook and stir 6 minutes. Add zucchini, pea pods and onions; cook and stir an additional 5 minutes. Add tomatoes, chives and dill. Season with salt and pepper. Heat until warmed through. Toss vegetable mixture with cooked pasta. Sprinkle with toasted sunflower kernels. Serve hot.

Makes 4 servings

*Favorite recipe from **National Sunflower Association***

Zesty Artichoke Basil Sauce

- 1 jar (6 ounces) marinated artichoke hearts, drained, reserving marinade
- 1 cup chopped onions
- 1 large clove garlic, minced
- 1 can (14½ ounces) CONTADINA® Recipe Ready Diced Tomatoes, undrained
- 1 can (6 ounces) CONTADINA® Tomato Paste
- 1 cup water
- 2 tablespoons chopped fresh basil
- ½ teaspoon salt

In medium saucepan, cook and stir onions and garlic in reserved marinade over medium heat 2 to 3 minutes or until tender. Chop artichoke hearts; add to saucepan with tomatoes, tomato paste, water, basil and salt. Bring to a boil; reduce heat to low. Simmer, uncovered, 20 minutes, stirring occasionally.

Makes 4 cups

Savory Caper and Olive Sauce: Omit artichoke hearts and basil. In medium saucepan, cook and stir onions and garlic in 2 tablespoons olive oil over medium heat 2 to 3 minutes. Add ¾ cup sliced and quartered zucchini, tomatoes, tomato paste, water, salt, 1 can (2¼ ounces) drained sliced pitted ripe olives and 2 tablespoons drained capers. Continue as directed.

Garden Primavera Pasta

- 6 ounces bow-tie pasta
- 1 jar (6 ounces) marinated artichoke hearts
- 2 cloves garlic, minced
- ½ teaspoon dried rosemary, crushed
- 1 green pepper, cut into thin strips
- 1 large carrot, cut into 3-inch julienne strips
- 1 medium zucchini, cut into 3-inch julienne strips
- 1 can (14½ ounces) DEL MONTE® Pasta Style Chunky Tomatoes
- 12 small pitted ripe olives (optional)

Cook pasta according to package directions; drain. Drain artichokes, reserving marinade. Toss pasta in 3 tablespoons artichoke marinade; set aside. Cut artichoke hearts into halves. In large skillet, cook garlic and rosemary in 1 tablespoon artichoke marinade. Add remaining ingredients, except pasta and artichokes. Cook, uncovered, over medium-high heat 4 to 5 minutes or until vegetables are tender-crisp and sauce is thickened. Add artichoke hearts. Spoon over pasta. Serve with grated Parmesan cheese, if desired. *Makes 4 servings*

Spinach-Stuffed Manicotti

8 manicotti shells, cooked and drained
1½ teaspoons olive oil
1 teaspoon minced fresh garlic
1½ cups canned or fresh tomatoes, chopped
1 teaspoon dried rosemary leaves, crushed
1 teaspoon dried sage leaves, crushed
1 teaspoon dried oregano leaves, crushed
1 teaspoon dried thyme leaves, crushed
1 package (10 ounces) frozen spinach, cooked, drained and squeezed dry
4 ounces ricotta cheese
1 slice whole wheat bread, torn into coarse crumbs
2 egg whites, slightly beaten

Preheat oven to 350°F. Heat oil in small saucepan over medium heat. Add garlic; cook and stir until lightly browned. Stir in tomatoes, rosemary, sage, oregano and thyme. Reduce heat to low; simmer 10 minutes, stirring occasionally.

Combine spinach, cheese and bread crumbs in medium bowl. Fold in egg whites. Stuff manicotti with spinach mixture. Spoon ⅓ of sauce into 13×9-inch baking dish. Arrange manicotti over sauce; cover with remaining sauce. Cover with foil. Bake 30 minutes or until hot and bubbly. Garnish as desired.

Makes 4 servings

Favorite recipe from **National Pasta Association**

Pasta Roll Ups

1 package (1.5 ounces) LAWRY'S® Original-Style Spaghetti Sauce Spices & Seasonings
1 can (6 ounces) tomato paste
2¼ cups water
2 tablespoons vegetable oil or butter
2 cups cottage cheese or ricotta cheese
1 cup (4 ounces) grated mozzarella cheese
¼ cup Parmesan cheese
2 eggs
½ to 1 teaspoon LAWRY'S® Garlic Salt
½ teaspoon dried basil (optional)
1 box (8 ounces) lasagna noodles, cooked

In medium saucepan, prepare Original-Style Spaghetti Sauce Spices & Seasonings with tomato paste, water and oil according to package directions. In large bowl, combine all remaining ingredients except noodles; blend well. Spread ¼ cup cheese mixture on entire length of each lasagna noodle; roll. Place seam side down in microwavable baking dish. Microwave on HIGH 6 to 7 minutes, until cheese begins to melt. Pour sauce over rolls and microwave on HIGH 1 minute, if necessary, to heat sauce.

Makes 6 servings

Presentation: Sprinkle with additional Parmesan or mozzarella cheese.

Hint: For quick microwavable meals, wrap prepared rolls individually and freeze. Sauce may be frozen in ¼ cup servings.

Spinach-Stuffed Manicotti

Three Cheese Vegetable Lasagna

1 large onion, chopped
3 cloves garlic, minced
1 teaspoon olive oil
1 can (28 ounces) no-salt-added tomato
   purée
1 can (14½ ounces) no-salt-added
   tomatoes, undrained and chopped
2 cups (6 ounces) sliced fresh
   mushrooms
1 zucchini, diced
1 large green bell pepper, chopped
2 teaspoons basil, crushed
1 teaspoon *each* salt and sugar
   (optional)
½ teaspoon *each* red pepper flakes and
   oregano, crushed
2 cups (15 ounces) SARGENTO® Light
   Ricotta Cheese
1 package (10 ounces) frozen chopped
   spinach, thawed and squeezed dry
2 egg whites
2 tablespoons (½ ounce) SARGENTO®
   Fancy Supreme® Shredded
   Parmesan Cheese
½ pound lasagna noodles, cooked
   according to package directions,
   without oil or salt
¾ cup (3 ounces) *each* SARGENTO®
   Preferred Light® Fancy Shredded
   Mozzarella and Mild Cheddar
   Cheese, divided

Spray large skillet with nonstick vegetable spray. Add onion, garlic and olive oil; cook over medium heat until tender, stirring occasionally. Add tomato purée, tomatoes, tomato liquid, mushrooms, zucchini, bell pepper, basil, salt, sugar, pepper flakes and oregano. Heat to a boil. Reduce heat; cover and simmer 10 minutes or until vegetables are crisp-tender.

Combine Ricotta cheese, spinach, egg whites and Parmesan cheese; mix well. Spread 1 cup sauce in bottom of 13×9-inch baking dish. Layer 3 lasagna noodles over sauce. Top with half of Ricotta cheese mixture and 2 cups of remaining sauce. Repeat layering with 3 more lasagna noodles, remaining Ricotta mixture and 2 cups sauce. Combine Mozzarella and Cheddar cheeses. Sprinkle ¾ cup cheese mixture over sauce. Top with remaining lasagna noodles and sauce. Cover with foil; bake at 375°F 30 minutes. Uncover; bake 15 minutes more. Sprinkle with remaining ¾ cup cheese mixture. Let stand 10 minutes before serving.

Makes 10 servings

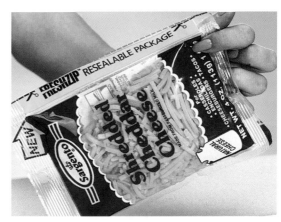

Always an industry leader, Sargento was among the first to introduce resealable packaging.

Three Cheese Vegetable Lasagna

Layered Pasta Ricotta Pie

Layered Pasta Ricotta Pie

¼ (1-pound) package CREAMETTE® Vermicelli
⅓ cup finely chopped onion
4 cloves garlic, finely chopped
1 tablespoon olive or vegetable oil
1 cup grated fresh Romano cheese
3 eggs
1 (15- or 16-ounce) container ricotta cheese
1 (10-ounce) package frozen chopped spinach, thawed and well drained
½ teaspoon salt
1 (26-ounce) jar CLASSICO® Di Sicilia (Ripe Olives & Mushrooms) Pasta Sauce

Preheat oven to 350°F. Break vermicelli into thirds; cook according to package directions. Drain. Meanwhile, in large skillet, cook onion and garlic in oil until tender; remove from heat. Add cooked vermicelli, *½ cup* Romano cheese and *1 egg;* mix well. Press into well-greased 9-inch springform pan. Combine *2 egg yolks,* ricotta, spinach, salt and remaining *½ cup* Romano cheese. Spread over pasta layer. In small mixer bowl, beat *2 egg whites* until stiff but not dry; fold into *1½ cups pasta sauce.* Pour over spinach mixture. Bake 50 to 60 minutes or until set; let stand 10 minutes. Heat remaining pasta sauce; serve with pie. Garnish as desired. Refrigerate leftovers.

Makes 6 to 8 servings

Lasagna Primavera

1 package (8 ounces) lasagna noodles
3 carrots, cut into ¼-inch slices
1 cup broccoli flowerets
1 cup zucchini, cut into ¼-inch slices
1 crookneck squash, cut into ¼-inch slices
2 (10-ounce) packages frozen chopped spinach, thawed
8 ounces ricotta cheese
1 jar (26 ounces) NEWMAN'S OWN® Marinara Sauce with Mushrooms
12 ounces shredded mozzarella cheese
½ cup grated Parmesan cheese

In 6-quart saucepan, bring 3 quarts water to a boil over high heat. Add lasagna noodles and cook 5 minutes. Add carrots; cook 2 more minutes. Add broccoli, zucchini and crookneck squash; cook 2 minutes more or until pasta is tender. Drain well.

Squeeze liquid out of spinach. Combine spinach with ricotta cheese. In 3-quart rectangular baking pan, spread ⅓ of Newman's Own® Marinara Sauce with Mushrooms. Line pan with lasagna noodles. Place half of vegetables, spinach mixture and mozzarella cheese on noodles. Pour half of remaining sauce over layers. Repeat layers and top with remaining sauce. Sprinkle with Parmesan cheese.

Place baking pan on 10×15-inch baking sheet lined with foil. Bake uncovered in 400°F oven 30 minutes or until hot in center. Let stand 10 minutes before serving. (Casserole may be prepared up to 2 days before baking and refrigerated, covered, until 1 hour before baking. If cold, bake 1 hour at 350°F.) Serve with Italian bread or rolls, green salad with Newman's Own® Light Italian Dressing and red wine. *Makes 8 servings*

Wild Rice Casserole

¼ pound butter
1 cup uncooked wild rice
½ cup slivered almonds
1 (8-ounce) can mushroom slices, drained
2 tablespoons chives or green onions
3 cups chicken broth

Preheat oven to 325°F. Combine butter, rice, almonds, mushrooms and chives in large saucepan. Cook, stirring constantly, over medium heat to brown rice. Place in medium casserole; add broth. Cover tightly and bake 1 hour. *Makes 6 servings*

*Favorite recipe from **Minnesota Cultivated Wild Rice Council***

Paul Newman's love of Italian food led him to create an enticing line of pasta sauces.
Photo courtesy of Newman's Own, Inc.

Guadalajara Rice

**3 tablespoons plus 2 teaspoons Chef
    Paul Prudhomme's MEAT MAGIC®
1 teaspoon dry mustard
1 teaspoon dried oregano leaves
1 pound ground round
1¼ cups finely chopped onions, divided
1¼ cups finely chopped green or yellow
    bell peppers, divided
1 cup finely chopped red bell peppers,
    divided
5 cups defatted beef stock or water,
    divided
1 cup finely chopped canned green
    chilies, divided
¾ cup chopped tomatoes
½ teaspoon minced garlic
2 cups uncooked rice (preferably
    converted)**

Combine Meat Magic®, mustard and oregano thoroughly in small bowl, being sure to break up any lumps.

In 4-quart saucepan (preferably not a nonstick type), combine meat and ½ cup onions, ½ cup green bell peppers and ½ cup red bell peppers, breaking up any big chunks of meat. Cover pan and cook 3 minutes over high heat. Stir well; cook 4 additional minutes. Stir again, breaking up any remaining chunks of meat. Add Meat Magic® mixture, stirring well; cook, uncovered, 2 minutes, stirring frequently and scraping the pan bottom well. Add 1 cup stock, stirring and scraping until any sediment is dissolved from pan bottom; cook until mixture is fairly dry, about 6 minutes, stirring and scraping occasionally. Add ½ cup green chilies, tomatoes and garlic; stir well. Cook 6 minutes, stirring and scraping continuously.

Stir in rice and remaining ¾ cup onions, ¾ cup green bell peppers, ½ cup red bell peppers and ½ cup chilies. Cook until mixture is sticking excessively, about 2 minutes, stirring constantly. Add remaining 4 cups stock, stirring well to dissolve any sediment from pan bottom. Cover pan and bring to a boil; stir and scrape well. Reduce heat to maintain a light simmer; re-cover pan. Cook 5 minutes, stirring and scraping frequently so mixture won't scorch. Stir once more; reduce heat to very low and re-cover pan. Continue cooking about 25 minutes more or until done. Remove from heat and serve immediately.

*Makes 6 (1½-cup) main-dish servings or
8 (1-cup) appetizer servings*

California Apricot Advisory Board

Discovered in China over 4,000 years ago, apricots made their way across the Persian empire to the Mediterranean where they continue to flourish.

Spanish missionaries introduced the golden fruit to the New World, and the first commercial orchard started in California in 1792. Ninety-seven percent of all apricots grown in the U.S. are from California.

Apricot Couscous Pilaf

Apricot Couscous Pilaf

½ tablespoon butter
½ tablespoon vegetable oil
½ cup thinly sliced green onions
½ cup finely diced red bell pepper
½ teaspoon ground cumin
 1 (16-ounce) can apricot halves,
     drained and diced
¼ teaspoon salt
¼ teaspoon ground black pepper
3½ cups cooked instant couscous or
     white or brown rice
 2 tablespoons chopped fresh coriander
     (cilantro) or parsley

Melt butter with oil over medium-high heat in large saucepan. Stir in onions, bell pepper and cumin. Sauté 5 minutes or until vegetables are tender. Add diced apricot, salt and pepper; cook 1 minute. Stir in cooked couscous or rice until all ingredients are well combined; cook, stirring constantly. Remove from heat; stir in coriander or parsley.

Serve with grilled or roasted poultry, meat or seafood. Use as stuffing for poultry or peppers. Perfect as light entrée with tossed salad and bread.   *Makes 8 servings*

*Favorite recipe from **California Apricot Advisory Board***

Muesli Savory Stuffing

4 ounces pork sausage
1 cup sliced mushrooms
½ cup chopped onion
¼ cup chopped celery
2 cups RALSTON® Brand Fruit Muesli
   cereal, crushed to 1½ cups
1 cup seasoned stuffing mix
¾ cup chicken broth
2 tablespoons chopped parsley
1 teaspoon poultry seasoning

Cook sausage in large skillet, over low heat, 5 minutes or until no longer pink, stirring occasionally; drain. Add mushrooms, onion and celery. Cook 2 to 3 minutes or until vegetables are crisp-tender. Stir in cereal, stuffing mix, broth, parsley and seasoning; mix well. Cook, covered, 5 minutes or until hot, stirring halfway through.

Makes 6 servings

Microwave Directions:* Microwave sausage in 2-quart microwave-safe dish on HIGH 2 minutes or until no longer pink, stirring halfway through; drain. Add mushrooms, onion and celery. Microwave on HIGH 2 minutes or until vegetables are crisp-tender. Stir in cereal, stuffing mix, broth, parsley and seasoning; mix well. Microwave on HIGH 2 minutes or until hot, stirring halfway through.

*Due to differences in microwave ovens, cooking time may need adjustment. These directions were developed using 625 to 700 watt ovens.

A small flour mill in Grand Forks, North Dakota, was almost a victim of the financial panic of 1893. Head miller, Tom Amidon, was able to sell the idea of producing a "breakfast porridge," called Cream of Wheat®. With no money to spend on package design, one of the mill owners found an illustration of a chef holding a saucepan over his shoulder. This chef was met with such great success that today he still appears as the product's widely known trademark.

Cheddar Spoonbread

1½ cups water
¾ cup Regular, Instant or Quick CREAM
   OF WHEAT® Cereal
1 cup shredded reduced-fat Cheddar
   cheese
½ cup milk
3 eggs, separated
¼ teaspoon ground black pepper

In large saucepan, over high heat, heat water to a boil; slowly sprinkle in cereal, stirring constantly. Return mixture to a boil; reduce heat. Cook and stir until thickened, about 2 to 3 minutes. Remove from heat; stir in cheese until melted, then milk, egg yolks and pepper. In small bowl, with electric mixer at high speed, beat egg whites until stiff peaks form; gently fold egg whites into cheese mixture. Pour into greased 8×8×2-inch baking dish. Bake at 375°F for 30 to 35 minutes or until set and browned. Serve immediately.

Makes 6 servings

*"Where the mail goes Cream of Wheat® goes"
was the ad for Nabisco's new breakfast porridge.*

Yorkshire Pudding

  2 eggs
  1 cup all-purpose flour
  ½ teaspoon salt
  ¾ cup milk
  ¼ cup water
  1 package (1.0 ounce) LAWRY'S®
     Seasoning Blend for Au Jus Gravy
1½ cups water
  ½ cup port wine
     Dash LAWRY'S® Seasoned Pepper
     Vegetable oil

In medium bowl, using electric beater, beat eggs until frothy. Reduce speed and gradually add flour and salt; beat until smooth. Slowly add milk and water; beat until blended. Increase speed to high and continue beating 10 minutes. Let stand 1 hour. In medium saucepan, prepare seasoning blend for Au Jus Gravy with water, wine and seasoned pepper according to package directions. Set aside. Preheat oven to 400°F. Coat 5-inch omelette pan with oil and place in oven. When pan is very hot, remove and pour off excess oil. In pan, place 1 tablespoon Au Jus Gravy and ½ cup batter. Bake 20 to 30 minutes until puffed and brown. Remove and wrap in foil. Repeat until all batter has been used.

Makes 4 Yorkshire Puddings (8 servings)

Presentation: Cut each pudding into quarters and serve with prime rib or roast beef. Serve remaining Au Jus Gravy over meat.

Hint: Pudding may be made ahead and reheated individually wrapped in foil.

Risotto Milanese

Risotto Milanese

4 to 5 cups beef or chicken stock,
 broth or bouillon, divided
⅓ cup minced onion
2 tablespoons diced GALBANI®
 Prosciutto di Parma
3 tablespoons extra virgin olive oil
1½ cups uncooked arborio rice
1 cup dry white wine
¼ cup CLASSICA™ Grated Parmesan
 cheese
½ teaspoon pepper
 Salt
2 tablespoons butter

Bring stock to a boil. Reduce heat. In separate large saucepan, sauté onion and Galbani® Prosciutto di Parma in olive oil until onion is tender; add rice. Cook 5 minutes, stirring constantly. Stir in wine. Cook until wine is absorbed, stirring constantly.

Add ½ cup stock; stir constantly until almost absorbed. Continue to repeat as absorbed, cooking until rice is tender, 20 to 25 minutes. Stir in Parmesan and pepper. Season with salt. Cook 2 to 3 minutes longer. Stir in butter.

Makes 4 servings

Premium® Stuffing

1 medium onion, minced
4 large stalks celery, chopped (about 1¼ cups)
⅓ cup margarine
80 PREMIUM® Crackers (any variety), coarsely broken (about 4 cups)
2 tablespoons chopped parsley
½ teaspoon ground sage
¼ teaspoon ground black pepper
1 cup chicken broth

In large skillet, over medium-high heat, cook onion and celery in margarine until tender; remove from heat. Stir in cracker crumbs, parsley, sage, pepper and broth. Use to stuff poultry or spoon into greased 1½-quart casserole and bake, covered, at 325°F for 40 minutes or until heated through.

Makes about 5 cups

Ritz® Cracker Stuffing

1 cup coarsely chopped broccoli or mushrooms
½ cup chopped onion
½ cup chopped celery
¼ cup margarine
4 Stay Fresh Packs RITZ® Crackers, coarsely crushed (about 7 cups crumbs)
2 cups walnuts, pecans or almonds, coarsely chopped
¼ cup snipped parsley
1 tablespoon poultry seasoning
½ teaspoon ground black pepper
1 (13¾-fluid ounce) can COLLEGE INN® Chicken Broth
2 eggs, beaten

In skillet, over medium heat, cook broccoli or mushrooms, onion and celery in margarine until tender.

In large bowl, combine cracker crumbs, nuts, parsley, poultry seasoning, pepper and vegetable mixture. Add broth and eggs, tossing until well combined. Spoon into 2-quart baking dish or pan; cover. Bake at 325°F for 30 to 40 minutes or until heated through. Or use as stuffing for turkey, chicken or pork.

Makes about 6 cups

Ritz® Crackers

In 1934, the National Biscuit Company (early Nabisco) made cracker history with a brand new entry. It was much crispier and its flavor was enhanced by a thin coat of coconut oil and a sprinkling of salt. Given the name "Ritz" because it was designed as a prestige item, this classy cracker is now one of the world's biggest-selling tidbit of its kind.

The Vegetable Garden

From garden to table, add pizazz to everyday vegetables. Let these delicious recipes be your inspiration for making the ordinary extraordinary.

Grilled Vegetables with Balsamic Vinaigrette

1 medium eggplant (about 1¼ pounds)
2 medium zucchini
2 to 3 medium yellow squash
2 medium red bell peppers
¾ cup olive oil
¼ cup balsamic vinegar
1 teaspoon salt
¼ teaspoon black pepper
1 clove garlic, minced
2 to 3 tablespoons finely chopped mixed fresh herbs

Trim, then slice eggplant, zucchini and yellow squash lengthwise into ¼- to ½-inch-thick slices. Core, seed and cut red peppers into 1-inch-wide strips. Place vegetables in deep serving platter or wide shallow casserole. Combine oil, vinegar, salt, pepper, garlic and herbs in small bowl. Pour vinaigrette over vegetables; turn to coat. Let stand 30 minutes or longer. Lift vegetables from vinaigrette, leaving vinaigrette that doesn't cling to vegetables in dish.

Oil hot grid to help prevent sticking. Grill vegetables, on covered grill, over medium KINGSFORD® briquets, 8 to 16 minutes or until fork-tender, turning once or twice. (Time will depend on the vegetable; eggplant takes the longest.) As vegetables are done, return them to platter, then turn to coat with vinaigrette. (Or, cut eggplant, zucchini and yellow squash into cubes, then toss with red peppers and vinaigrette.) Serve warm or at room temperature.   *Makes 6 servings*

Grilled Vegetables with Balsamic Vinaigrette

Honey Squash

2 acorn squash (about 6 ounces each)
¼ cup honey
2 tablespoons butter or margarine, melted
2 tablespoons chopped walnuts
2 tablespoons raisins
2 teaspoons Worcestershire sauce

Cut acorn squash lengthwise into halves; do not remove seeds. Place cut side up in baking pan or on baking sheet. Bake at 400°F 30 to 45 minutes or until soft. Remove seeds and fibers.

Combine honey, butter, walnuts, raisins and Worcestershire sauce; spoon into squash. Bake 5 to 10 minutes more or until lightly glazed. *Makes 4 servings*

Favorite recipe from **National Honey Board**

Creamed Spinach à la Lawry's®

4 bacon slices, finely chopped
1 cup finely chopped onions
¼ cup all-purpose flour
2 teaspoons LAWRY'S® Seasoned Salt
½ teaspoon LAWRY'S® Seasoned Pepper
½ teaspoon LAWRY'S® Garlic Powder with Parsley
1½ to 2 cups milk
2 packages (10 ounces each) frozen spinach, cooked and drained

In medium skillet, fry bacon until almost crisp. Add onions to bacon and cook until onions are tender, about 10 minutes. Remove from heat. Add flour, Seasoned Salt, Seasoned Pepper and Garlic Powder with Parsley; blend thoroughly. Gradually add milk, starting with 1½ cups, and stir over low heat until thickened. Add spinach and mix thoroughly. If too thick, add additional milk.
Makes 8 servings

Presentation: Serve with prime ribs of beef.

Spicy Baked Beans

6 bacon slices, cut up
2 cans (1 pound 12 ounces each) baked beans
½ cup firmly packed brown sugar
1 tablespoon bourbon
1 medium onion, chopped
1 tablespoon instant coffee
1 teaspoon dry mustard
¾ teaspoon LAWRY'S® Seasoned Salt
½ to ¾ teaspoon hot pepper sauce
1 can (1 pound 4 ounces) sliced pineapple

In small skillet, brown bacon until soft; drain fat and set aside. In 13×9×2-inch casserole, combine beans, brown sugar, bourbon, onion, coffee, mustard, Seasoned Salt and hot pepper sauce. Let stand at room temperature 30 minutes. Arrange bacon on bean mixture. Layer with pineapple slices. Bake, uncovered, in 375°F oven 40 minutes.
Makes 8 servings

Honey Squash

Roasted Fresh Tomatoes

6 large (about 3 pounds) Fresh Florida Tomatoes
2 tablespoons vegetable oil
½ teaspoon basil leaves, crushed
¼ teaspoon thyme leaves, crushed
¼ teaspoon salt
¼ teaspoon ground black pepper

Preheat oven to 425°F. Use tomatoes held at room temperature until fully ripe. Core tomatoes; cut into halves horizontally. Gently squeeze to remove seeds. Place cut side up on rack in broiler pan; set aside. In small bowl, combine oil, basil, thyme, salt and black pepper; brush over cut sides of tomatoes. Place tomatoes cut side down on broiler pan. Bake about 30 minutes or until well browned. Remove tomato skins, if desired. Serve hot, warm or cold. *Makes 4 to 6 servings*

Favorite recipe from **Florida Tomato Committee**

Lipton® California Mashed Potatoes

2 pounds all-purpose potatoes, peeled, if desired, and cut into chunks
Water
2 tablespoons chopped fresh parsley (optional)
1 envelope LIPTON® RECIPE SECRETS® Onion Soup Mix*
¾ cup milk, heated to boiling
½ cup sour cream

*Also terrific with Lipton® Recipe Secrets® Golden Onion, Golden Herb with Lemon or Savory Herb with Garlic Soup Mix.

In 3-quart saucepan, cover potatoes with water. Bring to a boil over high heat. Reduce heat to low and simmer 20 minutes or until potatoes are very tender; drain. Return potatoes to saucepan. Mash potatoes. Stir in parsley and onion soup mix blended with hot milk and sour cream.
Makes about 6 servings

Classica™ Fontina Potato Surprise

2½ pounds potatoes
3 tablespoons butter or margarine, melted
¼ cup CLASSICA™ Grated Parmesan cheese
1 egg
1 egg white
⅛ teaspoon salt
⅛ teaspoon ground nutmeg
4 tablespoons fine dry bread crumbs, divided
8 ounces CLASSICA™ brand Fontina, cut into chunks
¼ cup freshly grated sharp provolone cheese
¼ pound GALBANI® Prosciutto di Parma, cut into small pieces
2 tablespoons butter or margarine, cut into small pieces

Classica™ Fontina Potato Surprise

In large saucepan, cook potatoes in boiling water over medium-low heat until tender; drain. Cool slightly; peel and cut in half. Press potatoes through food mill or mash until smooth. Combine potatoes, melted butter, Classica™ grated Parmesan cheese, egg, egg white, salt and nutmeg in large bowl; mix until smooth. Set aside.

Sprinkle ½ of bread crumbs in well-buttered 9-inch-round baking dish. Tilt dish to coat.

Spread about ½ of potato mixture on bottom and side of dish.

Combine Classica™ Fontina, provolone and Galbani® Prosciutto di Parma in small bowl. Sprinkle over potato mixture in dish.

Cover with remaining potato mixture; sprinkle with remaining bread crumbs. Dot with pieces of butter.

Bake in preheated 350°F oven 40 minutes or until thin crust forms. Let stand 5 minutes.

Invert baking dish onto serving plate, tapping gently to remove. Serve immediately.

Makes 4 to 6 servings

Lemon Parmesan Cauliflower

1 medium head cauliflower
  Juice of 1 fresh SUNKIST® Lemon
2 to 3 tablespoons butter or margarine, melted
2 to 3 tablespoons grated Parmesan cheese
¼ teaspoon paprika
  Salt and pepper

In large saucepan, cook cauliflower in 1 inch boiling water with juice of ½ lemon 5 to 10 minutes for flowerets, 15 to 20 minutes for whole cauliflower or until tender; drain. To serve, sprinkle cauliflower with remaining juice of ½ lemon and butter. Combine Parmesan cheese and paprika; sprinkle over cauliflower. Sprinkle with salt and pepper to taste. Garnish with lemon cartwheel twists and parsley, if desired.

Makes 4 to 6 servings

Colorado Potato Devils

4 Colorado baking potatoes
  Salt and pepper
8 teaspoons whole seed or grainy mustard
6 ounces mushroom, pepper or regular Brie cheese
2 tablespoons finely chopped chives or green onion tops

Heat oven to 400°F. Prick potatoes in 5 or 6 places with tines of fork. Bake potatoes 50 to 60 minutes, until tender and skins are crisp. Cut potatoes crosswise into 4 thick slices. With melon baller or small spoon, scoop out a little potato from the center. Season with salt and pepper; spread each hollowed-out center with ½ teaspoon mustard. Cut up Brie into 16 chunks; place one piece in each center. Sprinkle with chives. Place on baking sheets. Bake at 400°F 15 to 20 minutes or until cheese has melted and browned in spots. Serve warm. *Makes 8 servings*

*Favorite recipe from **Colorado Potato Administrative Committee***

Colorado Potato Administrative Committee

In the late 18th century, local farmers in Colorado's San Luis Valley began growing potatoes because of the healthy, rich soil. Mother Nature still provides warm summer days and cool summer nights. This climate, combined with modern watering methods, produces excellent growing conditions to ensure outstanding potatoes.

From left to right: Colorado Hot & Spicy Ribbon Chips and Colorado Potato Devils

Colorado Hot & Spicy Ribbon Chips

2 pounds (4 to 6) Colorado baking
    potatoes
  Oil for frying
1 tablespoon chili powder
1 teaspoon salt
1 teaspoon garlic salt
¼ to ½ teaspoon cayenne pepper

With vegetable peeler, peel thin strips of potatoes lengthwise to make ribbons, or with knife, cut potatoes into very thin lengthwise slices. Place in 1 quart ice water; add 1 tablespoon salt. Heat about 1 inch oil in deep-fat fryer or heavy pan to 365°F. Combine chili powder, salt, garlic salt and cayenne pepper; set aside. Drain potatoes and pat dry with paper towels. Fry potatoes in batches until golden and crisp; remove to paper towels. Season with chili powder mixture. *Makes 8 to 12 servings*

*Favorite recipe from **Colorado Potato Administrative Committee***

Easy Glazed Yams

2 (17- or 23-ounce) cans yams or sweet
    potatoes, drained
¾ cup BAMA® Pineapple or Peach
    Preserves
½ to 1 cup CAMPFIRE® Miniature
    Marshmallows
¼ cup chopped nuts
1 tablespoon margarine or butter

Preheat oven to 350°F. Arrange yams in
ungreased 1½-quart baking dish. Spoon
preserves over yams; top with marshmallows,
nuts and margarine. Bake 25 minutes or
until hot. *Makes 4 to 6 servings*

Easy Family Beans

4 slices bacon
¼ cup chopped onion
2 cans (16 ounces each) HEINZ®
    Vegetarian Beans in Tomato Sauce
    or Pork 'N' Beans
¼ cup HEINZ® Tomato Ketchup
2 to 3 tablespoons light brown sugar
1 teaspoon HEINZ® Worcestershire
    Sauce
Dash garlic powder

In large skillet, cook bacon until crisp; drain
on paper towels and crumble. Drain fat from
skillet. In same skillet, sauté onion until
tender. Stir in bacon and remaining
ingredients. Simmer, uncovered, about 15
minutes or until desired consistency, stirring
occasionally.

Makes 6 (about 3½-cup) servings

Photo courtesy of Heinz U.S.A.

Easy Glazed Yams

Fast & Fresh Salads

Get rave reviews from these dazzling salads no matter what the occasion—a main attraction or a perfect accompaniment to any meal.

Hot Taco Salad

¾ **pound lean ground beef (80% lean)**
½ **cup chopped onion**
1 **package (6.8 ounces) RICE-A-RONI®**
   Beef Flavor
½ **cup salsa**
1 **teaspoon chili powder**
4 **cups shredded lettuce**
1 **medium tomato, chopped**
½ **cup (2 ounces) shredded Monterey**
   Jack or Cheddar cheese
½ **cup crushed tortilla chips (optional)**

1. In large skillet, brown ground beef and onion; drain. Remove from skillet; set aside.

2. In same skillet, prepare Rice-A-Roni® Mix as package directs.

3. Stir in meat mixture, salsa and chili powder; continue cooking over low heat 3 to 4 minutes or until heated through.

4. Arrange lettuce on serving platter. Top with rice mixture, tomato and cheese. Top with tortilla chips, if desired.

Makes 5 servings

Hot Taco Salad

Mr. & Mrs. Bridge's Salad

1 small orange
1 (8-ounce) bottle NEWMAN'S OWN®
    Olive Oil & Vinegar Dressing
2 tablespoons chopped parsley
2 tablespoons lemon juice
1 tablespoon honey
1 teaspoon grated, peeled fresh ginger
1 clove garlic, minced
1 pound beef flank steak
½ pound spinach (1 bunch)
1 (8-ounce) can sliced mushrooms
½ cup chopped green onions
½ cup coarsely chopped walnuts,
    toasted
1 medium red pepper
1 tablespoon olive oil

Cut orange in half; squeeze enough juice from half of orange to equal ¼ cup. Slice remaining orange half and reserve for garnish. In medium bowl, stir orange juice, Newman's Own® Olive Oil & Vinegar Dressing, parsley, lemon juice, honey, ginger and garlic; reserve ⅔ of dressing mixture.

With knife held in slanted position, almost parallel to work surface, cut flank steak crosswise into thin slices. In medium bowl, add steak slices to dressing mixture; toss to coat. Cover and refrigerate 30 minutes. Meanwhile, wash and drain spinach. Trim tough ends from spinach leaves; tear into bite-size pieces. On large platter, toss spinach, mushrooms, green onions and walnuts.

Thinly slice red pepper. Drain flank steak; discard marinade. In 12-inch nonstick skillet, heat olive oil over medium-high heat; add red pepper. Cook until tender-crisp; remove from skillet. Increase heat to high; add flank steak and cook about 5 minutes or until it is no longer pink, stirring constantly. Add red pepper and reserved dressing mixture; heat through. To serve, spoon warm beef mixture over spinach mixture. Garnish with reserved orange slices. *Makes 4 servings*

Shanghai Salad

3 tablespoons vegetable oil
1 teaspoon minced fresh ginger
1 clove garlic, minced
1½ cups cooked flank steak or other
    meat, cut into ½-inch strips
1½ cups fresh *or* 1 package (6 ounces)
    frozen snow peas, thawed and
    drained
1 can (8 ounces) sliced water
    chestnuts, drained
½ cup green onions, cut into ½-inch
    pieces
2 tablespoons dry sherry
1 tablespoon soy sauce
½ teaspoon TABASCO® pepper sauce
    Shredded lettuce

In large skillet, heat oil over high heat. Add ginger and garlic; cook 1 minute. Add remaining ingredients except lettuce; stir-fry over high heat until heated through. Spoon onto bed of shredded lettuce. Serve hot with additional TABASCO sauce, if desired.
Makes 3 to 4 servings

Tabasco®

Avery Island, located just above the Louisiana Gulf Coast, is the birthplace of Tabasco® brand pepper sauce. It isn't an island in the classic sense, but a salt dome— a 2,500-acre hill surrounded by marshes, swamps and bayous. Today, Tabasco sauce remains a high-quality product made from only three ingredients— peppers grown from Avery Island seed, Avery Island salt and pure, strong vinegar.

Taco Fajita Salad

Dressing
- 1 can (14½ ounces) whole tomatoes
- ¼ cup vegetable oil
- 2 tablespoons red wine vinegar
- 2 tablespoons lime juice
- 1 package (1.0 ounce) LAWRY'S® Fresh Salsa Spices & Seasonings

Salad
- 1 pound thinly sliced steak or boneless, skinless chicken breasts
- 1 tablespoon salad oil
- ½ cup LAWRY'S® Fajitas Skillet Sauce
- 1 can (15 ounces) pinto beans, drained and rinsed
- 2 cups shredded lettuce
- 1 onion, slivered
- 1 green bell pepper, diced
- 1 tomato, cut into wedges
  Tortilla chips

In food processor or blender, combine all dressing ingredients; blend 1 minute. Cover and chill. In medium skillet, brown meat in oil until no longer pink. Add Fajitas Skillet Sauce. Bring to a boil; reduce heat and simmer 3 to 5 minutes. On individual serving dishes, arrange meat strips and beans over bed of mixed lettuce, onion and bell pepper.
Makes 4 servings

Presentation: Garnish with tomato wedges and tortilla chips tucked around edges. Serve with dressing drizzled over or on the side.

Hint: Layer ingredients in pre-made tortilla basket with meat on top.

Golden Gate Chinese Chicken and Cabbage Sesame Salad

1½ **pounds boneless, skinless chicken breasts**
1½ **teaspoons salt-free lemon pepper**
¼ **teaspoon salt**
8 **cups thinly sliced napa cabbage**
1 **medium-size red bell pepper, cut into julienned strips**
1 **medium-size yellow bell pepper, cut into julienned strips**
½ **cup diagonally sliced green onions**
½ **cup sesame seeds, toasted**
½ **cup chopped dried apricots**
3½ **teaspoons grated fresh ginger, divided**
¼ **cup low-sodium chicken broth**
¼ **cup seasoned rice vinegar**
¼ **cup low-sodium soy sauce**
2 **tablespoons sugar**
2 **tablespoons dark sesame oil**
6 **napa cabbage leaves**
1½ **cups chow mein noodles**

Place chicken in microproof dish; sprinkle with lemon pepper and salt. Cover with wax paper and microwave on HIGH 8 to 10 minutes or until no longer pink in center, rotating dish half turn every 2 minutes. Or, poach chicken. Remove chicken from dish. Cool; discard liquid. Shred chicken into bite-size pieces. Combine chicken, sliced cabbage, red pepper, yellow pepper, onions, sesame seeds, apricots and 3 teaspoons ginger in large bowl. Toss well; cover and refrigerate until ready to serve. Combine broth, vinegar, soy sauce, sugar, oil and remaining ½ teaspoon ginger in small jar with lid; shake well. Pour over chicken and cabbage mixture; toss gently. Spoon onto individual plates lined with cabbage leaves. Sprinkle evenly with chow mein noodles. Serve immediately. *Makes 6 servings*

Favorite recipe from **National Broiler Council**

Curried Chicken and Chilean Fruit Salad

1 **barbecued or roasted chicken, about 2½ pounds, cooled**
½ **pound green seedless Chilean grapes, halved**
2 **Chilean Granny Smith apples, peeled, cored and diced**
1 **extra sweet onion, peeled and chopped**
½ **cup golden raisins**
 Juice of ½ lemon
½ **cup mayonnaise**
½ **cup dairy sour cream**
1 **tablespoon curry powder**
 Salt and pepper
 Leaf lettuce leaves
1 **cup slivered almonds, toasted**

Cut chicken meat from bones; discard skin. Combine first six ingredients. Whisk mayonnaise, sour cream and curry powder together in small bowl. Pour curried mayonnaise over salad; mix gently. Season to taste with salt and pepper. Line serving platter with lettuce leaves and spoon chicken salad on top. Sprinkle almonds over salad; serve. *Makes 6 to 8 servings*

Favorite recipe from **Chilean Fresh Fruit Association**

Golden Gate Chinese Chicken and Cabbage Sesame Salad

Chicken and Black Bean Salad

2 large limes
1 can (16 ounces) black beans, drained and rinsed
1 large tomato, cored and diced
1 cup carrots, peeled and diced
½ medium red onion, diced
½ cup loosely packed fresh cilantro leaves *or* ¼ cup loosely packed flat-leaf Italian parsley leaves and 1 tablespoon dried coriander
2½ tablespoons vegetable oil, divided
1 teaspoon sugar
½ teaspoon hot pepper sauce
1 pound COOKIN' GOOD® Tenderloins of Chicken Breast, thawed and cut in half crosswise
1 teaspoon chili powder

1. Grate 1 teaspoon lime peel; squeeze ½ cup juice.

2. In large bowl, combine black beans, tomato, carrots, onion and cilantro leaves; set aside.

3. In small bowl, whisk lime peel, lime juice, 1 tablespoon vegetable oil, sugar and hot pepper sauce; set aside.

4. In 10-inch skillet, cook chicken pieces in remaining 1½ tablespoons oil and chili powder over medium heat 6 minutes or until no longer pink, stirring frequently. Remove to plate; refrigerate to cool.

5. Combine cooled chicken, bean mixture and lime dressing in bowl; toss well to coat.
Makes 4 to 6 servings

Warm Chicken and Potato Salad with Mustard Dressing

1 pound COOKIN' GOOD® Boneless, Skinned Chicken Breasts
¾ pound small new red potatoes (about 1 to 1½ inches in diameter)
¼ teaspoon salt
Water
1 package (9 ounces) frozen or fresh Italian-style green beans
⅓ cup olive oil
1½ tablespoons white wine vinegar
1½ tablespoons grainy mustard
¼ teaspoon black pepper
⅛ teaspoon sugar
1 small red onion, sliced
½ cup sliced celery

1. Place chicken in large 12-inch skillet. Add potatoes and salt; cover with water. Bring to a boil over high heat. Reduce heat to low; cover and simmer 20 minutes, or until chicken is tender and juices run clear when pierced with fork and potatoes are tender, (potatoes may take a little longer). Remove to warm platter. When cool enough to handle, cut chicken into ¾-inch cubes and potatoes in quarters.

2. Return broth to a boil over high heat. Add green beans. Return to a boil; reduce heat to medium. Cover and cook 5 to 8 minutes. Drain; add to platter with chicken and potatoes.

3. In large bowl, whisk together olive oil, vinegar, mustard, pepper and sugar until well blended. Stir in chicken, potatoes, green beans, onion and celery. Toss until well coated with dressing. *Makes 4 servings*

Chicken and Black Bean Salad

Newman's Own®

For years, Paul Newman packaged homemade salad dressing in old wine bottles for Christmas gifts. One day, he and longtime friend, A. E. Hotchner, decided to market it. The overnight success of Newman's Own Salad Dressing led to expansion of the company's line of all-natural food products to include popcorn, spaghetti sauce, salsa and lemonade. Newman's Own has grown into a multimillion dollar business from which Paul Newman donates 100% of his after-tax profits to charitable and educational causes, including The Hole in the Wall Gang Camp, which he founded in 1988, for children with cancer and other serious blood-related illnesses.

Spinach, Turkey and Apple Salad

¼ cup NEWMAN'S OWN® Olive Oil and Vinegar Salad Dressing or NEWMAN'S OWN® Light Italian Salad Dressing
4 turkey cutlets, approximately ½ inch thick
4 cups spinach, washed, stems removed
2 Granny Smith apples, cored
¾ cup NEWMAN'S OWN® Olive Oil and Vinegar Salad Dressing or NEWMAN'S OWN® Light Italian Salad Dressing
⅓ cup crumbled blue cheese
¼ cup walnut halves

Prepare grill or heat broiler.

Brush turkey cutlets with ¼ cup Newman's Own® Salad Dressing; grill turkey cutlets over medium heat or broil as close as possible to heat source, until turkey is no longer pink. Set aside to cool.

Divide spinach among 4 plates. Thinly slice turkey and divide among spinach-lined plates. Thinly slice Granny Smith apples and place on top of turkey. Pour ¾ cup Newman's Own® Salad Dressing evenly over each plate. Top with crumbled blue cheese and walnut halves.   *Makes 4 servings*

Fruity Turkey Salad

Dressing

> 1 cup lowfat yogurt
> ¼ cup reduced calorie mayonnaise
> 2 tablespoons honey
> 1 teaspoon finely chopped crystallized
>   ginger
> ½ teaspoon salt
> ¼ teaspoon curry powder

Salad

> 2 cups cooked wild rice (⅔ cup raw)
> 2 cups cubed cooked turkey
> 1 cup diced nectarines
> ½ cup thinly sliced celery
>   Nectarine slices, optional garnish
>   Fresh greens, optional garnish

Combine dressing ingredients; cover and refrigerate to blend flavors. In large bowl, combine wild rice, turkey, nectarines and celery. Blend in dressing. Garnish, if desired.

Makes 4 servings

Favorite recipe from **Minnesota Cultivated Wild Rice Council**

Minnesota Cultivated Wild Rice Council

Wild rice is the only grain native to North America and has the prestige of being declared the Minnesota State Grain. Cultivated wild rice grows in paddies located in the north central part of the state that provide a natural habitat for many waterfowl species to feed and nest. Wild rice, once scarce and expensive, was served only on special occasions. However, with modern processing techniques and the abundance of wild rice, it is now used year-round in recipes from appetizers to desserts. Wild rice is a no fat, no preservatives source of fiber and other nutrients and is being incorporated into the diets of the health conscious. It is at the base of the food guide pyramid which suggests 6 to 11 daily servings of grains, bread, pasta and cereal.

Fresh Tomato and Shrimp Salad with Lemon Gremolata Dressing

**2 medium (10 ounces) fresh Florida
   Tomatoes
4 cups romaine lettuce in bite-sized
   pieces
12 ounces cooked, shelled and deveined
   shrimp
1 cup thinly sliced green bell pepper
¼ cup thinly sliced red onion
½ cup Lemon Gremolata Dressing
   (recipe follows)**

Use tomatoes held at room temperature until
fully ripe. Core tomatoes; cut into thin wedges
(makes about 2 cups). In large serving bowl,
place tomatoes, lettuce, shrimp, green
pepper and onion. Just before serving, toss
with Lemon Gremolata Dressing.

Makes 4 servings

Lemon Gremolata Dressing

**¼ cup chopped fresh parsley
1 teaspoon grated lemon peel
¾ teaspoon minced garlic
2 tablespoons fresh lemon juice
2 tablespoons olive oil
2 tablespoons water
2 teaspoons Dijon-style prepared
   mustard
1 teaspoon salt
¼ teaspoon ground black pepper
¼ teaspoon sugar**

In small bowl, whisk together all ingredients
until blended.   *Makes about ½ cup*

Favorite recipe from **Florida Tomato Committee**

Pizza Pasta Salad

**1 pound rotini, twists or other medium
   pasta shape, uncooked
¼ pound sliced pepperoni (about 1 cup)
¼ pound sliced provolone cheese
   (1 cup)
8 cherry tomatoes, cut in half
   (1¼ cups)
½ cup grated Parmesan cheese
½ cup Italian salad dressing
1 teaspoon Italian seasoning
½ teaspoon dehydrated garlic chips,
   soaked in 2 tablespoons water
2½ (7-inch-round) pita breads
1 green pepper**

Prepare pasta according to package
directions; drain and place in large bowl. Cut
each pepperoni slice into fourths and slice
provolone cheese into matchstick-size
pieces; add to pasta. Add cherry tomatoes,
Parmesan cheese, Italian dressing, Italian
seasoning, minced garlic and water; mix well.
Quarter pita bread rounds and place around
large platter. Top with pasta salad; garnish
with green pepper rings.

Makes 6 servings

Favorite recipe from **National Pasta Association**

*Fresh Tomato and Shrimp Salad with Lemon
Gremolata Dressing*

Smoked Turkey and Pepper Pasta Salad

¾ cup **MIRACLE WHIP®** Salad Dressing
1 tablespoon Dijon mustard
½ teaspoon dried thyme leaves
8 ounces fettuccini, cooked, drained
1 cup (8 ounces) diced **LOUIS RICH®** Hickory Smoked Breast of Turkey
¾ cup zucchini slices, cut into halves
½ cup red bell pepper strips
½ cup yellow bell pepper strips
Salt and black pepper

• Mix salad dressing, mustard and thyme in large bowl until well blended. Add pasta, turkey and vegetables; mix lightly. Season with salt and black pepper to taste.

• Cover; refrigerate at least 1 hour before serving. Add additional salad dressing before serving, if desired.   *Makes 6 servings*

Roasted Fresh Tomato Salad with Shells and Chicken

1½ cups small shell pasta, uncooked
3 cups Roasted Fresh Tomatoes (page 172)
1 cup (6 ounces) cooked chicken, cut in ½-inch cubes
1 cup frozen green peas, thawed
½ cup crumbled feta cheese
½ cup sliced ripe olives
¼ cup sliced scallions (green onions)
⅓ cup prepared ranch salad dressing

Cook pasta according to package directions; drain and rinse. Place in large bowl. Cut Roasted Fresh Tomatoes in chunks; add tomatoes, chicken, peas, feta cheese, olives and scallions. Pour salad dressing over all; toss to coat. Serve, if desired, on lettuce-lined plates sprinkled with parsley.

Makes 4 to 6 servings

Favorite recipe from **Florida Tomato Committee**

Miracle Whip® Salad Dressing, introduced in 1933, is an American classic. Key to its development was a new high-speed machine that mixed oil, eggs and a secret blend of spices into a fluffy, smooth consistency. Technically, Miracle Whip is different from mayonnaise since it contains less oil and also contains starch, but it can be used in any recipe calling for mayonnaise or salad dressing. Its tangy zip adds a wonderful flavor to a wide variety of dishes.

Smoked Turkey and Pepper Pasta Salad

Albacore Salad Puttanesca with Garlic Vinaigrette

Albacore Salad Puttanesca with Garlic Vinaigrette

2 cups cooked, chilled angel hair pasta
2 cups chopped, peeled plum tomatoes
1 can (4¼ ounces) chopped* ripe
   olives, drained
1 cup Garlic Vinaigrette Dressing
   (recipe follows)
1 can (6 ounces) STARKIST® Solid
   White Tuna, drained and flaked
¼ cup chopped fresh basil leaves

*If you prefer, olives may be sliced rather than chopped.

In large bowl, combine chilled pasta, tomatoes, olives and 1 cup Garlic Vinaigrette Dressing. Add tuna and basil leaves; toss. Serve immediately.　　*Makes 2 servings*

Garlic Vinaigrette Dressing

⅓ cup red wine vinegar
2 tablespoons lemon juice
1 to 2 cloves garlic, minced or pressed
1 teaspoon ground black pepper
   Salt to taste
1 cup olive oil

In small bowl, whisk together vinegar, lemon juice, garlic, pepper and salt. Slowly add oil, whisking continuously, until well blended.

Fresh Orange-Pasta Salad

Grated peel of ½ SUNKIST® Orange
Juice of 1 SUNKIST® Orange (⅓ cup)
3 tablespoons olive or vegetable oil
2 teaspoons chopped fresh dill weed *or*
½ teaspoon dried dill weed
¼ teaspoon seasoned salt
2 cups curly or spiral macaroni, cooked
and drained
2 SUNKIST® Oranges, peeled and cut
into half-cartwheel slices
2 cups broccoli flowerets, cooked and
drained
½ cup sliced celery
¼ cup sliced green onions

In large bowl, combine orange peel and juice, oil, dill and seasoned salt. Add remaining ingredients; toss gently. Cover and chill; stir occasionally.   *Makes 6 servings*

Pasta Salad with Pesto and Almonds

1 cup BLUE DIAMOND® Chopped
Natural Almonds
1 tablespoon butter
16 ounces corkscrew pasta
1 cup pesto
½ cup freshly grated Parmesan cheese
¼ cup white wine vinegar
¼ cup olive oil
½ teaspoon salt
¼ teaspoon white pepper
1 cup frozen green peas, thawed
4 green onions, sliced
4 ounces cooked ham, julienned
1 red bell pepper, diced

In small skillet, sauté almonds in butter over low heat until crisp; reserve. Cook pasta in salted, boiling water according to manufacturer's directions until just done. Meanwhile, combine pesto, cheese, vinegar, oil, salt and white pepper. When pasta is done, drain and toss hot pasta with peas and pesto dressing. Fold in onions, ham, bell pepper and toasted almonds.

Makes 4 to 6 servings

StarKist's® spokefish and all-time purveyor of good taste.

Colorful Grape, Pepper and Pasta Salad

8 ounces dry thin spaghetti, cooked
   Mustard Vinaigrette (recipe follows)
1 cup California seedless grapes
½ cup thinly sliced red or yellow bell
   pepper
2 tablespoons minced celery
2 tablespoons green onion
1 tablespoon chopped fresh tarragon*
   Salt and pepper to taste
¼ cup walnuts,** quartered
   Fresh tarragon sprigs, optional

*One-half teaspoon dried tarragon, crushed, may
be substituted.

**Walnuts may be omitted; substitute 1 tablespoon
walnut oil for 1 tablespoon olive oil in vinaigrette.

Combine cooked spaghetti and 3
tablespoons Mustard Vinaigrette; toss to coat
and cool. Add remaining ingredients including
vinaigrette; mix well. Serve in lettuce-lined
bowl; garnish with tarragon, if desired.
Makes 4 servings

Mustard Vinaigrette: Combine 3
tablespoons white wine vinegar, 2
tablespoons olive oil, 2 tablespoons Dijon-
style mustard, 1 clove minced garlic,
½ teaspoon sugar and ⅛ teaspoon pepper;
mix well. Makes about ⅓ cup.

*Favorite recipe from California Table Grape
Commission*

Warm Pasta and Spinach Salad

1 package (10 ounces) fresh spinach,
   washed, stems removed and torn
   into bite-size pieces
½ pound mushrooms, sliced
8 ounces MUELLER'S® Twists or Ziti,
   cooked, rinsed with cold water and
   drained
1 medium red onion, sliced
6 slices uncooked bacon, coarsely
   chopped
1 tablespoon ARGO® or KINGSFORD'S®
   Corn Starch
1 tablespoon sugar
1 teaspoon salt
½ teaspoon pepper
1 cup HELLMANN'S® or BEST FOODS®
   Real or Light Mayonnaise or Low
   Fat Mayonnaise Dressing
1 cup water
⅓ cup cider vinegar

In large serving bowl, toss spinach,
mushrooms, pasta and red onion. In medium
skillet, cook bacon over medium-high heat
until crisp. Remove with slotted spoon. Pour
off all but 2 tablespoons drippings. In small
bowl, mix corn starch, sugar, salt and pepper.
With wire whisk, stir corn starch mixture into
drippings in skillet until smooth. Stir in
mayonnaise until blended. Gradually stir in
water and vinegar. Over medium heat, bring
mixture to a boil; stir constantly. Boil 1 minute.
Pour over spinach mixture. Add bacon; toss
to coat well. Serve immediately.
Makes 8 to 10 servings

Party Pasta Salad

Party Pasta Salad

1 package (12 ounces) corkscrew pasta
1 can (20 ounces) DOLE® Pineapple
    Chunks in Juice
1 cup vegetable oil
½ cup distilled white vinegar
1 tablespoon Dijon mustard
1 tablespoon Worcestershire sauce
1 clove garlic, pressed
    Salt and pepper to taste
3 cups DOLE® Cauliflower florettes
3 cups DOLE® Broccoli florettes
1 DOLE® Red Bell Pepper, seeded,
    chunked
1 cup DOLE® Whole Natural Almonds,
    toasted

• Cook noodles according to package directions.

• Drain pineapple; reserve 3 tablespoons juice for dressing.

• For dressing, combine reserved juice, oil, vinegar, mustard, Worcestershire sauce, garlic, salt and pepper in screw-top jar; shake well.

• Combine noodles and cauliflower in large bowl. Pour dressing over salad; toss to coat.

• Cover and marinate in refrigerator overnight.

• Add broccoli, pineapple, red pepper and almonds; toss to coat.

Makes 12 to 15 servings

Southwest Ruffle Salad

⅔ cup HELLMANN'S® or BEST FOODS®
   Real or Light Mayonnaise or Low
   Fat Mayonnaise Dressing
⅓ cup sour cream
¼ cup chopped cilantro
2 tablespoons milk
2 tablespoons lime juice
1 fresh jalapeño pepper, seeded and
   minced
1 teaspoon salt
7 ounces MUELLER'S® Pasta Ruffles,
   cooked, rinsed with cold water and
   drained
2 large tomatoes, seeded and chopped
1 yellow bell pepper, chopped
1 zucchini, quartered lengthwise and
   thinly sliced
3 green onions, thinly sliced

In large bowl, combine mayonnaise, sour cream, cilantro, milk, lime juice, jalapeño pepper and salt. Add pasta, tomatoes, yellow bell pepper, zucchini and green onions; toss to coat well. Garnish as desired. Cover; refrigerate.   *Makes 6 to 8 servings*

Pasta Twists with Garden Vegetables

8 ounces uncooked rotelle macaroni
1 cup (8 ounces) WISH-BONE® Honey
   Dijon Dressing
2 medium tomatoes, finely chopped
1 medium green and/or red bell pepper,
   finely chopped
1 medium cucumber, sliced
½ small red onion, thinly sliced

Cook macaroni according to package directions; drain and rinse with cold water until completely cool.

In large salad bowl, combine honey Dijon dressing, tomatoes, green pepper, cucumber and red onion. Toss with macaroni; cover and chill.   *Makes 8 side-dish servings*

Roasted Tomato and Mozzarella Pasta Salad

3 cups (8 ounces) rotelle (corkscrew)
   pasta, uncooked
3 cups Roasted Fresh Tomatoes
   (page 172)
1 cup green bell pepper, cut into ½-inch
   pieces
¾ cup (4 ounces) mozzarella cheese,
   cut into ½-inch pieces
¼ cup chopped mild red onion
½ teaspoon salt
¼ teaspoon ground black pepper
⅓ cup prepared red wine vinaigrette
   salad dressing

Cook pasta according to package directions; rinse and drain. Place in large bowl. Cut Roasted Fresh Tomatoes in chunks; add to pasta. Add green pepper, mozzarella cheese, onion, salt and black pepper. Pour salad dressing over all; toss to coat. Serve garnished with basil leaves, if desired.
          Makes 4 servings

Favorite recipe from **Florida Tomato Committee**

Southwest Ruffle Salad

Santa Fe Rice Salad

1 package (6.9 ounces) RICE-A-RONI®
   With ⅓ Less Salt Chicken Flavor
3 tablespoons vegetable oil
2 cups chopped cooked chicken or
   turkey
1½ cups chopped tomatoes
1 cup frozen corn *or* 1 can (8 ounces)
   whole kernel corn, drained
½ cup chopped red or green bell pepper
¼ cup sliced green onions
2 to 3 tablespoons chopped cilantro or
   parsley
⅔ cup salsa or picante sauce
2 tablespoons lime or lemon juice

1. Prepare Rice-A-Roni® Mix as package directs, substituting 1 tablespoon oil for margarine. Cool 10 minutes.

2. In large bowl, combine prepared Rice-A-Roni®, chicken, tomatoes, corn, red pepper, onions and cilantro.

3. Combine salsa, lime juice and remaining 2 tablespoons oil. Pour over rice mixture; toss. Cover; chill 4 hours or overnight. Stir before serving. *Makes 5 servings*

Mediterranean Rice Salad

2 tablespoons vegetable oil, divided
1 pound large shrimp, peeled and
   deveined
1 large clove garlic, minced
2 green onions, sliced
2 cups water
1 cup long-grain rice
1 teaspoon salt
1 medium cucumber, diced
½ cup crumbled feta cheese

Spicy Vinaigrette

¼ cup olive oil
3 tablespoons cider vinegar
1 tablespoon Dijon mustard
1 teaspoon TABASCO® pepper sauce
1 teaspoon salt

In 3-quart saucepan over medium-high heat, in 1 tablespoon hot vegetable oil, cook half the shrimp until pink and tender. With slotted spoon, remove to large bowl. Repeat with remaining shrimp and oil. Reduce heat to medium. In drippings remaining in saucepan, cook garlic and green onions about 2 minutes, stirring frequently.

Add water, rice and salt to saucepan. Over high heat, heat to boiling. Reduce heat to low; cover and simmer 20 minutes or until rice is tender. Meanwhile, add cucumber and feta cheese to bowl containing shrimp.

Prepare Spicy Vinaigrette. In small bowl combine all vinaigrette ingredients. Add rice and vinaigrette to shrimp mixture and toss to mix well. *Makes 6 servings*

Santa Fe Rice Salad

California Table Grape Commission

Table grapes are a very important industry in the state of California which ranks third in worldwide production and supplies 97 percent of the domestically grown table grapes in the U.S. Unlike many fresh fruits, grapes are harvested only when the fruit is ripe. Grapes don't become any sweeter after they are clipped from the vine. Eleven major varieties of grapes are available from May until February, ranging in color from green and red to blue-black. Each has its own unique flavor and texture. The California Table Grape Commission is the promotional arm of the state's fresh grape industry.

Hand-Held Grape Salad with Couscous

1¼ cups chicken broth
1 tablespoon olive oil
1 cup couscous
1½ cups California seedless grapes
1 cup chopped parsley
1 cup peeled, chopped and seeded cucumber
½ cup chopped red or green bell pepper
¼ cup minced green onions
   Lemon Mustard Dressing (recipe follows)
8 large green or red lettuce leaves

Combine broth and olive oil in medium saucepan; bring to a boil over high heat. Add couscous. Stir; cover and remove from heat. Let stand 5 minutes. Stir to fluff and cool to room temperature. Add grapes, parsley, cucumber, red pepper, green onions and dressing; mix gently. Place ¼ cup mixture on each lettuce leaf; roll into cone shape and eat out of hand. *Makes 4 to 6 servings*

Lemon Mustard Dressing: Combine ¼ cup olive oil, 2 tablespoons lemon juice, 2 tablespoons white wine vinegar, 1 clove minced garlic, 1 teaspoon Dijon-style mustard, ½ teaspoon salt and ⅛ teaspoon black pepper; mix well. Makes ½ cup.

*Favorite recipe from **California Table Grape Commission***

Spinach, Bacon and Mushroom Salad

Spinach, Bacon and Mushroom Salad

1 large bunch (12 ounces) fresh
    spinach leaves, washed, drained
    and torn
¾ cup sliced fresh mushrooms
4 slices bacon, cooked and crumbled
¾ cup croutons
4 hard-cooked eggs, finely chopped
    Black pepper, to taste
¾ cup prepared HIDDEN VALLEY
    RANCH® Original Ranch® salad
    dressing

In medium salad bowl, combine spinach,
mushrooms and bacon; toss. Top with
croutons and eggs; season with pepper. Pour
salad dressing over all. *Makes 6 servings*

Nutty Rice Salad

4 cups long-grain rice, cooked
   (1½ cups uncooked)
1 green or red bell pepper, stemmed
   and chopped
1 cup frozen peas, thawed
1 can (6⅛ ounces) water-packed tuna,
   drained
½ cup chopped, toasted* California
   walnuts
½ cup chopped red onion
¼ cup chopped parsley
1 teaspoon dried tarragon *or*
   1 tablespoon chopped fresh
   tarragon
2 tablespoons nonfat yogurt
2 tablespoons olive oil
2 tablespoons lemon juice
1 teaspoon salt, or to taste
½ teaspoon freshly ground pepper
4 cups shredded iceberg lettuce

*Toasting walnuts is optional.

In large bowl, combine rice, green pepper,
peas, tuna, walnuts, onion, parsley and
tarragon; set aside. In tightly capped jar,
combine yogurt, olive oil, lemon juice, salt
and pepper; shake until well blended. Pour
over rice mixture; toss to combine. Place
lettuce on platter; mound rice mixture on top.

Makes 6 servings

*Favorite recipe from **Walnut Marketing Board***

Grape 'n Chicken Wild Rice Salad

4 cups cooked wild rice
2 cups cooked, cubed chicken breasts
½ cup thinly sliced green onions
1 can (8 ounces) sliced water
   chestnuts, drained
   Salt and pepper, to taste
   Dressing (recipe follows)
½ pound seedless green grapes, halved
⅔ cup cashews

In large bowl, combine wild rice, chicken,
onions, water chestnuts, salt and pepper;
toss with Dressing. Chill. Just before serving,
fold in grapes and cashews.

Makes 8 servings

Dressing

½ cup mayonnaise
1 teaspoon lemon juice
¼ cup milk
¼ teaspoon tarragon

Combine mayonnaise, lemon juice, milk and
tarragon in small bowl.

*Favorite recipe from **Minnesota Cultivated Wild
Rice Council***

Nutty Rice Salad

Red Cabbage Salad with Bel Paese®

1 small head red cabbage, shredded
8 ounces BEL PAESE® Cheese* cut into
　　small chunks
1 cup thinly sliced celery hearts
2 ounces fully cooked ham, cut into
　　small chunks (about ½ cup)
3 tablespoons extra-virgin olive oil
3 tablespoons fresh lemon juice

*Remove wax coating and moist, white crust from
cheese.

In large salad bowl, combine cabbage,
cheese, celery, ham, olive oil and lemon
juice; toss to coat.　　*Makes 4 to 6 servings*

BLT Salad Toss

1½ quarts torn lettuce
　1 cup cherry tomato halves
　½ cup chopped green pepper
　6 crisply cooked bacon slices,
　　　crumbled
　½ cup red onion rings
　1 cup MIRACLE WHIP® Salad Dressing
　½ cup (2 ounces) 100% Natural KRAFT®
　　　Shredded Sharp Cheddar Cheese

In 2-quart serving bowl, layer lettuce,
tomatoes, pepper, bacon and onion. Cover
with salad dressing, spreading to edge of
bowl to seal. Sprinkle with cheese. Cover;
chill. Toss lightly just before serving.
　　　　　　　Makes 4 to 6 servings

Black-Eyed Pea Jamboree

*Every July, a gala festival
honoring this unusual
lentil and its heritage is
held in Athens, Texas—
also known as the
Black-Eyed Pea
Capital of the
World! Thousands
of visitors take part in
the Jamboree, joining the Athenians in
celebrating the prosperity of growing
and processing black-eyed peas.*

Dilly Cucumbers

¾ cup REGINA® White Wine Vinegar
1 tablespoon sugar
1½ teaspoons dried dill weed
1½ quarts peeled and thinly sliced
　　cucumbers
1 cup thinly sliced onions, separated
　　into rings

In large bowl, whisk together vinegar, sugar
and dill until sugar is dissolved. Add
cucumbers and onions, tossing to coat well.

Refrigerate, covered, 6 hours or overnight,
stirring occasionally.　　*Makes 5 cups*

Encore Salad

1 cup olive oil
1½ cups white vinegar
¼ cup sugar
2 teaspoons salt
¾ teaspoon black pepper
1 clove garlic, minced
12 pearl onions or very small onions
1 cup water
1 small cauliflower, cut into flowerets
1 can beets, drained, cut into quarters
1 green pepper, cut into ½-inch strips
1 (6-ounce) can ripe olives, drained, halved
2 cups black-eyed peas, canned, rinsed and drained

Combine oil, vinegar, sugar, salt, pepper and garlic in medium saucepan. Bring to a boil over high heat, stirring constantly; cool 5 minutes. Add onions and water; bring to a boil. Cover and reduce heat; simmer 2 minutes or until onions are tender. Drain. Add cauliflower, beets, green pepper, olives and black-eyed peas; refrigerate 8 hours, stirring occasionally. *Makes 10 to 12 servings*

Favorite recipe from **Black-Eyed Pea Jamboree— Athens, Texas**

Spinach Salad

¼ pound sliced bacon
½ cup sliced scallions
2 tablespoons all-purpose flour
1 cup COLLEGE INN® Beef or Chicken Broth
⅓ cup red wine vinegar
8 cups spinach leaves, torn
2 cups sliced fresh mushrooms

In large skillet, over medium-high heat, cook bacon until crisp. Drain, reserving ¼ cup drippings. Crumble bacon; set aside. In reserved drippings, over medium heat, cook scallions until tender. Stir in flour; cook 1 minute. Stir in broth and vinegar; heat to a boil. Reduce heat; cook until slightly thickened.

In large bowl, mix spinach leaves and mushrooms. Pour hot dressing over salad, tossing to coat well. Sprinkle with reserved bacon pieces. Serve immediately.
Makes 8 servings

Cartwheel Salad

1 small head iceberg lettuce, torn into bite-size pieces
1 small head romaine lettuce, torn into bite-size pieces
1 cup chopped tomato
¼ cup sliced black olives
¼ cup shoestring beets
¼ cup sliced radishes
1 can (8 ounces) garbanzo beans, drained
1 bottle (8 ounces) LAWRY'S® White Wine Vinaigrette Dressing or Creamy Mexican Dressing con Cilantro (page 212)
Tortilla strips

Have ingredients prepared and chilled. In large, shallow salad bowl, make bed with lettuce. Arrange tomato, olives, beets, radishes and beans on lettuce in cartwheel design. To serve, toss salad with White Wine Vinaigrette Dressing. Place salad on individual plates and top with tortilla strips.
Makes 6 to 8 servings

Great American Potato Salad

1 cup MIRACLE WHIP® Salad Dressing
1 teaspoon KRAFT® Pure Prepared
    Mustard
½ teaspoon celery seed
½ teaspoon salt
⅛ teaspoon pepper
4 cups cubed cooked potatoes
2 hard-cooked eggs, chopped
½ cup chopped onion
½ cup celery slices
½ cup chopped sweet pickle

Combine salad dressing, mustard, celery seed, salt and pepper; mix well. Add remaining ingredients; mix lightly. Cover; chill.
Makes 6 servings

California Black Bean Salad

1 can (15 ounces) black beans, drained
    and rinsed
1 can (12 ounces) whole kernel corn,
    drained
1 medium tomato, chopped
½ cup chopped red onion
½ cup chopped green bell pepper
½ teaspoon LAWRY'S® Garlic Powder
    with Parsley
  Spicy Mexican Dressing
    (page 212)

In large bowl, combine beans, corn, tomato, onion, bell pepper and Garlic Powder with Parsley; blend well. Toss with dressing; refrigerate 15 minutes. *Makes 6 servings*

Gloria's Pesto Salad

Dressing

1 cup mayonnaise
2 tablespoons prepared pesto

Salad

4 cups peeled diced potatoes, cooked
½ cup chopped celery
½ cup sliced green onions
½ cup diced red bell pepper
1½ cups (6 ounces) Wisconsin Monterey
    Jack cheese, cubed
1 tablespoon grated Wisconsin
    Parmesan cheese

In small bowl, combine dressing ingredients; set aside. In medium bowl, combine potatoes, celery, onions, pepper and Monterey Jack cheese. Add dressing. Toss lightly. Sprinkle with Parmesan cheese. Chill.
Makes 6 servings

Tip: Wisconsin Style Havarti® cheese delivers the same creamy texture when substituted for Monterey Jack cheese in this recipe.

*Favorite recipe from **Wisconsin Milk Marketing Board***

Great American Potato Salad

Colorado Potato & Prosciutto Salad

1¼ pounds round, red-skin Colorado potatoes, unpeeled (about 4 potatoes)
½ pound green beans, trimmed, sliced into approximately 2½-inch lengths
1 red or green bell pepper, cored, seeded and cut into slivers
1½ cups cooked corn kernels, fresh or frozen and thawed
6 ounces mozzarella cheese, cut into ½-inch cubes
3 ounces thinly sliced prosciutto or ham, torn into strips
3 green onions, sliced
⅓ cup olive oil
¼ cup lemon juice
2 tablespoons water
1 or 2 cloves garlic, minced
1 tablespoon chopped fresh thyme *or* 1½ teaspoons dried thyme leaves
Salt and pepper

Cook potatoes until tender. Cool; slice ½ inch thick, then cut into quarters. Cook green beans until tender; cool. In large serving bowl, combine potatoes, beans, red pepper, corn, cheese, prosciutto and green onions. In small bowl, whisk together oil, lemon juice, water, garlic and thyme. Season with salt and pepper to taste. Pour dressing over potato mixture and toss to coat. Serve immediately or refrigerate.

Makes about 8 cups (6 to 8 servings)

Favorite recipe from **Colorado Potato Administrative Committee**

Chilean Nectarine, Grape and Raspberry Salad

4 ripe Chilean nectarines
1 small bunch red seedless Chilean grapes
1 small bunch green seedless Chilean grapes
2 medium zucchini
½ cup olive oil
2 tablespoons raspberry vinegar
Salt and black pepper
Leaf lettuce leaves
1 cup Chilean raspberries

Halve nectarines and cut into wedges. Pull grapes from stems; there should be about 1 cup of red and 1 cup of green. Cut zucchini into sticks. Whisk together olive oil and raspberry vinegar in small bowl; season to taste with salt and pepper. Line 4 salad plates with lettuce leaves and arrange nectarine slices, grapes, zucchini sticks and raspberries decoratively on top. Drizzle with dressing.   *Makes 4 servings*

Favorite recipe from **Chilean Fresh Fruit Association**

Colorado Potato & Prosciutto Salad

Curried Chilean Nectarine, Sweet Onion and Grape Salad

6 ripe Chilean nectarines
1 extra sweet onion
1 cup seedless green Chilean grapes
1 cup seedless red Chilean grapes
Leaf lettuce leaves
8 ounces dairy sour cream
1 teaspoon curry powder
2 tablespoons chopped fresh cilantro
Additional cilantro sprigs for garnish

Cut nectarines into wedges. Peel onion and slice very thin. Cut grapes in half. Line 4 plates with lettuce leaves and arrange fruit and onion slices on top. Stir sour cream until smooth; blend in curry powder and chopped cilantro. Spoon dressing over each salad and garnish with cilantro sprigs.

Makes 4 servings

Favorite recipe from **Chilean Fresh Fruit Association**

Lemon Pear Zest

1 can (16 ounces) Bartlett pear halves
½ lemon, thinly sliced
3 tablespoons lemon juice
2 teaspoons white vinegar
1 tablespoon chopped parsley

Drain pears; reserve ½ cup liquid. Cut pear halves in thirds lengthwise. Place pears and lemon slices in medium bowl. Combine reserved pear liquid, lemon juice and vinegar; mix well. Bring to a boil. Pour over pears. Cover and refrigerate several hours or overnight. Sprinkle with chopped parsley just before serving and stir gently.

Makes 6 servings

Tip: Serve with grilled meat or whitefish.

Favorite recipe from **Pacific Coast Canned Pear Service**

Citrus Vinaigrette

¼ cup KARO® Light Corn Syrup
¼ cup orange juice
¼ cup cider vinegar
¼ teaspoon grated lime peel
2 tablespoons lime juice
1 tablespoon Dijon mustard
½ teaspoon ground cumin
½ teaspoon salt
½ cup MAZOLA® Corn Oil

In medium bowl, combine corn syrup, orange juice, vinegar, lime peel, lime juice, mustard, cumin and salt. With wire whisk or fork, gradually blend in corn oil. Cover and refrigerate several hours or overnight. Toss with salad greens or serve over sliced avocado or fruit. *Makes about 1⅓ cups*

Basic Olive Oil Vinaigrette

⅓ cup wine or cider vinegar
¼ teaspoon salt
¼ teaspoon black pepper
1 cup FILIPPO BERIO® Extra Virgin Olive Oil

Whisk together vinegar, salt and pepper in small bowl. Slowly whisk in oil until well blended. Serve with salad greens.

Makes 10 servings

Basic Olive Oil Vinaigrette

• **Herb Vinaigrette:** Prepare as directed. Stir in 1 teaspoon *each* dried mustard, basil and tarragon leaves.

• **Balsamic Vinaigrette:** Prepare as directed substituting balsamic vinegar for the wine vinegar. Stir in 1 tablespoon of minced shallots and ¼ teaspoon dried marjoram leaves.

• **Chive Vinaigrette:** Prepare as directed. Stir in 2 teaspoons minced fresh chives.

• **Creamy Dijon Vinaigrette:** Prepare as directed; whisk in 2 teaspoons Dijon mustard and ½ tablespoon mayonnaise.

• **Honey-Dijon Vinaigrette:** Prepare as directed; whisk in 1 tablespoon Dijon mustard and 2 tablespoons honey.

• **Mint Vinaigrette:** Prepare as directed. Stir in 2 tablespoons chopped fresh mint.

• **Parmesan Vinaigrette:** Prepare as directed. Stir in 1 tablespoon Parmesan cheese.

Italian Herb Dressing

⅔ cup vegetable oil
⅓ cup HEINZ® Gourmet Wine or
    Distilled White Vinegar
1 clove garlic, split
1 teaspoon dry mustard
½ teaspoon salt
½ teaspoon dried basil leaves, crushed
½ teaspoon dried oregano leaves,
    crushed
¼ teaspoon crushed red pepper

Combine all ingredients in jar; cover and shake vigorously. Refrigerate until chilled to blend flavors. Remove garlic; shake again before serving over tossed green salads.

Makes 1 cup

Honey Orange Dressing

½ cup plain yogurt
¼ cup honey
¼ cup mayonnaise
¾ teaspoon grated orange peel
¼ teaspoon dry mustard
3 tablespoons orange juice
1½ teaspoons vinegar

Whisk together yogurt, honey, mayonnaise, orange peel and mustard in small bowl until blended. Gradually mix in orange juice and vinegar. Cover and refrigerate until ready to serve. *Makes about 1 cup*

Favorite recipe from **National Honey Board**

Creamy Mexican Dressing con Cilantro

¾ cup dairy sour cream
⅓ cup mayonnaise
⅓ cup buttermilk
1 tablespoon lemon juice
1 tablespoon water
½ teaspoon LAWRY'S® Seasoned Salt
¼ teaspoon basil
¼ teaspoon dry mustard
¼ teaspoon LAWRY'S® Seasoned
    Pepper
⅛ teaspoon LAWRY'S® Garlic Powder
    with Parsley
⅛ teaspoon oregano
3 to 4 tablespoons minced cilantro

In medium bowl, combine all ingredients with wire whisk or fork; blend well. Refrigerate several hours to blend flavors.

Makes about 1½ cups

Spicy Mexican Dressing

¾ cup Italian-style salad dressing
2 teaspoons chopped cilantro
½ to ¾ teaspoon hot pepper sauce
½ teaspoon LAWRY'S® Seasoned
    Pepper
½ teaspoon chili powder

In medium bowl, combine all ingredients; blend well. *Makes 3 cups*

Presentation: Serve dressing with California Black Bean Salad (page 206).

Italian Herb Dressing

Best Brunches & Lunches

Celebrate all occasions with an impressive array of taste sensations. These irrestible recipes are perfect for a bountiful late-morning brunch or leisurely midday lunch.

Western Omelet

½ cup finely chopped red or green bell pepper
½ cup cubed cooked potato
2 slices turkey bacon, diced
¼ teaspoon dried oregano leaves
2 teaspoons FLEISCHMANN'S® Margarine, divided
1 cup EGG BEATERS® Real Egg Product
Fresh oregano sprig, for garnish

In 8-inch skillet, over medium heat, sauté bell pepper, potato, turkey bacon and dried oregano in 1 teaspoon margarine until tender.* Remove from skillet; keep warm.

In same skillet, over medium heat, melt remaining 1 teaspoon margarine. Pour Egg Beaters® into skillet. Cook, lifting edges to allow uncooked portion to flow underneath. When almost set, spoon vegetable mixture over half of omelet. Fold other half over vegetable mixture; slide onto serving plate. Garnish with fresh oregano.

Makes 2 servings

*For frittata, sauté vegetables and turkey bacon in 2 teaspoons margarine. Pour Egg Beaters® evenly into skillet over prepared vegetables. Cook without stirring for 4 to 5 minutes or until cooked on bottom and almost set on top. Carefully turn frittata; cook for 1 to 2 minutes more or until done. Slide onto serving platter; cut into wedges to serve.

Western Omelet

Party Popovers

3 eggs
1 cup all-purpose flour
1 cup milk
2 tablespoons butter, melted
½ teaspoon salt
2 teaspoons instant minced onion
    Easy Creamed Eggs Elegant (recipe
    follows)

Place eggs, flour, milk, butter and salt in blender container or small mixing bowl. Cover and blend or beat at medium speed until smooth. Stir in onion. Fill lightly greased popover pans, muffin cups or 6-ounce custard cups half full. Bake in preheated 425°F oven until brown and firm, 35 to 40 minutes.* Remove from pans immediately. For each serving, fill each of 2 popovers with about ⅓ cup Easy Creamed Eggs Elegant.
    Makes 1 dozen popovers or 6 servings

*For crisper popovers, prick side of each with wooden pick. Turn off oven and let stand in oven additional 5 minutes.

*Favorite recipe from **American Egg Board***

Easy Creamed Eggs Elegant

1 cup sliced celery
¼ cup butter
¼ cup all-purpose flour
½ teaspoon salt
2 cups milk
½ cup (2 ounces) shredded Cheddar
    cheese
6 hard-cooked eggs,* wedged
¾ cup diced cooked turkey, chicken or
    ham *or* 1 can (5 to 6¾ ounces)
    boned chicken, undrained
1 can (2 ounces) sliced mushrooms
    with liquid
2 tablespoons sherry, optional
1 teaspoon instant minced onion

*To hard-cook, put eggs in single layer in saucepan. Add enough tap water to come at least 1 inch above eggs. Cover and quickly bring just to boiling. Turn off heat. If necessary, remove pan from burner to prevent further boiling. Let eggs stand, covered, in the hot water 15 to 17 minutes for large eggs. (Adjust time up or down by about 3 minutes for each size larger or smaller.) Immediately run cold water over eggs or put them in ice water until completely cooled.

In medium saucepan over medium heat, cook celery in butter until crisp-tender, about 3 to 5 minutes. Blend in flour and salt. Cook, stirring constantly, until mixture is smooth and bubbly. Stir in milk all at once. Cook and stir until mixture boils and is smooth and thickened. Remove from heat. Stir in cheese until melted. Stir in remaining ingredients. Cook over low heat until heated through.
    Makes 6 servings

*Favorite recipe from **American Egg Board***

GREY POUPON®

Undoubtedly, the mustard capital of the world is Dijon in eastern France. The French were passionate about mustard, considering it the condiment of kings. In 1777, Monsieur Grey developed a secret recipe for a strong mustard made with white wine. He formed a partnership with Monsieur Poupon, who supplied financial backing. The two men revolutionized the business by introducing the first automatic mustard machines, freeing workers from the backbreaking chore of grinding the seeds. The creamy mustard their partnership yielded remains the standard by which Dijon mustards are judged.

Italian Baked Frittata

1 cup broccoli flowerettes
½ cup sliced mushrooms
½ red pepper, cut into rings
2 green onions, sliced into 1-inch pieces
1 tablespoon margarine
8 eggs
¼ cup GREY POUPON® Dijon or COUNTRY DIJON® Mustard
¼ cup water
½ teaspoon Italian seasoning
1 cup (4 ounces) shredded Swiss cheese

In 10-inch ovenproof skillet, over medium-high heat, cook broccoli, mushrooms, red pepper and green onions in margarine until tender-crisp, about 5 minutes. Remove from heat.

In small bowl, with electric mixer at medium speed, beat eggs, mustard, water and Italian seasoning until foamy; stir in cheese. Pour mixture into skillet over vegetables. Bake at 375°F for 20 to 25 minutes or until set. Serve immediately.   *Makes 4 servings*

Country Fare Breakfast with Wisconsin Fontina

¼ cup butter
2 cups frozen hash brown potatoes
¼ cup finely chopped onion
6 eggs, beaten
¾ teaspoon salt
⅛ teaspoon pepper
2 tablespoons milk
¼ cup chopped parsley, divided
1 cup (4 ounces) shredded Wisconsin Fontina cheese, divided
1 cup cubed cooked turkey

Melt butter in 10-inch ovenproof skillet; add potatoes and onion. Cook, covered, over medium heat 15 minutes until tender and lightly browned; stir occasionally. Beat together eggs, salt, pepper and milk; stir in 3 tablespoons parsley and ½ cup cheese. Pour egg mixture over potatoes; sprinkle with turkey. Bake, uncovered, in preheated 350°F oven for 20 minutes or until eggs are set. Sprinkle remaining ½ cup cheese over eggs; return to oven for about 2 minutes until cheese is melted. Remove from oven and garnish with remaining 1 tablespoon parsley. Cut into wedges and serve with salsa, if desired. *Makes 6 servings*

Note: Ham may be substituted for turkey.

Favorite recipe from **Wisconsin Milk Marketing Board**

Hearty Breakfast Custard Casserole

1 pound (2 medium-large) Colorado baking potatoes
Salt and pepper
8 ounces bulk low-fat sausage, cooked and crumbled, *or* 6 ounces finely diced lean ham *or* 6 ounces turkey bacon, cooked and crumbled
⅓ cup julienne-sliced roasted red pepper *or* 2-ounce jar sliced pimentos
3 eggs
1 cup low-fat milk
3 tablespoons chopped chives or green onion tops, *or* ¾ teaspoon dried thyme or oregano leaves
Salsa and low-fat yogurt (optional)

Heat oven to 375°F. Butter 8- or 9-inch square baking dish or other small casserole. Peel potatoes and slice very thin; arrange half of potatoes in prepared baking dish. Sprinkle with salt and pepper. Cover with half of sausage or ham. Arrange remaining potatoes on top; sprinkle with salt and pepper. Top with remaining sausage and red pepper. Beat eggs, milk and chives until blended. Pour over potatoes. Cover baking dish with aluminum foil and bake 35 to 45 minutes, or until potatoes are tender. Uncover and bake 5 to 10 minutes more. Serve with salsa and yogurt, if desired. *Makes 4 to 5 servings*

Favorite recipe from **Colorado Potato Administrative Committee**

Country Fare Breakfast with Wisconsin Fontina

Cheese-Bacon Soufflé

Grated Parmesan cheese
2 tablespoons butter
¼ cup chopped green onions
2 tablespoons all-purpose flour
¼ teaspoon salt
⅛ teaspoon pepper
⅛ teaspoon garlic powder
1 cup milk
1 cup (4 ounces) shredded Cheddar
   cheese
3 egg yolks, slightly beaten
3 egg whites
¼ teaspoon cream of tartar
6 slices bacon, cooked, drained and
   crumbled

Preheat oven to 350°F. Butter 1½-quart soufflé dish or casserole. Sprinkle enough Parmesan cheese in dish to coat bottom and side evenly; remove any excess. Melt butter in medium-sized saucepan. Sauté green onions until tender, about 3 minutes. Blend in flour, salt, pepper and garlic powder. Remove from heat; stir in milk. Heat to boiling, stirring constantly. Boil and stir 1 minute. Remove from heat and stir in cheese until melted. If necessary, return to low heat to finish melting cheese. *(Do not boil.)* Blend a little of hot mixture into egg yolks; return all to saucepan. Blend thoroughly; set aside. Beat egg whites until frothy. Add cream of tartar and beat until soft peaks form. Fold cheese sauce into egg whites. Fold in bacon. Turn into prepared soufflé dish. Bake 40 to 45 minutes. Serve immediately. *Makes 2 servings*

*Favorite recipe from **American Dairy Association***

Crowd-Sized Spinach Soufflé

Butter
Grated Parmesan cheese
2 cups milk
½ cup quick-cooking tapioca
4 teaspoons instant minced onion
1 tablespoon instant chicken bouillon
⅛ teaspoon ground nutmeg
1 cup (4 ounces) shredded Swiss
   cheese
8 eggs, separated
1 teaspoon cream of tartar
2 packages (10 ounces each) frozen
   chopped spinach, thawed and well-
   drained

Butter bottom and sides of 13×9×2-inch baking dish. Dust with Parmesan cheese. Set aside.

In medium saucepan, stir together milk, tapioca, onion, bouillon and nutmeg. Let stand 10 minutes. Cook over medium-high heat, stirring constantly, until mixture boils and is thickened. Stir in Swiss cheese until melted. Set aside.

In large bowl, beat egg whites with cream of tartar at high speed until stiff but not dry, just until whites no longer slip when bowl is tilted. Thoroughly blend egg yolks and spinach into reserved sauce. Gently, but thoroughly, fold yolk mixture into whites. Carefully pour into prepared dish. Bake in preheated 350°F oven 30 to 40 minutes or until puffy, delicately browned and soufflé shakes slightly when oven rack is gently moved back and forth. Serve immediately. *Makes 8 servings*

*Favorite recipe from **American Egg Board***

Crab & Shrimp Quiche

Crab & Shrimp Quiche

6 slices BORDEN® Process American
    Cheese Food
2 tablespoons sliced green onion
2 tablespoons chopped pimiento
1 tablespoon all-purpose flour
1 (6-ounce) can ORLEANS® or HARRIS®
    Crab Meat, drained
1 (4¼-ounce) can ORLEANS® Shrimp,
    drained and soaked as label directs
1½ cups BORDEN® or MEADOW GOLD®
    Half-and-Half
3 eggs, beaten
1 (9-inch) unbaked pastry shell

Place rack in lowest position in oven; preheat oven to 425°F. Cut *4 slices* cheese food into pieces. In large bowl, toss cheese food pieces, onion and pimiento with flour. Add crab meat, shrimp, half-and-half and eggs. Pour into pastry shell. Bake 20 minutes. Reduce oven temperature to 325°F; bake 20 minutes longer or until set. Arrange remaining *2 slices* cheese food on top of quiche. Let stand 10 minutes before serving. Garnish as desired. Refrigerate leftovers.

Makes one 9-inch quiche

Cheese-Turkey Crêpes

2 frozen Basic Crêpes (recipe follows)
½ cup frozen whole green beans
4 slices (1 ounce each) Muenster cheese, cut in half
2 slices (1 ounce each) deli-style turkey breast, each cut into 4 pieces
½ can (16 ounces) whole berry cranberry sauce

Thaw crêpes as directed in Basic Crêpes recipe. Preheat oven to 350°F. Cook green beans according to package directions; drain. To assemble, place half the cheese down center of each crêpe (pale side up). Top with turkey and beans. Fold opposite edges to overlap filling. Place, seam side down, in buttered 8-inch square baking dish. Bake 15 to 18 minutes or until cheese is melted. Meanwhile, heat cranberry sauce in small saucepan over low heat, stirring frequently. To serve, spoon sauce over each crêpe. Serve immediately. *Makes 2 servings*

Notes: Place remaining ½ can cranberry sauce in covered plastic container. Store in refrigerator for use later in week.

Leftover or deli slices of ham or chicken breast may be substituted for turkey. No other changes need be made since green beans and Muenster cheese harmonize with any of the meats.

*Favorite recipe from **American Dairy Association***

Basic Crêpes

1 cup all-purpose flour
1½ cups milk
2 eggs
1 tablespoon butter, melted
¼ teaspoon salt
Butter

In small bowl, combine flour, milk, eggs, 1 tablespoon butter and salt; beat with rotary beater or wire whisk until blended. Heat lightly buttered 6-inch skillet or crêpe pan. Remove from heat; spoon in about 2 tablespoons batter. Lift and tilt skillet to spread batter evenly. Return to heat; brown on one side only. To remove, invert pan over paper toweling; remove crêpe. Repeat with remaining batter, buttering skillet as needed. To freeze, layer crêpes between 2 sheets of waxed paper. Overwrap with aluminum foil; freeze. Crêpes can be kept frozen 2 to 4 months. To defrost, remove only number needed. Keep crêpes covered with waxed paper; let thaw at room temperature about 1 hour. *Makes 16 to 18 crêpes*

*Favorite recipe from **American Dairy Association***

Roman Meal® Pancakes

1⅓ cups all-purpose flour
1 tablespoon baking powder
½ teaspoon salt
2 tablespoons sugar
½ cup ROMAN MEAL® Cereal
1½ cups milk (may use skim or 2%)
2 tablespoons vegetable oil
3 egg whites (*or* 1 whole egg)

Preheat griddle. In medium bowl, combine flour, baking powder, salt, sugar and cereal. Beat milk and oil with egg whites (or whole egg); add to dry ingredients and beat well. Pour batter by ¼ cup portions onto hot, lightly greased griddle. When surface bubbles and edges lose their sheen, turn and bake other side.

Makes 12 to 15 (4- to 5-inch) pancakes

Chilean Fresh Fruit Association

Nothing perks up jaded winter appetites like the taste of fresh summer fruit. Top quality nectarines, peaches, plums, apricots, grapes and berries arrive in our supermarkets from December through May, thanks to Chile's lush fruit-producing valleys. Chile's growing season is opposite our own—their summer is our winter. And, as the season advances, different fruit becomes available. The fruit is not held in cold storage but is sent by advanced shipping and handling methods to arrive in prime condition.

Roman Meal® Waffles

1⅓ cups all-purpose flour
2 tablespoons sugar
1 tablespoon baking powder
½ teaspoon salt
⅔ cup ROMAN MEAL® Cereal
1½ cups milk (may be skim milk)
⅓ cup vegetable oil
2 stiffly beaten egg whites

Preheat waffle iron. In medium bowl, combine flour, sugar, baking powder, salt and cereal. Mix together milk and oil; add all at once to dry ingredients. Mix well. Fold in egg whites. Pour batter onto hot waffle iron.

Makes 8 to 10 waffles, 4½ inches each

Morning Compote of Chilean Fruit

½ cup honey
Grated zest of ½ orange
Juice of 1 orange
3 ripe Chilean pears, cut into wedges
6 ripe Chilean plums, cut into wedges
1 cup red seedless Chilean grapes
1 cup green seedless Chilean grapes

Combine honey, orange zest and orange juice in large saucepan. Bring to a boil and add pears, plums, red and green grapes. Return to a boil; reduce heat and partially cover pan. Let simmer for 5 minutes; fruit will give off a lot of juice. Cool and refrigerate overnight. Serve with vanilla-flavored yogurt.

Makes 6 servings

*Favorite recipe from **Chilean Fresh Fruit Association***

America's Favorite Cheddar Beef Burgers

1 pound ground beef
⅓ cup A.1.® Steak Sauce
1 medium onion, cut into strips
1 medium green or red bell pepper, cut into strips
1 tablespoon margarine
4 ounces Cheddar cheese, sliced
4 hamburger rolls
4 tomato slices

In medium bowl, combine ground beef and 3 tablespoons steak sauce; shape mixture into 4 patties. Set aside.

In medium skillet, over medium heat, cook onion and pepper in margarine until tender, stirring occasionally. Stir in remaining steak sauce; keep warm.

Grill burgers over medium heat 4 minutes on each side or until done. When almost done, top with cheese; grill until cheese melts. Spoon 2 tablespoons onion mixture onto each roll bottom; top each with burger, tomato slice, some of remaining onion mixture and roll top.   *Makes 4 servings*

Lipton® Onion Burgers

1 envelope LIPTON® RECIPE SECRETS® Onion Soup Mix*
2 pounds ground beef
½ cup water

*Also terrific with Lipton® Recipe Secrets® Beefy Onion, Onion-Mushroom or Italian Herb with Tomato Soup Mix.

In large bowl, combine soup mix, beef and water; shape into 8 patties. Grill or broil until done.   *Makes about 8 servings*

Suggestion: Serve with lettuce, tomato, pickles and potato salad.

Wisconsin Cheese Burgers

3 pounds ground beef
½ cup dry bread crumbs
2 eggs, beaten
1¼ cups (5 ounces) your favorite shredded Wisconsin cheese, Pepper Havarti cheese, shredded, Blue cheese, crumbled, or Basil & Tomato Feta cheese, crumbled

In large bowl, combine beef, bread crumbs and eggs; mix well, but lightly. Divide mixture into 24 balls; flatten each on waxed paper to 4 inches across. Place 1 heaping tablespoonful cheese on each of 12 patties. Top with remaining patties, carefully pressing edges to seal. Grill patties 4 inches from coals, turning only once, 6 to 9 minutes on each side or until no longer pink. To keep cheese between patties as it melts, do not flatten burgers with spatula while grilling.
          Makes 12 servings

Caution: Cheese filling may be very hot if eaten immediately after cooking.

Favorite recipe from **Wisconsin Milk Marketing Board**

America's Favorite Cheddar Beef Burger

Sloppy Joes

Sloppy Joes

1 pound lean ground beef
½ cup chopped onion
⅓ cup chopped green pepper
1 bottle (12 ounces) HEINZ® Chili Sauce
¼ cup water
1 to 2 tablespoons brown sugar
1 tablespoon HEINZ® Worcestershire
    Sauce
¼ teaspoon salt
⅛ teaspoon pepper
    Sandwich buns

In large saucepan, cook beef, onion and green pepper until green pepper is tender; drain, if necessary. Stir in chili sauce, water, sugar, Worcestershire sauce, salt and pepper; simmer 10 minutes, stirring occasionally. Serve in sandwich buns.

Makes 6 to 8 servings

It all began 126 years ago in one boy's garden in Sharpsburg, Pennsylvania. That is where young Henry J. Heinz tended a vegetable garden outside his family's home. His hard work quickly led to a surplus which he sold to his neighbors. At 16, he was selling to grocers in Pittsburgh and by 25, he had begun a modest enterprise that is now the international corporation which bears his name. He was also the first in the industry to package his products in clear glass bottles so the consumer could see the quality and pureness of the product.

Meatball Hero Sandwiches

½ **pound ground beef**
¼ **pound hot Italian sausage, casings removed**
¼ **cup seasoned dry bread crumbs**
1 **egg**
½ **teaspoon salt**
1 **(15-ounce) can HUNT'S® Ready Tomato Sauces Original Garlic**
1 **teaspoon sugar**
2 **tablespoons grated Parmesan cheese**
4 **(6-inch) hero rolls**

In small bowl, combine ground beef, sausage, bread crumbs, egg and salt. Form mixture into 12 (1½-inch) balls. Place meatballs on foil-lined baking sheet. Bake in preheated 375°F oven 25 minutes; drain. In large saucepan, stir together Hunt's® ready tomato sauces original garlic and sugar. Add meatballs; simmer, covered, 10 minutes. Stir in cheese. Spoon 3 meatballs and sauce onto each roll. *Makes 4 servings*

Chili Dogs

½ **pound lean ground beef**
1 **cup chopped onions**
1 **(6-ounce) can HUNT'S® Tomato Paste No Salt Added**
1 **cup water**
2 **tablespoons chili powder**
1 **tablespoon prepared yellow mustard**
½ **teaspoon garlic powder**
½ **teaspoon ground cumin**
¼ **teaspoon sugar**
⅛ **teaspoon crushed red pepper**
1 **pound turkey hot dogs**
10 **hot dog buns**

In skillet, brown beef and onions. Stir in tomato paste, water, chili powder, mustard, garlic powder, cumin, sugar and crushed red pepper; heat through. Meanwhile, heat or grill hot dogs. To serve, place hot dogs in buns; spoon chili down center of each.
Makes 10 chili dogs

Philadelphia Cheese Steak Sandwiches

2 cups sliced red or green bell peppers (about 2 medium)
1 small onion, thinly sliced
1 tablespoon vegetable oil
½ cup A.1.® BOLD Steak Sauce
1 teaspoon prepared horseradish
8 ounces thinly sliced beef sandwich steaks
4 long sandwich rolls, split
4 ounces thinly sliced mozzarella cheese

In medium saucepan, over medium heat, sauté bell peppers and onion in oil until tender. Stir in steak sauce and horseradish; keep warm.

In lightly greased medium skillet, over medium-high heat, cook sandwich steaks until done. On roll bottoms, portion beef, pepper mixture and cheese.

Broil sandwich bottoms 4 inches from heat source 3 to 5 minutes or until cheese melts; replace tops. Serve immediately.

Makes 4 sandwiches

Chicken Po' Boy Sandwich

½ cup fat free, cholesterol free mayonnaise
1 tablespoon Dijon mustard
2 teaspoons cider vinegar
½ teaspoon dried thyme
¼ teaspoon ground red pepper
3½ tablespoons all-purpose flour
2 green onions, minced
1 teaspoon paprika
1 pound COOKIN' GOOD® Tenderloins of Chicken Breast, thawed
2 tablespoons vegetable oil, divided
1 long loaf Italian or French bread
½ head red leaf lettuce
1 large tomato, sliced

1. In small bowl, combine mayonnaise, mustard, vinegar, thyme and ground red pepper; set aside.

2. In plastic bag or on wax paper, combine flour, green onions and paprika. Add chicken, a few pieces at a time, tossing to coat with flour mixture. Repeat with remaining chicken pieces.

3. In 10-inch skillet over medium heat, heat 1 tablespoon vegetable oil. Cook half of chicken pieces 3 to 4 minutes or until no longer pink, turning once. Repeat with remaining 1 tablespoon oil and chicken pieces.

4. To serve, cut bread in half horizontally. Place lettuce leaves on bottom half of bread. Arrange chicken pieces and tomato slices on top of lettuce. Spread mayonnaise mixture on top half of bread. Replace top of bread. Cut bread crosswise into 4 pieces.

Makes 4 servings

Philadelphia Cheese Steak Sandwich

Soft Shell Chicken Tacos

¾ **pound boneless, skinless chicken breasts**
1 **teaspoon ground cumin**
1 **can (8 ounces) stewed tomatoes**
⅓ **cup salsa**
1 **green onion, thinly sliced**
8 **(7-inch) flour tortillas, warmed**
1 **cup shredded lettuce**
1 **medium tomato, chopped**
1 **cup (4 ounces) SARGENTO®
   Preferred Light® Shredded Cheese
   For Tacos**
¼ **cup chopped fresh cilantro (optional)**

Place chicken in single layer in skillet; season with cumin. Pour tomatoes and salsa over chicken. Simmer, uncovered, 15 minutes or until chicken is tender, turning once. Remove chicken; save liquid in skillet. Cool and shred chicken; add to skillet with green onion. Cook 2 minutes or until most of the liquid is absorbed. Divide chicken mixture evenly down center of each tortilla. Top with shredded lettuce, chopped fresh tomato and taco cheese. Add cilantro; fold and serve immediately.   *Makes 4 servings*

Sargento

It was in Plymouth, in the heart of Wisconsin's dairyland, that Leonard Gentine, Sr. launched the Plymouth Cheese Counter in the late 1940s. Gentine noticed there was a great demand for smaller-sized packaged cheese products versus the larger bulk sizes sold in retail stores. To satisfy this demand, Gentine went into partnership with Joseph Sartori and formed the Sargento Cheese Company in 1953. Consumer-sized packages of Mozzarella, Provolone and Romano were the company's first products. As consumers expressed more interest in convenience products, Sargento was the first company to introduce shredded and sliced natural cheeses, and the first zippered resealable packaging for perishable food products.

Tuna Melt

Tuna Melt

**1 can (12 ounces) STARKIST® Solid
    White or Chunk Light Tuna, drained
    and flaked**
⅓ cup mayonnaise
1½ tablespoons sweet pickle relish
1½ tablespoons chopped onion
½ tablespoon mustard
3 English muffins, split and toasted
6 tomato slices, halved
**6 slices American, Cheddar, Swiss or
    Monterey Jack cheese**
Fresh fruit (optional)

In medium bowl, combine tuna, mayonnaise, pickle relish, onion and mustard; mix well. Spread about ⅓ cup on each muffin half. Top with tomato slice and cheese slice. Broil 4 to 5 minutes or until cheese melts. Serve with fresh fruit, if desired.　*Makes 6 servings*

Pesto Pita Pizzas

1 envelope (½ ounce) pesto sauce mix
½ cup water
¼ cup tomato sauce, preferably no salt added
4 (6-inch) rounds pita bread or ready-made pizza crusts
½ cup (2 ounces) grated reduced fat Monterey Jack cheese
½ cup (2 ounces) chopped California walnuts
1 teaspoon dried mixed Italian herbs or Italian seasoning

Combine pesto sauce mix and water; blend well. (Omit the oil called for in package directions.) Microwave on HIGH 3 minutes, stirring once, or boil on stovetop 3 minutes.

Preheat oven to 450°F. Stir tomato sauce into pesto mix and spread each pita or pizza crust with about 2 tablespoons of sauce. Sprinkle each with 2 tablespoons cheese and 2 tablespoons walnuts. Sprinkle each pizza lightly with Italian herbs. Place on baking sheet and bake 8 to 10 minutes, or until sauce is bubbling and cheese is melted.

Makes 4 pizzas

Favorite recipe from **Walnut Marketing Board**

Pesto Pita Pizza

Cheesy Tortilla Trap™

1 flour tortilla (6 or 8 inches)
2 KRAFT® American Singles Pasteurized Process Cheese Food
Salsa

• Place tortilla on microwavable plate. Place process cheese food on half of tortilla. Fold tortilla in half to cover process cheese food. Cover.

• Microwave on HIGH 25 to 40 seconds or until process cheese food begins to melt.

• Let stand, covered, 1 minute or until cool enough to eat. Fold in half again. Serve with salsa. *Makes 1 serving*

Top of Stove: • Place tortilla in medium skillet on medium heat. Place process cheese food on half of tortilla. Fold tortilla in half to cover process cheese food. • Heat 1 minute on each side. • Fold in half again. Serve with salsa.

Oven: • Heat oven to 350°F. • Place process cheese food on half of tortilla. Fold tortilla in half to cover process cheese food. • Bake 2 to 3 minutes or until process cheese food begins to melt. • Fold in half again. Serve with salsa.

Variation: Top process cheese food with sliced red and green peppers. Continue as directed.

Grilled Pizza

2 loaves (1 pound each) frozen bread
    dough, thawed*
Olive oil
K.C. MASTERPIECE® Barbecue Sauce
    or pizza sauce
Seasonings: finely chopped garlic
    and fresh or dried herbs
Toppings: any combination of
    slivered ham, shredded barbecued
    chicken and grilled vegetables,
    such as thinly sliced mushrooms,
    zucchini, yellow squash, bell
    peppers, eggplant, pineapple
    chunks, tomatoes
Salt and black pepper
Cheese: any combination of
    shredded mozzarella, Provolone,
    Monterey Jack, grated Parmesan or
    crumbled feta

*Substitute your favorite pizza crust recipe. Dough
for 1 large pizza will make 4 individual ones.

Divide each loaf of dough into 4 balls. Roll
on cornmeal-coated or lightly floured surface
and pat out dough to ¼-inch thickness to
make small circles. Brush each circle with oil.

Arrange hot KINGSFORD® briquets on one
side of grill. Oil hot grid to help prevent
sticking. Vegetables, such as mushrooms,
zucchini, yellow squash, bell peppers and
eggplant need to be grilled until tender before
using them as toppings. (See Note.)

Place 4 circles directly above medium
Kingsford® briquets. (The dough will not fall
through the grid.) Grill circles, on uncovered
grill, until dough starts to bubble in spots on
top and bottom gets lightly browned. Turn

over using tongs. Continue to grill until other
side is lightly browned, then move crusts to
cool part of grill.

Brush each crust lightly with barbecue sauce;
top with garlic and herbs, then meat or
vegetables. Season with salt and pepper,
then top with cheese. Cover pizzas and grill,
about 5 minutes until cheese melts, bottom of
crust is crisp and pizza looks done. Repeat
with remaining dough.

Makes 8 individual pizzas

Note: Vegetables such as mushrooms,
zucchini, yellow squash, bell peppers and
eggplant should be grilled before adding to
pizza. If used raw, they will not have enough
time to cook through. To grill, thread cut-up
vegetables on skewers. Brush lightly with oil.
Grill vegetables, on uncovered grill, over hot
Kingsford® briquets, until tender, turning
frequently.

Ham & Pineapple Pizza: Brush crust lightly
with K.C. Masterpiece® Barbecue Sauce and
top with minced garlic, slivered ham, grilled
bell peppers, pineapple chunks and shredded
mozzarella or Monterey Jack cheese.

Veggie-Herb Pizza: Brush crust lightly with
pizza sauce and top with finely chopped
basil, minced garlic and grilled mushrooms,
zucchini and green bell pepper. Sprinkle with
grated Parmesan cheese.

Tomato-Feta Pizza: Top crust with minced
garlic and crumbled dried herbs or minced
fresh herbs, such as oregano, rosemary and
basil. Top with chopped fresh tomato, slivered
red onion and coarsely chopped olives.
Sprinkle with grated Parmesan cheese and
crumbled feta cheese.

Grilled Pizzas

New York Style Deluxe Cheese Pizza

Dough

   1 package active dry yeast
   1 tablespoon sugar
   ¼ cup warm water (105°–115°F)
3½ cups unbleached all-purpose flour
   1 tablespoon salt
   ¼ cup olive oil
   ¾ cup warm water (approximately)

   8 ounces pizza sauce
15 ounces Wisconsin Whole Milk
      Mozzarella, shredded
   5 ounces Wisconsin Provolone,
      shredded
40 slices pepperoni
1½ ounces Wisconsin Parmesan, grated
   1 tablespoon dried oregano

To make dough: In small bowl, combine yeast, sugar and ¼ cup warm water. Stir well to combine. Set aside for 5 minutes. In large bowl, combine flour and salt. Add olive oil to yeast mixture and stir well. Add oil/yeast mixture to flour mixture and add additional warm water. Knead dough in mixing bowl until a compact ball is formed. Turn out dough onto work surface and knead vigorously 5 to 6 minutes. Put 1 teaspoon olive oil in bowl. Place dough in bowl and turn twice to coat. Cover bowl with plastic wrap and kitchen towel and set in warm place until doubled in bulk, about 1½ hours.

After dough has doubled, punch down and turn out onto work surface. Knead dough for 2 minutes. (Note: Yield is about 26 ounces of dough. Recipe uses only 20 ounces. Extra dough can be frozen for later use.) Press dough into flat, lightly oiled 16-inch diameter pizza pan (or 16-inch pizza screen).

To assemble pizza: Spread pizza sauce on dough to within ½ inch of edge. Top sauce with Mozzarella, Provolone and pepperoni. Bake pizza in preheated 500°F oven 8 to 10 minutes or until crust is browned and cheese is bubbly and lightly speckled. Just before serving, sprinkle top of pizza with Parmesan cheese and oregano.   *Makes 1 pizza*

*Favorite recipe from **Wisconsin Milk Marketing Board***

Golden Gate Open Face Sandwich

   4 ounces crab-style surimi seafood
      blend
   ¼ cup chopped red bell pepper
   2 tablespoons green onion slices
   1 teaspoon lemon juice
   1 (8-ounce) package HEALTHY
      CHOICE® Fat Free Natural Fancy
      Shredded Mozzarella Cheese
      Fat-free mayonnaise
   6 sourdough bread slices, toasted
   1 cup alfalfa sprouts

Combine seafood, pepper, onion, lemon juice and half of cheese with ¼ cup mayonnaise; mix lightly. For each sandwich, spread slice of bread with 2 teaspoons mayonnaise; top with 2 tablespoons sprouts, ⅓ cup seafood mixture and ½ ounce of remaining cheese. Bake at 350°F, 10 minutes.

Makes 6 servings

Paul Newman has fun in the kitchen creating his famed sauces.
Photo courtesy of Newman's Own, Inc.

Bagelroonies

6 onion bagels
6 tablespoons soft-spread margarine
1 (14-ounce) jar NEWMAN'S OWN®
    Sockarooni™ Sauce
1 (8-ounce) package Canadian bacon
    slices
1 (16-ounce) package mozzarella
    cheese, shredded (2 cups)
Freshly grated Parmesan cheese

Cut bagels in half; spread with margarine. Spoon Newman's Own® Sockarooni™ Sauce on bagel halves, approximately 3 tablespoons per bagel half. Chop Canadian bacon slices and place over sauce. Sprinkle liberally with shredded mozzarella cheese. If desired, shake grated Parmesan cheese over bagels. Broil until cheese melts and bubbles.

Makes 6 servings

The Bountiful Bread Basket

Fill your kitchen with the enticing aroma of home-baked breads. This oven-loving collection of heartwarming recipes is abounding with homemade goodness.

Mott's® Morning Glory Bread

2½ cups all-purpose flour
2 teaspoons baking powder
1 teaspoon baking soda
½ teaspoon salt
½ teaspoon cinnamon
¼ teaspoon nutmeg
¼ teaspoon allspice
¾ cup granulated sugar
¾ cup light brown sugar
1 tablespoon GRANDMA'S® Molasses
3 egg whites
½ cup MOTT'S® Chunky Apple Sauce
1 tablespoon vegetable oil
¾ cup grated carrots
½ cup raisins
⅓ cup crushed pineapple, drained
¼ cup shredded coconut

1. Preheat oven to 375°F. Spray 8½×4½×3-inch loaf pan with nonstick cooking spray.

2. In medium bowl, combine flour, baking powder, baking soda, salt and spices.

3. In separate large bowl, mix together sugars, molasses, egg whites, apple sauce and vegetable oil.

4. Add flour mixture to apple sauce mixture and stir until mixture is combined. Fold in carrots, raisins, pineapple and coconut.

5. Pour batter into prepared pan and bake 45 to 50 minutes or until toothpick inserted in center comes out clean.

Makes 18 servings

From left to right: Mott's® Lemon Poppy Seed Tea Loaf (page 240) and Mott's® Morning Glory Bread

Mott's® Lemon Poppy Seed Tea Loaf

2 tablespoons vegetable oil
⅔ cup MOTT'S® Natural Apple Sauce
1 cup granulated sugar
1 whole egg
2 egg whites, slightly beaten
1 teaspoon vanilla
2½ cups all-purpose flour
2 teaspoons baking powder
½ teaspoon baking soda
½ teaspoon salt
¼ cup poppy seed
1 tablespoon grated lemon peel
⅓ cup skim milk

Lemon Syrup

¼ cup lemon juice
¼ cup granulated sugar

1. Preheat oven to 350°F. Spray 9×5×4-inch loaf pan with nonstick cooking spray.

2. In large bowl, combine oil, Mott's® Natural Apple Sauce, 1 cup granulated sugar, egg, beaten egg whites and vanilla.

3. In separate medium bowl, combine flour, baking powder, baking soda, salt, poppy seed and lemon peel.

4. Add flour mixture to apple sauce mixture alternately with skim milk. Mix until ingredients are thoroughly moistened.

5. Pour batter into prepared pan. Bake 30 to 35 minutes or until toothpick inserted in center comes out clean. Cool loaf in pan on cooling rack.

6. Heat lemon juice and ¼ cup granulated sugar in small saucepan until sugar dissolves. Remove from heat and cool.

7. Remove cake from pan and return to cooling rack. Pierce loaf all over with metal skewer. Brush loaf with prepared lemon syrup. Let stand until cool. Slice thinly to serve. *Makes 20 servings*

Mott's was founded in 1842 when Sam R. Mott began making cider and vinegar in a small mill in Bouckville, New York. These products caught the fancy of his neighbors and as demand grew so did the size of his mill. In 1900, Mott merged with the W.B. Duffy Cider Company. Sam Mott quickly incorporated Duffy's method for preserving apple cider in wood which further increased the size of the market. In 1930, apple sauce was added to the Mott's line. Today, Mott's produces over 13 million cases of apple juice and apple sauce every year.

Colorful Veg-All® Cornbread

Colorful Veg-All®
Cornbread

1 (8½-ounce) box cornbread mix
1 (16-ounce) can VEG-ALL® Mixed
  Vegetables, drained
1 cup shredded Cheddar cheese
½ cup chopped onion
⅓ cup milk
1 egg, slightly beaten

Combine cornbread mix, vegetables, cheese, onion, milk and egg. (Leftover chopped, cooked ham or sausage can be added.) Spoon into lightly greased 8×8-inch pan. Bake in preheated 400°F oven 25 minutes. Cool 5 minutes before cutting.

Makes 6 to 8 servings

Mott's® Cinnamania Bread

½ cup GRANDMA'S® Molasses
½ cup water
1 cup chopped dates
1 (4-ounce) container red cinnamon
   imperial candies
½ cup MOTT'S® Natural Apple Sauce
2 egg whites
1 teaspoon baking soda
1 teaspoon baking powder
3 teaspoons cinnamon
½ cup unprocessed bran
1½ cups whole wheat flour

Topping

¼ cup MOTT'S® Natural Apple Sauce
½ teaspoon cinnamon
¼ cup crushed walnuts

1. Preheat oven to 350°F. Spray
8½×4½×2½-inch loaf pan with nonstick
cooking spray.

2. Combine Grandma's® Molasses, water,
dates and candies in microwavable bowl.
Microwave for 4 minutes on HIGH power or
until boiling. Stir in ½ cup Mott's® Natural
Apple Sauce and let mixture cool
approximately 15 minutes. Stir in egg whites.

3. In separate large bowl, mix together
baking soda, baking powder, 3 teaspoons
cinnamon, bran and wheat flour. Pour in
molasses mixture and stir just until
moistened.

4. Pour batter into prepared loaf pan.
Prepare Topping. Mix together ¼ cup Mott's®
Natural Apple Sauce and ½ teaspoon
cinnamon. Spread evenly over top of batter
with back of spoon. Sprinkle crushed walnuts
on top. Bake for 1 hour or until knife inserted
in center comes out clean.

Makes 9 servings

Cherry Marketing Institute

*Cherries have pleased
the palates of food
lovers for centuries.
Cherries are available
throughout the year
either frozen, dried,
canned or in juice. As
an added bonus, they are low in
calories and sodium, while high in
vitamins and minerals.*

Cherry Banana Bread

1 jar (10 ounces) maraschino cherries
1¾ cups all-purpose flour
½ teaspoon salt
1½ teaspoons baking powder
½ teaspoon baking soda
⅓ cup butter or margarine, softened
⅔ cup firmly packed brown sugar
2 eggs
1 cup mashed, ripe bananas
½ cup chopped macadamia nuts
1 tablespoon raw brown sugar
   (optional)

Drain maraschino cherries, reserving 2
tablespoons juice. Cut cherries in quarters;
set aside.

Combine flour, salt, baking powder and
baking soda; set aside.

Cherry Banana Bread

In medium bowl, combine butter, ⅔ cup brown sugar, eggs and reserved cherry juice; mix with electric mixer on medium speed until ingredients are thoroughly combined. Add flour mixture and mashed bananas alternately, beginning and ending with flour mixture. Stir in cherries and nuts. Lightly spray 9×5×3-inch loaf pan with nonstick cooking spray. Spread batter evenly in pan. Sprinkle batter with raw brown sugar.

Bake in preheated 350°F oven about 1 hour, or until golden brown and wooden pick inserted in center comes out clean. Remove from pan and cool on wire rack. Store in tightly covered container or foil.

Makes 1 loaf, about 16 slices

Favorite recipe from **Cherry Marketing Institute, Inc.**

Generations of Americans have depended on Libby's Solid Pack Pumpkin for the very best holiday pumpkin pies—in fact, for many people, a slice of Libby's Famous Pumpkin Pie is the only way to finish the eagerly awaited holiday meal. Libby began its pumpkin processing operations in 1929 after years of research to develop their own strain of pumpkin that is meaty, sweet and less watery than pumpkins found at the local market. Minimal processing during canning yields a 100% pure product that is always high quality.

Pumpkin Pecan Bread

1 cup butter, softened
1 cup granulated sugar
1 cup packed dark brown sugar
4 eggs
1 cup LIBBY'S® Solid Pack Pumpkin
2¾ cups all-purpose flour
1 tablespoon pumpkin pie spice
2 teaspoons baking powder
1 teaspoon baking soda
½ teaspoon salt
1 cup pecans, finely chopped

CREAM butter, granulated sugar and brown sugar in large mixer bowl until light. Add eggs, one at a time, beating well after each addition. Beat in pumpkin.

COMBINE flour, pumpkin pie spice, baking powder, baking soda, salt and pecans in small bowl. Add to pumpkin mixture; mix just until blended.

SPOON into 2 greased and floured 8½×4½-inch loaf pans.

BAKE in preheated 350°F oven for 1 hour 10 minutes, or until wooden pick inserted in center comes out clean. Cool for 10 minutes. Remove from pans; cool on wire racks.

Makes 2 loaves

Cherry Oatmeal Muffins

1 cup individually quick frozen tart
    cherries
1⅛ cups quick-cooking oats, uncooked
1 cup buttermilk
1 egg, beaten
¾ cup firmly packed brown sugar
½ cup solid vegetable shortening,
    melted and cooled
1 cup all-purpose flour
1½ teaspoons baking powder
½ teaspoon salt

Cut cherries in half; set aside. In large bowl, combine oats and buttermilk; mix well. Let stand 1 hour.

In another large bowl, combine egg, brown sugar and shortening. Add egg mixture to oats mixture. Mix with electric mixer on low speed 30 seconds; scrape side of bowl.

Cherry Oatmeal Muffiins

In small bowl, combine flour, baking powder and salt. Add flour mixture to oats mixture; mix until ingredients are moistened. Fold in cherries with spoon or rubber spatula.

Fill 12 greased muffin cups two-thirds full. Bake in preheated 400°F oven 15 to 20 minutes.   *Makes 12 muffins*

Note: 1 cup canned tart cherries, well drained and halved, or 1 cup chopped dried cherries may be substituted for 1 cup individually quick frozen tart cherries.

*Favorite recipe from **Cherry Marketing Institute, Inc.***

Biscuits

2 cups sifted all-purpose flour
3 teaspoons baking powder
1 teaspoon salt
⅓ CRISCO® Stick or ⅓ cup Crisco
    all-vegetable shortening
¾ cup milk

1. **Heat** oven to 425°F. **Combine** flour, baking powder and salt in bowl. **Cut** in shortening using pastry blender (or 2 knives) until mixture resembles coarse meal. **Add** milk; **stir** with fork until blended.

2. **Transfer** dough to lightly floured surface. **Knead** gently 8 to 10 times. **Roll** dough ½ inch thick. **Cut** with floured 2-inch-round cutter.

3. **Bake** on ungreased cookie sheet for 12 to 15 minutes.

Makes 12 to 16 (2-inch) biscuits

The Original Kellogg's®
All-Bran Muffin™

1¼ cups all-purpose flour
 ½ cup sugar
 1 tablespoon baking powder
 ¼ teaspoon salt
 2 cups KELLOGG'S® ALL-BRAN® Cereal
1¼ cups milk
 1 egg
 ¼ cup vegetable oil
    Vegetable cooking spray

1. Stir together flour, sugar, baking powder and salt. Set aside.

2. In large mixing bowl, combine Kellogg's® All-Bran® cereal and milk. Let stand about 5 minutes or until cereal softens. Add egg and oil. Beat well. Add flour mixture, stirring only until combined. Portion batter evenly into twelve 2½-inch muffin-pan cups coated with cooking spray.

3. Bake at 400°F about 20 minutes or until lightly browned. Serve warm.

Makes 12 muffins

Crisco® was packaged in glass jars during World War II because of metal shortages.

Cherry Cheese Muffins

1 package (17¼ ounces) frozen puff
    pastry, thawed
2½ cups Northwest sweet cherries, pitted
    and halved
½ cup sugar
1 tablespoon cornstarch
1 teaspoon grated orange peel
    Cheese Filling (recipe follows)
    Egg Glaze (recipe follows)

Roll each pastry sheet into 15×10-inch
rectangle. Cut each sheet into 6 (5×5-inch)
squares. Arrange in muffin pans. Combine
cherries, sugar, cornstarch and orange peel;
mix thoroughly. Fill pastry with 3 to 4
tablespoons Cheese Filling; divide cherry
mixture evenly and spoon over filling. Pull
corners of pastry to center and pinch to
partially seal. Brush with Egg Glaze. Bake in
preheated 400°F oven 20 to 25 minutes or
until pastry has puffed and cherry filling is
thick and bubbly. *Makes 12 muffins*

Cheese Filling: Beat 1 package (8 ounces)
cream cheese, softened, ¼ cup sugar, 1 egg
and 2 tablespoons orange juice until smooth.
Makes about 1¾ cups

Egg Glaze: Combine 1 egg, beaten, and 1
tablespoon water; mix thoroughly.

Favorite recipe from **Northwest Cherry Growers**

Apple 'n Walnut Spiced Muffins

1 cup raisins
2 cups all-purpose flour
1 cup oatmeal
⅔ cup sugar
2½ teaspoons baking powder
½ teaspoon salt
½ teaspoon ground cinnamon
½ teaspoon ground allspice
¼ teaspoon ground nutmeg
4 to 5 small apples
1 egg
2 egg whites
¼ cup canola oil or vegetable oil
½ cup chopped California walnuts

Preheat oven to 350°F. Grease muffin tins or
spray with nonstick cooking spray.

Pour hot water over raisins in small bowl and
let sit 10 minutes; drain well and set aside.

Meanwhile, in medium bowl, combine flour,
oatmeal, sugar, baking powder, salt,
cinnamon, allspice and nutmeg. Stir and toss
to combine; set aside.

Peel and core apples. Grate coarsely—you
need about 2 generous cups, lightly pressed
down. Combine grated apples, egg, egg
whites, oil and walnuts; beat to blend. Add to
combined dry ingredients and raisins; stir just
until blended and moistened—batter will be
very stiff. Spoon into prepared muffin tins,
filling about three-quarters full. Bake 20 to 25
minutes, or until wooden pick inserted in
muffin comes out clean. Cool 5 minutes in
pan; remove and serve warm.
Makes 12 muffins

Favorite recipe from **Walnut Marketing Board**

Good Old American White Rolls

5 to 5½ cups all-purpose flour
2 packages RED STAR® Active Dry
   Yeast or QUICK•RISE™ Yeast
2 tablespoons sugar
4 tablespoons nonfat dry milk
2 teaspoons salt
1½ cups water
1 tablespoon shortening or oil
3 tablespoons melted butter
2 teaspoons honey

Preheat oven to 400°F. In large mixer bowl, combine 2½ cups flour, yeast, sugar, milk and salt; mix well. In saucepan, heat water and shortening until very warm (120°–130°F; shortening does not need to melt). Add to flour mixture. Blend at low speed until moistened; beat 3 minutes at medium speed. By hand, gradually stir in enough remaining flour to make firm dough. Knead on floured surface until smooth and elastic 5 to 8 minutes. Place in greased bowl, turning to grease top. Cover; let rise in warm place until doubled, about 45 minutes (30 minutes for Quick•Rise™ Yeast).

Punch down dough. Divide dough into 2 parts. Divide each part into 6 to 12 equal pieces (depending on what size, 1 ounce or 2 ounces, finished product is desired). Round into smooth balls. Place on greased cookie sheet. Cover; let rise in warm place until about doubled, 25 to 30 minutes (15 to 20 minutes for Quick•Rise™ Yeast). Bake at 400°F for 10 to 12 minutes until golden brown. Mix melted butter and honey together; brush rolls with honey-butter mixture. Remove from cookie sheet and cool.

Makes 12 to 24 rolls

Pecan Sticky Buns

Dough*

4½ to 5½ cups all-purpose flour, divided
½ cup granulated sugar
1½ teaspoons salt
2 packages active dry yeast
¾ cup warm milk (105° to 115°F)
½ cup warm water (105° to 115°F)
¼ cup (½ stick) MAZOLA® Margarine or
   butter, softened
2 eggs

Glaze

½ cup KARO® Light or Dark Corn Syrup
½ cup packed light brown sugar
¼ cup (½ stick) MAZOLA® Margarine or
   butter
1 cup pecans, coarsely chopped

Filling

½ cup firmly packed light brown sugar
1 teaspoon cinnamon
2 tablespoons MAZOLA® Margarine or
   butter, melted

***To use frozen bread dough:** Thaw two 1-pound loaves frozen bread dough in refrigerator overnight. Press loaves together and roll to 20×12-inch rectangle; complete as recipe directs.

For Dough: In large bowl combine 2 cups flour, sugar, salt and yeast. Stir in milk, water and ¼ cup margarine until blended. Stir in eggs and enough additional flour (about 2 cups) to make a soft dough. Knead on floured surface until smooth and elastic, about 8 minutes. Cover dough and let rest on floured surface 10 minutes.

Pecan Sticky Buns

For Glaze: Meanwhile, in small saucepan over low heat stir corn syrup, ½ cup brown sugar and ¼ cup margarine until smooth. Pour into 13×9×2-inch baking pan. Sprinkle with pecans; set aside.

For Filling: Combine ½ cup brown sugar and cinnamon; set aside. Roll dough to 20×12-inch rectangle. Brush dough with 2 tablespoons melted margarine; sprinkle with filling. Starting from long side, roll up jelly-roll fashion. Pinch seam to seal. Cut into 15 slices. Place cut side up in prepared pan. Cover tightly. Refrigerate 2 to 24 hours.

To bake, preheat oven to 375°F. Remove pan from refrigerator. Uncover pan and let stand at room temperature 10 minutes. Bake 28 to 30 minutes or until tops are browned. Invert onto serving tray. Serve warm or cool completely.   *Makes 15 rolls*

For Chocolate Lovers Only

Rediscover the world of delectable chocolate. From decadent cakes and pies to sumptuous brownies and fudge, these sinful pleasures will surely satisfy any die-hard chocoholic.

Wellesley Fudge Cake

4 squares BAKER'S® Unsweetened Chocolate
1¾ cups sugar, divided
½ cup water
1⅔ cups flour
1 teaspoon baking soda
¼ teaspoon salt
½ cup (1 stick) butter or margarine, softened
3 eggs
¾ cup milk
1 teaspoon vanilla

HEAT oven to 350°F.

MICROWAVE chocolate, ½ cup sugar and water in large microwavable bowl on HIGH 1 to 2 minutes or until chocolate is almost melted, stirring halfway through heating time. Stir until chocolate is completely melted; cool.

MIX flour, baking soda and salt; set aside. Beat butter and remaining 1¼ cups sugar in large bowl with electric mixer on medium speed until light and fluffy. Add eggs, 1 at a time, beating well after each addition. Add flour mixture alternately with milk, beating after each addition until smooth. Stir in chocolate mixture and vanilla. Pour into 2 greased and floured 9-inch round cake pans.

BAKE 30 to 35 minutes or until cake springs back when lightly touched. Cool 10 minutes; remove from pans. Cool on wire racks. Frost as desired. *Makes 12 servings*

From top to bottom: German Sweet Chocolate Cake (page 252) and Wellesley Fudge Cake

Baker's Chocolate

In 1765, an Irish immigrant named John Hannon received financial help from Dr. James Baker when he started milling chocolate in Dorchester, Massachusetts. In 1852, a new kind of chocolate was introduced, Baker's German's sweet chocolate, named for Samuel German, who helped perfect this delectable sweet chocolate.

German Sweet Chocolate Cake

1 package (4 ounces) BAKER'S®
    GERMAN'S Sweet Chocolate
½ cup water
2 cups all-purpose flour
1 teaspoon baking soda
¼ teaspoon salt
1 cup (2 sticks) butter or margarine,
    softened
2 cups sugar
4 egg yolks
1 teaspoon vanilla
1 cup buttermilk
4 egg whites
    Classic Coconut-Pecan Filling and
    Frosting (page 254)

HEAT oven to 350°F. Line bottoms of 3 (9-inch) round cake pans with waxed paper.

MICROWAVE chocolate and water in large microwavable bowl on HIGH 1½ to 2 minutes or until chocolate is almost melted, stirring halfway through heating time. *Stir until chocolate is completely melted.*

MIX flour, baking soda and salt; set aside. Beat butter and sugar in large bowl with electric mixer on medium speed until light and fluffy. Add egg yolks, 1 at a time, beating well after each addition. Stir in chocolate mixture and vanilla. Add flour mixture alternately with buttermilk, beating after each addition until smooth.

BEAT egg whites in another large bowl with electric mixer on high speed until they form stiff peaks. Gently stir into batter. Pour batter into prepared pans.

BAKE 30 minutes or until cake springs back when lightly touched in center. Immediately run spatula between cakes and sides of pans. Cool in pans 15 minutes. Remove from pans. Peel off waxed paper. Cool completely on wire racks.

SPREAD Classic Coconut-Pecan Filling and Frosting between layers and over top of cake.

Makes 12 servings

Hershey®s introduced Hershey's Kisses Milk Chocolates in 1907, Hershey's Kisses with Almonds Chocolates in 1990, and Hershey's Hugs Chocolates and Hershey's Hugs with Almonds Chocolates in 1993.

Senior Hall of Milton Hershey School in the 1940s.
Photo courtesy of Hershey Foods Corporation

Hot Fudge Pudding Cake

- 1¼ cups granulated sugar, divided
- 1 cup all-purpose flour
- 7 tablespoons HERSHEY'S Cocoa, divided
- 2 teaspoons baking powder
- ¼ teaspoon salt
- ½ cup milk
- ⅓ cup butter or margarine, melted
- 1½ teaspoons vanilla extract
- ½ cup packed light brown sugar
- 1¼ cups hot water
  Whipped topping

Heat oven to 350°F. In bowl, stir together ¾ cup granulated sugar, flour, 3 tablespoons cocoa, baking powder and salt. Stir in milk, butter and vanilla; beat until smooth. Pour batter into 8- or 9-inch square baking pan. Stir together remaining ½ cup granulated sugar, brown sugar and remaining 4 tablespoons cocoa; sprinkle mixture evenly over batter. Pour hot water over top; do not stir. Bake 35 to 40 minutes or until center is almost set. Let stand 15 minutes; spoon into dessert dishes, spooning sauce from bottom of pan over top. Garnish with whipped topping, if desired.

Makes about 8 servings

Old-Fashioned Chocolate Cake

¾ cup (1½ sticks) butter or margarine, softened
1⅔ cups sugar
3 eggs
1 teaspoon vanilla extract
2 cups all-purpose flour
⅔ cup HERSHEY₃S Cocoa
1¼ teaspoons baking soda
1 teaspoon salt
¼ teaspoon baking powder
1⅓ cups water
½ cup finely crushed hard peppermint candy (optional)
One-Bowl Buttercream Frosting (page 273)
Additional crushed hard peppermint candy (optional)

Heat oven to 350°F. Grease and flour two 9-inch round baking pans or one 13×9×2-inch baking pan. In large mixer bowl, combine butter, sugar, eggs and vanilla; beat on high speed of electric mixer 3 minutes. Stir together flour, cocoa, baking soda, salt and baking powder; add alternately with water to butter mixture. Blend just until combined; add candy, if desired. Pour batter into prepared pans. Bake 30 to 35 minutes or until wooden pick inserted in center comes out clean. Cool 10 minutes; remove from pans to wire racks. Cool completely. Frost with One-Bowl Buttercream Frosting. Just before serving, garnish with peppermint candy, if desired.
Makes 8 to 10 servings

Classic Coconut-Pecan Filling and Frosting

1 can (12 ounces) evaporated milk
1½ cups sugar
¾ cup (1½ sticks) butter or margarine
4 egg yolks, slightly beaten
1½ teaspoons vanilla
1 package (7 ounces) BAKER'S® ANGEL FLAKE® Coconut (about 2⅔ cups)
1½ cups chopped pecans

STIR milk, sugar, butter, egg yolks and vanilla in large saucepan. Cook over medium heat until mixture thickens and is golden brown, about 12 minutes, stirring constantly. Remove from heat.

STIR in coconut and pecans. Cool to room temperature and of spreading consistency.
Makes about 4¼ cups or enough to fill and frost top of 1 (3-layer) cake, frost tops of 2 (13×9-inch) cakes or frost 24 cupcakes

Chocolate Mayonnaise Cake

2 cups all-purpose flour
⅔ cup unsweetened cocoa
1¼ teaspoons baking soda
¼ teaspoon baking powder
3 eggs
1⅔ cups sugar
1 teaspoon vanilla
1 cup HELLMANN'S® or BEST FOODS® Real or Light Mayonnaise or Low Fat Mayonnaise Dressing
1⅓ cups water

Chocolate Mayonnaise Cake

Grease and flour bottoms of two 9×1½-inch round cake pans. In medium bowl, combine flour, cocoa, baking soda and baking powder; set aside. In large bowl with mixer at high speed, beat eggs, sugar and vanilla, scraping bowl occasionally, 3 minutes or until smooth and creamy. Reduce speed to low; beat in mayonnaise until blended. Add flour mixture in 4 additions alternately with water, beginning and ending with flour mixture. Pour into prepared pans. Bake in 350°F oven 30 to 35 minutes or until cake springs back when touched lightly in center. Cool in pans on wire racks 10 minutes. Remove from pans; cool completely on racks. Fill and frost as desired.

Makes 1 (9-inch) layer cake

Chocolate Intensity

Cake

> 1 package (8 ounces) NESTLÉ®
>   Unsweetened Chocolate Baking
>   Bars
> 1½ cups granulated sugar
> ½ cup butter, softened
> 3 eggs
> 2 teaspoons vanilla extract
> ⅔ cup all-purpose flour
>   Powdered sugar (optional)

Coffee Crème Anglaise Sauce

> 4 egg yolks
> ⅓ cup granulated sugar
> 1 tablespoon TASTER'S CHOICE®
>   Freeze Dried Instant Coffee
> 1½ cups milk
> 1 teaspoon vanilla extract

For Cake: In small saucepan over low heat, melt baking bars; stir until smooth. Cool to lukewarm. In small bowl, beat sugar, butter, eggs and vanilla 4 minutes or until thick. Blend in melted chocolate. Gradually beat in flour. Spread into greased 9-inch springform pan. Bake in preheated 350°F oven 25 to 28 minutes. Wooden pick inserted in center will be moist. Cool in pan on wire rack 15 minutes. Remove side of pan; cool completely. Sprinkle with powdered sugar. Serve with 3 to 4 tablespoons sauce.

For Coffee Crème Anglaise Sauce: In small bowl, whisk egg yolks. In medium saucepan, combine sugar and coffee; stir in milk. Cook over medium heat, stirring constantly, until mixture comes to a simmer. Remove from heat. Gradually whisk ½ of hot milk mixture into yolks; return to saucepan. Continue cooking, stirring constantly, 3 to 4 minutes or until mixture is slightly thickened. Strain into small bowl; stir in vanilla. Cover with plastic wrap; chill. *Makes 1 (9-inch) cake*

Chocolate Intensity

Rich Chocolate Cake with Raspberry Sauce

> 2 cups frozen raspberries in syrup,
>   thawed, puréed and strained
> 1 tablespoon cornstarch
> 2 cups all-purpose flour
> 1⅓ cups skim milk
> 1 cup sugar
> ⅔ cup FLEISCHMANN'S® Margarine,
>   softened
> 1 cup EGG BEATERS® Real Egg
>   Product
> ⅔ cup unsweetened cocoa
> 1½ teaspoons vanilla extract
> 1½ teaspoons baking powder
> ½ teaspoon baking soda
>   Mint sprigs, for garnish

In small saucepan, over medium-high heat, cook raspberries and cornstarch, stirring constantly until mixture thickens and begins to boil; chill.

In medium bowl, with electric mixer at low speed, mix remaining ingredients until blended. Beat at high speed 3 minutes. Spread batter in lightly greased 13×9×2-inch baking pan. Bake at 350°F 30 to 35 minutes or until toothpick inserted in center comes out clean. Cool in pan 10 minutes. Remove and cool on wire rack. Cut into 16 pieces. Serve topped with raspberry sauce and mint sprigs.

Makes 16 servings

Chocolate Cream Torte

1 package DUNCAN HINES® Moist
    Deluxe Devil's Food Cake Mix
1 package (8 ounces) cream cheese,
    softened
½ cup sugar
1 teaspoon vanilla extract
1 cup finely chopped pecans
1 cup whipping cream, chilled
    Strawberry halves, for garnish
    Mint leaves, for garnish (optional)

1. Preheat oven to 350°F. Grease and flour two 8- or 9-inch round cake pans.

2. Prepare, bake and cool cake following package directions for basic recipe. Chill layers for ease in splitting.

3. Place cream cheese, sugar and vanilla extract in small bowl. Beat at low speed with electric mixer until smooth. Add pecans; stir until blended. Set aside. Beat whipping cream in small bowl until stiff peaks form. Fold whipped cream into cream cheese mixture.

4. To assemble, split each cake layer in half horizontally. Place one cake layer on serving plate. Spread top with one fourth of filling. Repeat with remaining layers and filling. Garnish with strawberry halves and mint leaves, if desired. Refrigerate until ready to serve.   *Makes 12 to 16 servings*

Mr. Duncan Hines (top photo), founder of Duncan Hines, was a famous traveling restaurant critic in the 1930s. Duncan Hines introduced its "New Fudge Marble Cake Mix" in 1957 (bottom photo).

Chocolate Cream Torte

Blue Diamond was formed in 1910 by a group of 230 enterprising almond growers to market California's largest food export. Today, over 4,000 growers own this company that exports almonds to all 50 states and more than 90 foreign countries.

Almond Chocolate Torte with Raspberry Sauce

Torte

2½ cups **BLUE DIAMOND® Blanched Whole Almonds, toasted, divided**
9 ounces **semi-sweet chocolate**
¼ cup **butter**
6 eggs, **beaten**
¾ cup **sugar**
2 tablespoons **all-purpose flour**
¼ cup **brandy** *or* 2 teaspoons **brandy extract**

Chocolate Glaze

6 tablespoons **water**
3 tablespoons **sugar**
3 ounces **semi-sweet chocolate**
1 tablespoon **brandy** *or* 1 teaspoon **brandy extract**

Raspberry Sauce

2 packages (10 ounces each) **frozen raspberries, thawed**
Sugar

In food processor or blender, finely grind 1 cup almonds. Generously grease 9-inch round cake pan. Sprinkle side and bottom with 2 tablespoons ground almonds; set aside. Melt 9 ounces chocolate and butter in top of double boiler over simmering water. In large bowl, beat together eggs and ¾ cup sugar. Beat in chocolate mixture. Beat in flour, remaining ground almonds and ¼ cup brandy. Pour into prepared pan. Bake at 350°F 25 minutes or until toothpick inserted in center comes out almost clean. Cool 10 minutes. Invert torte onto wire rack; remove pan. Cool completely.

Meanwhile, prepare Chocolate Glaze. In small saucepan, combine water and 3 tablespoons sugar; simmer until sugar dissolves. Add 3 ounces chocolate and 1 tablespoon brandy. Simmer a few minutes until chocolate melts and glaze coats back of spoon. Pour glaze over torte, spreading over top and side with spatula. Transfer torte to serving plate. Allow glaze to set.

Meanwhile, prepare Raspberry Sauce. Purée raspberries and strain through fine sieve. Add sugar to taste. To garnish torte, arrange remaining 1½ cups whole almonds, points toward center, in circle around outer edge. Working towards center, repeat circles, overlapping almonds slightly. To serve, pour small amount of Raspberry Sauce on each plate and top with a slice of torte.

Makes 10 to 12 servings

Chocolate Macadamia Nut Pie

Chocolate Macadamia Nut Pie

- 3 squares (1 ounce each) semisweet chocolate
- ¼ cup **MAZOLA®** Margarine
- ½ cup heavy cream
- ½ cup **KARO®** Light Corn Syrup
- 3 eggs, slightly beaten
- ⅓ cup sugar
- ⅓ cup packed brown sugar
- 1 jar (3½ ounces) macadamia nuts, coarsely chopped and toasted (¾ cup)
- 1 baked (9-inch) pie crust
  Whipped cream (optional)

Preheat oven to 350°F. In 1-quart saucepan combine chocolate and margarine; stir over low heat until melted and smooth. Remove from heat. Stir in cream and corn syrup until well blended. In medium bowl beat eggs and sugars until well mixed. Stir in chocolate mixture until well blended. Add nuts. Pour into pie crust. Bake 40 minutes or until knife inserted halfway between center and edge comes out clean. Cool on wire rack. If desired, serve with whipped cream.

Makes 1 (9-inch) pie

Chocolate Mudslide Frozen Pie

1 cup NESTLÉ® TOLL HOUSE® Semi-Sweet Chocolate Morsels
1 teaspoon instant coffee granules
1 teaspoon hot water
¾ cup sour cream
½ cup granulated sugar
1 teaspoon vanilla extract
1 (9-inch) prepared chocolate crumb crust
1½ cups heavy whipping cream
1 cup powdered sugar
¼ cup NESTLÉ® Toll House® Baking Cocoa
2 tablespoons NESTLÉ® TOLL HOUSE® Semi-Sweet Chocolate Mini Morsels

MELT 1 cup morsels in small, heavy saucepan over lowest possible heat. When morsels begin to melt, remove from heat; stir. Return to heat for a few seconds at a time, stirring until smooth. Remove from heat; cool for 10 minutes.

COMBINE coffee and water in medium bowl. Add sour cream, granulated sugar and vanilla; stir until sugar is dissolved. Stir in melted chocolate until smooth. Spread into crust; chill.

BEAT cream, powdered sugar and cocoa in small mixer bowl until stiff peaks form. Spread or pipe over chocolate layer. Sprinkle with mini morsels. Freeze at least 6 hours or until firm.   *Makes 8 servings*

Fudge Brownie Pie

1 (9-inch) unbaked pastry shell, lightly pricked
1 cup (6 ounces) semi-sweet chocolate chips
¼ cup margarine or butter
1 (14-ounce) can EAGLE® BRAND Sweetened Condensed Milk (NOT evaporated milk)
½ cup biscuit baking mix
2 eggs
1 teaspoon vanilla extract
1 cup chopped nuts

Preheat oven to 375°F. Bake pastry shell 10 minutes; remove from oven. *Reduce oven temperature to 325°F.* In small saucepan, over low heat, melt chips with margarine, stirring frequently until smooth. In large mixer bowl, beat chocolate mixture with sweetened condensed milk, biscuit mix, eggs and vanilla until smooth. Add nuts. Pour into prepared pastry shell. Bake 35 to 45 minutes or until center is set. Cool. Serve warm or at room temperature. Garnish as desired. Store ungarnished pie covered at room temperature.   *Makes 1 (9-inch) pie*

Chocolate Mudslide Frozen Pie

 *It's been called the ® King of Cookies.* Oreo Chocolate Sandwich Cookies, more than 75 years old, reign supreme as the number-one-selling cookie in America. The origin of the name of this famous cookie remains somewhat of a puzzle. One theory is that "oreo," which is the Greek word for mountain, was chosen because in early tests the cookie resembled a mountain. Others say the name is derived from "or," the French word for gold, a color used in early package designs. Whatever the genesis, some two hundred billion of these cookies have been produced—enough, if piled on top of one another, to reach to the moon and back three times.

Oreo® Mud Pie

26 OREO® Chocolate Sandwich Cookies
2 tablespoons margarine, melted
1 pint chocolate ice cream, softened
2 pints coffee ice cream, softened
½ cup heavy cream, whipped
¼ cup chopped walnuts
½ cup chocolate fudge topping

Finely roll 12 cookies; mix with margarine. Press crumb mixture on bottom of 9-inch pie plate; stand remaining 14 cookies around edge of plate. Place in freezer 10 minutes or until firm. Evenly spread chocolate ice cream into prepared crust. Scoop coffee ice cream into balls; arrange over chocolate layer. Freeze 4 hours or until firm.

To serve, top with whipped cream, walnuts and fudge topping.   *Makes 8 servings*

Chocolate Mousse Brownies

Brownie

½ cup butter or margarine
1 (12-ounce) package semi-sweet chocolate chips
2 cups JACK FROST® Granulated Sugar
1¼ cups all-purpose flour
2 teaspoons vanilla
½ teaspoon baking powder
½ teaspoon salt
3 large eggs
½ cup chopped pecans

In large microwave-safe bowl, melt butter and chocolate chips on HIGH 90 seconds, stirring every 30 seconds.

Stir in sugar, flour, vanilla, baking powder, salt and eggs; beat until smooth. Stir in pecans. Spread into buttered 13×9-inch baking pan; set aside.

Mousse Topping

1 (6-ounce) package semi-sweet chocolate chips
¾ cup whipping cream
3 large eggs
1½ teaspoons vanilla
½ cup JACK FROST® Granulated Sugar
¼ teaspoon salt
1 cup chopped pecans

In microwave-safe bowl, melt chocolate chips and cream on HIGH 90 seconds, stirring every 30 seconds; cool slightly.

In medium bowl, beat eggs, vanilla, sugar and salt with electric mixer at medium speed until foamy; stir in chocolate mixture.

Pour mousse topping mixture over brownie; sprinkle with pecans. Bake in preheated 350° oven 50 to 55 minutes. Let cool 2 hours in pan on wire rack before cutting into squares.

Makes 48 brownies

Extra Moist & Chunky Brownies

1 (8-ounce) package cream cheese, softened
1 cup sugar
1 egg
1 teaspoon vanilla extract
¾ cup all-purpose flour
1 (3⅜-ounce) package ROYAL® Chocolate or Dark 'n' Sweet Chocolate Pudding & Pie Filling
4 (1-ounce) semisweet chocolate squares, chopped

Microwave Directions: In large bowl, with electric mixer at high speed, beat cream cheese, sugar, egg and vanilla until smooth; blend in flour and pudding mix. Spread batter into greased 8×8-inch microwavable dish; sprinkle with chocolate. Shield corners of dish with foil. Microwave at HIGH for 8 to 10 minutes or until toothpick inserted in center comes out clean, rotating dish ½ turn every 2 minutes. Cool completely in pan. Cut into squares. *Makes about 16 brownies*

In 1925, the Royal Baking Powder Company introduced its six-flavor line of Royal Gelatin Desserts. The company soon was to pioneer in the development of a "quick-setting gelatin" and a process for creating "sealed-in, real fruit" flavors.

Mott's® Marble Brownies

½ cup unsweetened cocoa powder
½ cup plus 2 tablespoons all-purpose
    flour, divided
1 teaspoon baking powder
½ teaspoon salt
2 tablespoons margarine
1½ cups plus ¼ cup granulated sugar,
    divided
3 egg whites, divided
½ cup MOTT'S® Natural Apple Sauce
1½ teaspoons vanilla extract, divided
4 ounces fat-free cream cheese

1. Preheat oven to 350°F. Spray 8-inch
square baking pan with nonstick cooking
spray.

2. In medium bowl, sift together cocoa
powder, ½ cup flour, baking powder and salt.

3. In large bowl, beat margarine and 1½ cups
sugar with electric mixer at medium speed
until blended. Whisk in 2 egg whites, apple
sauce and 1 teaspoon vanilla extract. Stir in
flour mixture until combined.

4. In small bowl, beat cream cheese and
¼ cup sugar with electric mixer at medium
speed until well blended. Stir in remaining
egg white, 2 tablespoons flour and ½
teaspoon vanilla extract.

5. Pour brownie mixture into prepared pan.
Spoon cream cheese mixture on top of
brownie mixture. Cut through both mixtures
with knife to create marbled design.

6. Bake 35 to 40 minutes or until firm. Cool
on wire rack 15 minutes; cut into 12 bars.

Makes 12 servings

Among the treasures Columbus *brought back to King Ferdinand were a few brown beans, probably cocoa beans. No one knew what to do with them until Cortes visited Mexico where he drank a brew made from such beans. The Aztecs called it "cacahuatl," or "gift from the gods." Cortes brought the chocolate back to Spain and eventually the drink was introduced to the rest of Europe. In 1765, an Irish immigrant, John Hannon, started milling chocolate in Dorchester, Massachusetts. Without the expensive import costs, the price went down and chocolate became a popular drink.*

One Bowl® Brownies

4 squares BAKER'S® Unsweetened
    Chocolate
¾ cup (1½ sticks) butter or margarine
2 cups sugar
3 eggs
1 teaspoon vanilla
1 cup flour
1 cup coarsely chopped nuts (optional)

One Bowl® Brownies

HEAT oven to 350°F (325°F for glass baking dish). Line 13×9-inch baking pan with foil extending over edges to form handles. Grease foil.

MICROWAVE chocolate and butter in large microwavable bowl on HIGH 2 minutes or until butter is melted. **Stir until chocolate is completely melted.**

STIR sugar into chocolate mixture until well blended. Mix in eggs and vanilla until well blended. Stir in flour and nuts until well blended. Spread in prepared pan.

BAKE for 30 to 35 minutes or until toothpick inserted into center comes out with fudgy crumbs. **DO NOT OVERBAKE.** Cool in pan. Lift out of pan onto cutting board. Cut into squares.   *Makes about 24 brownies*

Tips

• For cakelike brownies, stir in ½ cup milk with eggs and vanilla. Increase flour to 1½ cups.

Quick & Easy Fudgey Brownies

4 bars (1 ounce each) HERSHEY®S Unsweetened Baking Chocolate, broken into pieces
¾ cup (1½ sticks) butter or margarine
2 cups sugar
3 eggs
1½ teaspoons vanilla extract
1 cup all-purpose flour
1 cup chopped nuts (optional)
Quick & Easy Chocolate Frosting (recipe follows, optional)

Heat oven to 350°F. Grease 13×9×2-inch baking pan. In large microwave-safe bowl, place chocolate and butter. Microwave at HIGH 1½ to 2 minutes or until chocolate is melted and mixture is smooth when stirred. Add sugar; stir with spoon until well blended. Add eggs and vanilla; mix well. Add flour and nuts, if desired; stir until well blended. Spread into prepared pan. Bake 30 to 35 minutes or until wooden pick inserted in center comes out almost clean. Cool in pan on wire rack. Frost with Quick & Easy Chocolate Frosting, if desired. Cut into squares.
Makes about 24 brownies

Quick & Easy Chocolate Frosting

3 bars (1 ounce each) HERSHEY®S Unsweetened Baking Chocolate, broken into pieces
1 cup miniature marshmallows
½ cup (1 stick) butter or margarine, softened
⅓ cup milk
2½ cups powdered sugar
½ teaspoon vanilla extract

In medium saucepan over low heat, melt chocolate, stirring constantly. Add marshmallows; stir frequently until melted. (Mixture will be very thick and will pull away from side of pan.) Spoon mixture into small mixer bowl; beat in butter. Add milk gradually, beating until smooth. Add powdered sugar and vanilla; beat to desired consistency.
Makes about 2¼ cups frosting

Hershey®s Syrup Snacking Brownies

½ cup (1 stick) butter or margarine, softened
1 cup sugar
1½ cups (16-ounce can) HERSHEY®S Syrup
4 eggs
1¼ cups all-purpose flour
1 cup HERSHEY®S Semi-Sweet Chocolate Chips

Heat oven to 350°F. Grease 13×9×2-inch baking pan. In large mixer bowl, beat butter and sugar. Add syrup, eggs and flour; beat well. Stir in chocolate chips. Pour batter into prepared pan. Bake 30 to 35 minutes or until brownies begin to pull away from sides of pan. Cool completely in pan on wire rack. Cut into bars. *Makes about 36 brownies*

Quick & Easy Fudgey Brownies

268

Double-Decker Fudge

1 cup REESE'S® Peanut Butter Chips
1 cup HERSHEY₂S Semi-Sweet
   Chocolate Chips or HERSHEY₂S
   MINI CHIPS® Semi-Sweet Chocolate
2¼ cups sugar
1 jar (7 ounces) marshmallow creme
¾ cup evaporated milk
¼ cup (½ stick) butter or margarine
1 teaspoon vanilla extract

Line 8-inch square pan with foil, extending foil over edges of pan. Measure peanut butter chips into one medium bowl and chocolate chips into second medium bowl. In heavy 3-quart saucepan, combine sugar, marshmallow creme, evaporated milk and butter. Cook over medium heat, stirring constantly, until mixture boils; boil and stir 5 minutes. Remove from heat; stir in vanilla. Immediately stir ½ of hot mixture (1½ cups) into peanut butter chips until chips are completely melted; quickly pour into prepared pan. Stir remaining ½ of hot mixture into chocolate chips until chips are completely melted. Quickly spread over top of peanut butter layer. Cool; refrigerate 1½ hours or until firm. Remove from pan; place on cutting board. Peel off foil; cut into 1-inch squares. Store tightly covered in refrigerator.

Makes about 5 dozen pieces or
about 2 pounds candy

Peanut Butter Fudge: Omit chocolate chips; place 1⅔ cups (10-ounce package) Reese's® Peanut Butter Chips in large bowl. Cook fudge mixture as directed above; add to chips, stirring until chips are completely melted. Pour into prepared pan; cool to room temperature.

Rich Cocoa Fudge

3 cups sugar
⅔ cup HERSHEY₂S Cocoa or
   HERSHEY₂S European Style Cocoa
⅛ teaspoon salt
1½ cups milk
¼ cup (½ stick) butter or margarine
1 teaspoon vanilla extract

Line 8- or 9-inch square pan with foil; butter foil. In heavy 4-quart saucepan, stir together sugar, cocoa and salt; stir in milk. Cook over medium heat, stirring constantly, until mixture comes to a full rolling boil. Boil, without stirring, to 234°F or until syrup, when dropped into very cold water, forms a soft ball which flattens when removed from water. (Bulb of candy thermometer should not rest on bottom of saucepan.) Remove from heat. Add butter and vanilla. DO NOT STIR. Cool at room temperature to 110°F (lukewarm). Beat with wooden spoon until fudge thickens and loses some of its gloss. Spread quickly into prepared pan; cool. Cut into squares.

Makes about 36 pieces or 1¾ pounds

Nutty Rich Cocoa Fudge: Beat cooked fudge as directed. Immediately stir in 1 cup chopped almonds, pecans or walnuts; quickly spread into prepared pan.

High Altitude Directions: Increase milk to 1⅔ cups. Use soft-ball cold water test for doneness or test and read thermometer in boiling water; subtract difference from 212°F. Then subtract that number from 234°F. This is the soft-ball temperature for your altitude and thermometer.

From left to right: Nutty Rich Cocoa Fudge
and Double-Decker Fudge

Carnation® Famous Fudge

2 tablespoons butter or margarine
⅔ cup undiluted CARNATION®
Evaporated Milk
1½ cups granulated sugar
¼ teaspoon salt
2 cups (4 ounces) miniature
marshmallows
1½ cups (9 ounces) NESTLÉ® TOLL
HOUSE® Semi-Sweet Chocolate
Morsels
½ cup chopped pecans or walnuts
1 teaspoon vanilla extract

COMBINE butter, evaporated milk, sugar and salt in medium, heavy saucepan. Bring to a boil over medium heat, stirring constantly. Boil 4 to 5 minutes, stirring constantly. Remove from heat.

STIR in marshmallows, morsels, nuts and vanilla. Stir vigorously 1 minute or until marshmallows are melted. Pour into foil-lined 8×8-inch baking pan; chill until firm. Cut into 1½×1½-inch squares.

Makes about 2 pounds

Milk Chocolate Fudge: Substitute 2 cups (11½-ounce package) Nestlé® Toll House® Milk Chocolate Morsels for Semi-Sweet Morsels.

Butterscotch Fudge: Substitute 2 cups (12-ounce package) Nestlé® Toll House® Butterscotch Flavored Morsels for Semi-Sweet Morsels.

Mint Chocolate Fudge: Substitute 1½ cups (10-ounce package) Nestlé® Toll House® Mint Flavored Chocolate Morsels for Semi-Sweet Morsels.

Carnation

Your Grocery Boy will deliver **Carnation Milk** FROM CONTENTED COWS

Nestlé Food Company opened a brand new plant in 1993 to meet demands of a market that consumes 10 million cases of evaporated milk each year.

Foolproof Dark Chocolate Fudge

3 cups (18 ounces) semi-sweet chocolate chips
1 (14-ounce) can EAGLE® BRAND Sweetened Condensed Milk (NOT evaporated milk)
Dash salt
1 cup chopped nuts
1½ teaspoons vanilla extract

In large heavy saucepan, over low heat, melt chips with sweetened condensed milk and salt, stirring frequently until smooth. Remove from heat; stir in nuts and vanilla. Spread evenly into aluminum foil-lined tree-shaped mold or 9-inch square pan. Chill 2 hours or until firm. Place fudge on cutting board; peel off foil. Garnish as desired or cut into squares. Store loosely covered at room temperature.   *Makes about 2 pounds*

Microwave: In 1-quart glass measure with handle, combine chips with sweetened condensed milk and salt. Cook on HIGH 3 minutes or until chips melt, stirring after each 1½ minutes. Stir in nuts and vanilla. Proceed as above.

Tip: For ease in cutting fudge and cleaning pan, line pan with foil before preparing fudge; lightly grease foil. When fudge has cooled, lift from pan; cut fudge into squares.

Peanut Butter Fudge Sauce

½ cup KARO® Light or Dark Corn Syrup
½ cup SKIPPY® Creamy Peanut Butter
¼ cup heavy or whipping cream
½ cup semisweet chocolate chips

In 1½-quart microwavable bowl combine corn syrup, peanut butter and cream. Microwave on HIGH 1½ minutes or until boiling. Add chocolate chips; stir until melted. Serve warm over ice cream. Store in refrigerator.
Makes about 1¼ cups

Note: To reheat, microwave uncovered on LOW (30%) about 1½ minutes, just until pourable.

One-Bowl Buttercream Frosting

6 tablespoons butter or margarine, softened
2⅔ cups powdered sugar
½ cup HERSHEY'S Cocoa
⅓ cup milk
1 teaspoon vanilla extract

In small mixer bowl, beat butter. Add powdered sugar and cocoa alternately with milk; beat to spreading consistency (additional milk may be needed). Blend in vanilla.   *Makes about 2 cups frosting*

Cakes for All Occasions

Make every occasion special with scrumptious cakes and cheesecakes suitable for festive birthday parties, family holidays, special dinner parties or casual gatherings.

Carrot Layer Cake

Cake

- 1 package DUNCAN HINES® Moist Deluxe Yellow Cake Mix
- 4 eggs
- ½ cup CRISCO® Oil or CRISCO® PURITAN® Canola Oil
- 3 cups grated carrots
- 1 cup finely chopped nuts
- 2 teaspoons ground cinnamon

Cream Cheese Frosting

- 1 (8-ounce) package cream cheese, softened
- ¼ cup butter or margarine, softened
- 2 teaspoons vanilla extract
- 4 cups confectioners sugar

1. Preheat oven to 350°F. Grease and flour 2 (8- or 9-inch) round baking pans.

2. **For cake,** combine cake mix, eggs, oil, carrots, nuts and cinnamon in large bowl. Beat at low speed with electric mixer until moistened. Beat at medium speed for 2 minutes. Pour into pans. Bake at 350°F for 35 to 40 minutes or until toothpick inserted in centers comes out clean. Cool.

3. **For frosting,** place cream cheese, butter and vanilla extract in large bowl. Beat at low speed until smooth and creamy. Add confectioners sugar gradually, beating until smooth. Add more sugar to thicken or milk or water to thin frosting, as needed. Fill and frost cooled cake. Garnish with whole pecans. *Makes 12 to 16 servings*

Carrot Layer Cake

Super Moist Carrot Cake

1 cup JACK FROST® Granulated Sugar
1 cup JACK FROST® Light Brown
    Sugar, packed
2 cups all-purpose flour
1 teaspoon baking powder
1 teaspoon baking soda
1 teaspoon salt
1 teaspoon cinnamon
3 cups finely shredded carrots
1½ cups vegetable oil
4 eggs
2 teaspoons vanilla
½ cup chopped walnuts
½ cup raisins
    Cream Cheese Frosting (recipe
    follows)

Preheat oven to 325°F. In large mixer bowl, combine sugars, flour, baking powder, baking soda, salt and cinnamon. Add carrots, oil, eggs and vanilla; beat 2 to 3 minutes at medium speed with electric mixer. Stir in nuts and raisins. Pour into greased and floured 13×9-inch* baking pan; bake 50 to 60 minutes. Cool on rack. Frost with Cream Cheese Frosting.** Refrigerate until serving.
Makes 1 (13×9-inch) cake

*Two 9-inch baking pans can be used. Reduce baking time to 40 minutes.

**To frost two 9-inch cakes, double frosting recipe.

Cream Cheese Frosting

1 (3-ounce) package cream cheese,
    softened
¼ cup butter or margarine, softened
1 teaspoon vanilla
1½ cups JACK FROST® Confectioners
    Sugar

In large bowl, beat cream cheese, butter and vanilla until light and fluffy. Gradually add confectioners sugar, beating until smooth. Spread over cooled cake.

Mott's® Peppermint Cake

Cake

2¼ cups cake flour
2 teaspoons baking powder
1 teaspoon salt
½ teaspoon baking soda
1½ cups granulated sugar
2 tablespoons margarine
½ cup MOTT'S® Natural Apple Sauce
½ cup skim milk
4 egg whites
1 teaspoon vanilla extract

Peppermint Frosting

1½ cups granulated sugar
¼ cup water
2 egg whites
¼ teaspoon cream of tartar
½ teaspoon peppermint extract
½ ounce crushed starlight candies

1. Preheat oven to 375°F. Spray 9-inch round cake pan with nonstick cooking spray.

2. **To prepare Cake,** in medium bowl, combine flour, baking powder, salt and baking soda. In large bowl, beat 1½ cups sugar and margarine with electric mixer at medium speed until blended. Whisk in apple sauce, milk, 4 egg whites and vanilla extract.

3. Add flour mixture to apple sauce mixture; stir until well blended. Pour into prepared cake pan.

4. Bake 35 to 40 minutes or until toothpick inserted in center comes out clean. Cool

Mott's® Peppermint Cake

completely on wire rack. Split cake horizontally in half to make 2 layers.

5. **To prepare Peppermint Frosting,** in top of double boiler, whisk together 1½ cups sugar, water, 2 egg whites and cream of tartar. Cook, whisking occasionally, over simmering water 4 minutes or until mixture is hot and sugar is dissolved. Remove from heat; stir in peppermint extract. Beat with

electric mixer at high speed 3 minutes or until mixture forms stiff peaks.

6. Place 1 cake layer on serving plate. Spread with layer of Peppermint Frosting. Top with second cake layer. Frost top and side with remaining frosting. Sprinkle top and side of cake with crushed candies. Cut into 12 slices. Refrigerate leftovers.

Makes 12 servings

Apple Praline Bundt Cake

Apple Praline Bundt Cake

1 can (20 ounces) sliced apples,
   drained
½ cup granulated sugar
½ cup packed light brown sugar
1 cup vegetable oil
4 eggs
1½ cups all-purpose flour
2 teaspoons ground cinnamon
1½ teaspoons baking powder
1½ teaspoons baking soda
1½ teaspoons dried mint
¼ teaspoon ground nutmeg
¾ cup chopped walnuts, divided
Praline Sauce (recipe follows)

Preheat oven to 350°F.

Finely chop apples to measure 1½ cups; place apples in large bowl, reserving remaining slices. Add sugars and oil. Add eggs, one at a time. Add combined flour, cinnamon, baking powder, baking soda, mint and nutmeg; mix well. Add ½ cup walnuts.

Spoon batter into greased and floured 12-cup fluted cake pan. Bake 50 minutes or until cake begins to pull away from side of pan. Cool cake in pan on wire rack 10 minutes; remove from pan and cool on wire rack.

Pierce warm cake with long-tined fork; spoon half of Praline Sauce over cake. Arrange remaining apple slices on top of cake; spoon remaining Praline Sauce over apples and sprinkle with remaining ¼ cup walnuts.

Makes 10 to 12 servings

Praline Sauce

6 tablespoons margarine or butter
¾ cup packed light brown sugar
¼ cup brandy or apple juice

Heat margarine in small saucepan until melted; stir in brown sugar and brandy. Heat to boiling; reduce heat and simmer until sauce is thickened to the consistency of honey, 5 to 8 minutes.

Makes about ⅔ cup

*Favorite recipe from **Canned Food Information Council***

Apple Facts

Apples are grown in temperate zones throughout the world and have been cultivated for at least 3,000 years. Apple varieties number well into the thousands.

Kentucky Bourbon Cake

4 cups unsifted flour
2 teaspoons ground nutmeg
1½ teaspoons baking powder
3 cups chopped pecans
2 cups (1 pound) mixed candied fruit
1 (16-ounce) jar BAMA® Orange Marmalade
1½ cups raisins
1½ cups margarine or butter, softened
2 cups granulated sugar
6 eggs
½ cup light molasses
¾ cup bourbon
Confectioners' sugar (optional)

Preheat oven to 300°. Sift or stir together flour, nutmeg and baking powder; set aside. In large bowl, combine pecans, candied fruit, marmalade and raisins; add 1 cup flour mixture. Toss to coat well. In large mixer bowl, beat margarine and granulated sugar until fluffy. Add eggs, one at a time, beating well after each addition. Stir in molasses. Add remaining flour mixture alternately with bourbon. Stir in fruit mixture. Turn into well-greased waxed paper-lined 10-inch tube pan. Bake 2½ to 3 hours or until wooden pick inserted near center comes out clean. Cool 10 minutes. Remove from pan. Cool thoroughly. If desired, wrap cake in cloth dampened with bourbon; store tightly covered at room temperature. Before serving, garnish with confectioners' sugar, if desired.

Makes one 10-inch cake

Apricot Nectar Bundt Cake

    3 cups all-purpose flour
    1 teaspoon salt
    ½ teaspoon baking soda
    ½ teaspoon baking powder
    ½ teaspoon ground nutmeg
    1 cup butter, softened
    1 to 1½ cups granulated sugar
    4 large eggs, let stand at room
        temperature 20 minutes
    1 teaspoon vanilla extract
    1¼ cups apricot nectar
        Apricot Glaze (recipe follows)
        Canned or fresh apricot slices and
        whipped cream

Heat oven to 325°F. Grease and flour 10-inch Bundt or tube pan. Combine flour, salt, baking soda, baking powder and nutmeg; set aside. Beat butter until creamy; beat in sugar, ¼ cup at a time, until combined. Beat in eggs, one at a time, until light and fluffy. Beat in vanilla. Beat in one-third of combined dry ingredients; beat in half of nectar. Beat in remaining dry ingredients; beat in remaining nectar until batter is smooth. Pour batter into prepared cake pan; smooth evenly. Tap pan on counter to prevent air holes. Bake until toothpick inserted in center of cake comes out almost clean, about 50 minutes. Cool on wire rack 10 minutes. Remove cake from pan; place on rack over baking sheet or waxed paper. Brush half of Apricot Glaze over warm cake; let soak in. Brush on remaining glaze; cool. Serve cake slices with 2 canned or fresh apricot halves and 2 tablespoons whipped cream.

Makes 12 servings

Apricot Glaze: Stir together 1 cup sifted confectioner's sugar and ¼ cup nectar until smooth.

*Favorite recipe from **California Apricot Advisory Board***

Sock-It-To-Me Cake

Streusel Filling

    1 package DUNCAN HINES® Moist
        Deluxe Butter Recipe Golden Cake
        Mix, divided
    2 tablespoons packed brown sugar
    2 teaspoons ground cinnamon
    1 cup finely chopped pecans

Cake

    4 eggs
    1 cup dairy sour cream
    ⅓ cup CRISCO® Oil or CRISCO®
        PURITAN® Oil
    ¼ cup water
    ¼ cup granulated sugar

Glaze

    1 cup confectioners sugar
    1 tablespoon milk

1. Preheat oven to 375°F. Grease and flour 10-inch tube pan.

2. **For streusel filling,** combine 2 tablespoons cake mix, brown sugar and cinnamon in medium bowl. Stir in pecans. Set aside.

3. **For cake,** combine remaining cake mix, eggs, sour cream, oil, water and granulated sugar in large bowl. Beat at medium speed with electric mixer for 2 minutes. Pour two-

Sock-It-To-Me Cake

thirds of batter into pan. Sprinkle with streusel filling. Spoon remaining batter evenly over filling. Bake at 375°F for 45 to 55 minutes or until toothpick inserted in center comes out clean. Cool in pan 25 minutes. Invert onto serving plate. Cool completely.

4. **For glaze,** combine confectioners sugar and milk in small bowl. Stir until smooth. Add more milk to thin glaze as needed. Drizzle over cake. *Makes 12 to 16 servings*

Tip: For quick glaze, heat ½ cup Duncan Hines® Vanilla Frosting in small saucepan over medium heat, stirring constantly, until thin.

Cappuccino Cake

½ cup (3 ounces) chocolate chips
½ cup chopped hazelnuts, walnuts or
  pecans
1 (18.25-ounce) package yellow cake
  mix
¼ cup instant espresso coffee powder
2 teaspoons ground cinnamon
1¼ cups water
3 eggs
⅓ cup FILIPPO BERIO® Pure or Extra
  Light Tasting Olive Oil
  Powdered sugar
1 (15-ounce) container ricotta cheese
2 teaspoons granulated sugar
  Additional ground cinnamon

Preheat oven to 325°F. Grease 10-inch
(12-cup) Bundt pan or 10-inch tube pan
with olive oil. Sprinkle lightly with flour.

In small bowl, combine chocolate chips and
hazelnuts. Spoon evenly into bottom of
prepared pan.

In large bowl, combine cake mix, coffee
powder and 2 teaspoons cinnamon. Add
water, eggs and olive oil. Beat with electric
mixer at low speed until dry ingredients are
moistened. Beat at medium speed 2 minutes.
Pour batter over topping in pan.

Bake 60 minutes or until toothpick inserted in
center comes out clean. Cool on wire rack 15
minutes. Remove from pan. Place cake,
fluted side up, on serving plate. Cool
completely. Sprinkle with powdered sugar.

In medium bowl, combine ricotta cheese and
granulated sugar. Sprinkle with additional
cinnamon. Serve alongside slices of cake.
Serve with cappuccino, espresso or your
favorite coffee, if desired.

Makes 12 to 16 servings

Olive Oil Pound Cake

2¼ cups all-purpose flour
1¼ teaspoons salt
1 teaspoon baking powder
¾ cup FILIPPO BERIO® Extra Light
  Tasting Olive Oil
1½ cups sugar
2 tablespoons orange juice
2 teaspoons vanilla
3 eggs
⅔ cup milk

Preheat oven to 325°F. Grease 2
(6¾×3½-inch) loaf pans with olive oil.

In medium bowl, combine flour, salt and
baking powder.

In large bowl, place olive oil. Slowly beat in
sugar, orange juice and vanilla with electric
mixer at medium speed until blended. Add
eggs, one at a time, beating well after each
addition. Add milk; beat 2 minutes. Gradually
beat flour mixture into olive oil mixture until
well blended. Pour batter equally into
prepared pans.

Bake 50 to 55 minutes or until golden brown
and toothpick inserted in centers comes out
clean. Cool on wire racks 15 minutes.
Remove from pans; cool completely on wire
racks. *Makes 2 small loaves*

Cappuccino Cake

Mr. Rabbit Cut-Up Cake

2¼ cups BAKER'S® ANGEL FLAKE®
 Coconut, divided
 Red food coloring
2 baked 9-inch round cake layers,
 cooled
2⅔ cups Fluffy Seven Minute Frosting
 (recipe follows)
2 green starlight mints (for eyes)
2 green gumdrops (for eyes)
 Red licorice (for whiskers and mouth)
1 small purple gumdrop (for nose)
 Red licorice sticks (to outline bowtie)
 Chewy candies (for bowtie)

TINT ¼ cup of coconut pink using red food coloring.

LEAVE one cake whole; cut remaining cake as shown in illustration.

USING small amount of frosting to hold pieces together, arrange cake on serving tray as shown in photograph.

FROST cake with remaining frosting. Sprinkle center of bunny's ears with pink coconut. Sprinkle remaining 2 cups white coconut over bunny's head and outer edges of ears.

DECORATE cake as shown in photograph using remaining ingredients.
Makes 12 to 16 servings

Fluffy Seven Minute Frosting

2 egg whites
1½ cups sugar
 Dash of salt
½ cup water
1 tablespoon light corn syrup
1 teaspoon vanilla

MIX egg whites, sugar, salt, water and corn syrup in top of double boiler. Beat about 1 minute to blend thoroughly.

PLACE over boiling water; beat constantly on high speed of electric mixer until frosting stands in stiff peaks, about 7 minutes, scraping down side occasionally with rubber scraper.

REMOVE from boiling water. Immediately pour into large bowl. Add vanilla; beat until thick enough to spread, about 1 minute.
Makes about 5⅓ cups

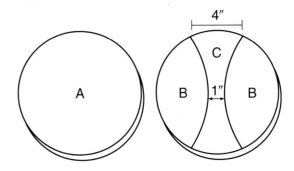

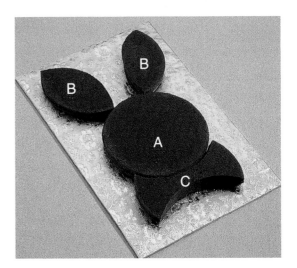

Mr. Rabbit Cut-Up Cake

Lemon Angel Cake Roll

1 (14½- or 16-ounce) package angel
    food cake mix
    Confectioners' sugar
1 (14-ounce) can EAGLE® Brand
    Sweetened Condensed Milk
    (NOT evaporated milk)
⅓ cup REALEMON® Lemon Juice from
    Concentrate
2 teaspoons grated lemon peel
    (optional)
4 to 6 drops yellow food coloring
    (optional)
1 (4-ounce) container frozen nondairy
    whipped topping, thawed (1¾ cups)
½ cup flaked coconut, tinted yellow,* if
    desired

*To tint coconut: Combine coconut, ½ teaspoon
water and 2 drops yellow food coloring in small
plastic bag or bowl; shake or mix well.

Preheat oven to 350°. Line 15×10-inch jelly-
roll pan with aluminum foil, extending foil
1 inch over ends of pan. Prepare cake mix as
package directs. Spread batter evenly into
prepared pan. Bake 30 minutes or until top
springs back when lightly touched.
Immediately turn onto towel sprinkled with
confectioners' sugar. Peel off foil; beginning
at narrow end, roll up cake with towel, jelly-
roll fashion. Cool thoroughly. Meanwhile, in
medium bowl, combine sweetened
condensed milk, ReaLemon® brand, peel and
food coloring if desired; mix well. Fold in
whipped topping. Unroll cake; trim edges.
Spread with half the lemon filling; reroll.
Place on serving plate, seam side down;
spread remaining filling over roll. Garnish with
coconut. Chill thoroughly. Store in refrigerator.
Makes 8 to 10 servings

Borden

*When he perfected his process for
condensing milk, Gail Borden had
never heard of germs or Louis Pasteur
or even artificial refrigeration. But the
sight of children dying aboard an
immigrant ship because of drinking
impure milk haunted him. His years
of experimentation led to an eventual
patent for condensing milk. The
condensed milk remained wholesome
for long periods of time without
refrigeration. Gail Borden then
founded the New York Condensed Milk
Company in 1857, later to become the
Borden Company.*

Mott's® Magic Apple Roll

2 cups MOTT'S® Natural Apple Sauce
½ teaspoon ground cinnamon
4 egg whites
¾ cup granulated sugar
⅔ cup all-purpose flour
¾ teaspoon baking powder
¼ teaspoon salt
1 teaspoon vanilla extract
1 tablespoon powdered sugar

1. Preheat oven to 400°F. Spray 15×10×1-inch jelly-roll pan with nonstick cooking spray. Line with waxed paper; spray with cooking spray. Pour apple sauce into pan, spreading evenly. Sprinkle with cinnamon.

2. In large bowl, beat egg whites with electric mixer at high speed until foamy. Gradually add granulated sugar, beating until mixture is thick and light.

3. In small bowl, sift together flour, baking powder and salt. Fold into egg white mixture with vanilla. Gently pour batter over apple sauce mixture, spreading evenly.

4. Bake 15 to 18 minutes or until lightly browned. Cool on wire rack 5 minutes. Invert cake, apple side up, onto clean, lint-free dish towel sprinkled with powdered sugar; peel off waxed paper. Trim edges of cake. Starting at narrow end, roll up cake. Place, seam side down, on serving plate. Cool completely. Sprinkle top with powdered sugar. Cut into 10 slices. *Makes 10 servings*

Pudding Poke Cake

1 package (2-layer size) yellow or chocolate cake mix
2 packages (4-serving size each) JELL-O Instant Pudding & Pie Filling, any flavor
4 cups cold milk

PREPARE and bake cake mix as directed on package for 13×9-inch pan. Remove from oven. Immediately poke holes down through cake to pan with round handle of wooden spoon. (Or poke holes with a plastic drinking straw, using a turning motion to make large holes.) Holes should be at 1-inch intervals.

POUR cold milk into large bowl. Add pudding mix. Beat with wire whisk 2 minutes. Quickly, before pudding mixture thickens, pour about ½ of thin pudding mixture evenly over warm cake and into holes to make stripes. Allow remaining pudding mixture to thicken slightly. Spoon over top of cake, swirling to "frost" cake.

REFRIGERATE at least 1 hour. Store cake in refrigerator. *Makes 15 servings*

Flag Cake

2 pints strawberries
1 package (12 ounces) pound cake, cut
  into 8 slices
1⅓ cups blueberries, divided
1 tub (8 ounces) COOL WHIP Whipped
  Topping, thawed

SLICE 1 cup strawberries; set aside. Halve
remaining strawberries; set aside.

LINE bottom of 12×8-inch baking dish with
cake slices. Top with 1 cup sliced
strawberries, 1 cup blueberries and all of
whipped topping.

PLACE strawberry halves and remaining
⅓ cup blueberries over whipped topping
to create a flag design.

REFRIGERATE until ready to serve.

Makes 15 servings

Flag Cake

Mott's® Pineapple Upside Down Cake

1 (8-ounce) can crushed pineapple in
  juice, undrained
2 tablespoons margarine, melted and
  divided
½ cup packed light brown sugar
6 whole maraschino cherries
1½ cups all-purpose flour
2 tablespoons baking powder
¼ teaspoon salt
1 cup granulated sugar
½ cup MOTT'S® Natural Apple Sauce
1 whole egg
3 egg whites, beaten until stiff

1. Preheat oven to 375°F. Spray 8×8-inch
baking pan with nonstick cooking spray. Drain
pineapple; reserve juice.

2. Spread 1 tablespoon melted margarine
evenly in bottom of prepared pan. Sprinkle
with brown sugar; top with pineapple. Slice
cherries in half. Arrange cherries, cut side up,
so that when cake is cut, each piece will have
cherry half in center.

3. In small bowl, combine flour, baking
powder and salt. In large bowl, combine
granulated sugar, apple sauce, whole egg,
remaining 1 tablespoon melted margarine
and reserved pineapple juice.

4. Add flour mixture to apple sauce mixture;
stir until well blended. Fold in egg whites.
Gently pour batter over fruit, spreading
evenly.

5. Bake 35 to 40 minutes or until lightly
browned. Cool on wire rack 10 minutes.
Invert cake onto serving plate. Serve warm or
cool completely. Cut into 12 pieces.

Makes 12 servings

Pumpkin Apple Gingerbread

3½ cups all-purpose flour
1 tablespoon baking powder
2½ teaspoons ground ginger
½ teaspoon baking soda
½ teaspoon salt
½ teaspoon pumpkin pie spice
1 cup butter or margarine, softened
1 cup granulated sugar
½ cup packed brown sugar
4 eggs
1¾ cups (16-ounce can) LIBBY'S® Solid Pack Pumpkin
½ cup molasses
1 large pippin or Granny Smith apple, peeled, cored and shredded (about 1 cup)
Powdered sugar
Hard Sauce (recipe follows)

COMBINE flour, baking powder, ginger, baking soda, salt and pumpkin pie spice in medium bowl.

CREAM butter, granulated sugar and brown sugar in large mixer bowl until light and fluffy. Add eggs, two at a time, beating well after each addition. Add pumpkin, molasses and apple; beat well. Add flour mixture; mix until well blended.

SPOON batter into well-greased and floured 12-cup Bundt pan. Bake in preheated 350°F oven 1 hour or until wooden pick comes out clean. Cool on wire rack for 15 minutes; remove from pan. Dust with powdered sugar before serving warm with Hard Sauce.

Makes 12 servings

Hard Sauce: Beat 1 cup softened butter, 4 cups sifted powdered sugar and 2 teaspoons vanilla extract in small mixer bowl until smooth.

Note: Recipe may also be made in two 8- or 9-inch round cake pans or one 13×9-inch pan. Bake in preheated 350°F oven 40 to 45 minutes.

Mott's® Guilt-Free Black Forest Dessert

3 cups all-purpose flour
2½ cups sugar
⅓ cup unsweetened cocoa powder
2 teaspoons baking soda
1 teaspoon salt
2 cups cold water
¾ cup MOTT'S® Natural Apple Sauce
2 whole eggs *or* ½ cup egg substitute
2 tablespoons apple-cider vinegar
1 tablespoon vanilla extract
1 (1.4-ounce) package sugar-free instant chocolate pudding
2 cups skim milk
1 (20-ounce) can light cherry pie filling
Frozen light nondairy whipped topping, thawed (optional)

1. Preheat oven to 350°F. Spray 13×9-inch pan with nonstick cooking spray.

2. In medium bowl, combine flour, sugar, cocoa, baking soda and salt. In large bowl, combine water, apple sauce, eggs, vinegar and vanilla.

Mott's® Guilt-Free Black Forest Dessert

3. Add flour mixture to apple sauce mixture; stir until well blended. Pour batter into prepared pan. Bake 45 minutes or until toothpick inserted in center of cake comes out clean. Cool completely on wire rack.

4. Prepare pudding mix according to package directions using 2 cups skim milk.

5. Spread top of cake with pudding; refrigerate until set. Top evenly with dollops of pie filling; spread over pudding. Cut into 10 pieces. Serve with whipped topping, if desired. Refrigerate leftovers.

Makes 10 servings

Grandma's Favorite Molasses Fruitcake

2 California-Arizona oranges
1 cup light molasses
1 package (15 ounces) raisins
1 package (8 ounces) dates, chopped
2 containers (16 ounces each) glacé fruit mix
1¼ cups granulated sugar
1 cup butter or margarine, softened
6 eggs
3 cups all-purpose flour
1½ teaspoons ground cinnamon
1 teaspoon baking soda
1 teaspoon ground nutmeg
½ teaspoon ground allspice
½ teaspoon ground cloves
1 cup freshly squeezed orange juice
2 cups nut halves
Powdered sugar

Cut oranges into large chunks. In blender or food processor, finely chop oranges to measure 1⅓ cups. In large saucepan, combine chopped oranges, molasses, raisins and dates; bring to a boil. Reduce heat and simmer 5 to 10 minutes. Remove from heat; stir in fruit mix. Set aside.

Preheat oven to 300°F. In large bowl, cream together sugar and butter. Beat in eggs, one at a time. Sift together flour, cinnamon, baking soda, nutmeg, allspice and cloves. Add to creamed mixture alternately with orange juice. Stir batter into molasses-fruit mixture. Add nuts. Divide batter; spoon 8 cups batter into *well-greased* 10-inch Bundt or tube pan. With remaining 6 cups batter, make 2 dozen cupcakes *or* 8 dozen mini fruitcakes. Bake 2 hours or until toothpick inserted in center comes out clean. Cool 10 minutes. Remove from pan; cool on wire rack. To serve, sprinkle with powdered sugar. Garnish with orange pieces and candied cherries, if desired.

Favorite recipe from **Sunkist Growers**

Western Golden Fruitcake

1 cup butter or margarine, softened
2 cups sugar
4 eggs
4 cups all-purpose flour
1½ teaspoons baking soda
1 cup buttermilk
½ cup freshly squeezed orange juice
2 cups pecan or walnut halves
1 package (8 ounces) dates, chopped
8 ounces candied cherries, halved
8 ounces candied pineapple chunks
Grated peel of 2 fresh oranges
Fresh Orange Glaze or Fresh Lemon Glaze (recipes follow)

Preheat oven to 300°F. In large bowl, cream together butter and sugar. Beat in eggs, one at a time. Sift together flour and baking soda. Add to creamed mixture alternately with buttermilk and orange juice, beating until smooth. Stir in nuts, dates, cherries, pineapple and orange peel. Divide batter; spoon 7½ cups into *well-greased* 10-inch Bundt or tube pan and spoon remaining 2½ cups batter into *well-greased* 7½×3½×2¼-inch loaf pan. Bake both cakes 2 hours or until toothpick inserted in center comes out clean. Cool 10 minutes. Remove from pans; cool on wire racks. To serve, drizzle cakes with Fresh Orange Glaze or Fresh Lemon Glaze and garnish with nut halves, if desired.

Fresh Orange Glaze: In small bowl, combine 1 cup confectioners' sugar, 1 teaspoon freshly grated orange peel and 1½ to 2 tablespoons freshly squeezed orange juice.

Fresh Lemon Glaze: In small bowl, combine 1 cup confectioners' sugar, 1 teaspoon freshly grated lemon peel and 1½ to 2 tablespoons freshly squeezed lemon juice.

Favorite recipe from **Sunkist Growers**

Holiday Fruit Cake

```
 1 (16-ounce) package HONEY MAID®
     Grahams, finely rolled (about
     5 cups crumbs)
 ½ teaspoon ground cinnamon
 ½ teaspoon ground allspice
 ¼ teaspoon ground cloves
 ¾ cup seedless raisins
 1 cup pitted dates, snipped
12 ounces mixed candied fruit
     (about 1½ cups)
 1 cup PLANTERS® Walnut Pieces,
     chopped
 ½ cup orange juice
 ⅓ cup light corn syrup
```

In large bowl, combine crumbs, cinnamon, allspice, cloves, raisins, dates, candied fruit and walnuts. Stir together orange juice and corn syrup; add to crumb mixture, blending until moistened. Press firmly into foil-lined 8½×4½×2½-inch loaf pan; cover tightly. Store at least 2 days in refrigerator before serving. Cake will keep several weeks in refrigerator.   *Makes 1 (8-inch) loaf*

PLANTERS®

Amedeo Obici immigrated to Pennsylvania from his native Italy at the young age of 12. At the age of 19, he opened a fruit stand that also had a peanut roaster. He developed a system to turn the roaster automatically instead of by hand and also conceived the idea of salting the peanuts to enhance the flavor. In 1906, in partnership with a fellow immigrant, Mario Peruzzi, the Planters Nut & Chocolate Company was formed. In 1916, as a way to enhance the popularity of the peanut, the partners offered a prize for the best sketch suitable for the company trademark. The winning design, an animated peanut, was submitted by a schoolboy. Later a commercial artist added a top hat, monocle and cane, and Mr. Peanut was born.

Classic Sour Cream Cheesecake

Classic Sour Cream Cheesecake

1½ cups shortbread cookie crumbs
    (about 24 cookies)
2 tablespoons margarine or butter,
    melted
3 (8-ounce) packages cream cheese,
    softened
1 (14-ounce) can EAGLE® Brand
    Sweetened Condensed Milk
    (NOT evaporated milk)
4 eggs
1 (8-ounce) container BORDEN® or
    MEADOW GOLD® Sour Cream
1 tablespoon vanilla extract

Preheat oven to 350°. Combine crumbs and margarine; press firmly on bottom of 9-inch springform pan. In large mixer bowl, beat cheese until fluffy. Gradually beat in sweetened condensed milk until smooth. Beat in eggs then sour cream and vanilla. Pour into prepared pan. Bake 50 to 55 minutes or until lightly browned around edge (center will be slightly soft). Cool. Chill. Just before serving, remove side of springform pan. Garnish with cherry pie filling, if desired. Refrigerate leftovers.

Makes one 9-inch cheesecake

Creamy Strawberry Cheesecake

½ cup **NABISCO**® Graham Cracker Crumbs
1 cup sugar
2 tablespoons margarine, melted
1 (24-ounce) container lowfat cottage cheese (1% milkfat)
2 cups **EGG BEATERS**® Real Egg Product
2 (8-ounce) packages light cream cheese (Neufchâtel), softened
½ teaspoon almond extract (optional)
2 cups sliced strawberries
Mint sprig, for garnish

In small bowl, combine crumbs, 2 tablespoons sugar and margarine; press on bottom of 9-inch springform pan. Set aside.

In electric blender or food processor, purée cottage cheese and ½ cup egg product, scraping down side of container as necessary. In large bowl, with mixer at high speed, beat cream cheese, ¾ cup sugar, cottage cheese mixture, almond extract and remaining 1½ cups egg product until smooth; pour over crust in pan.

Bake at 325°F for 1 hour or until puffed and set. Cool on rack 15 minutes. Carefully run metal spatula around edge of cheesecake to loosen. Chill at least 3 hours.

In electric blender, purée 1 cup strawberries and remaining 2 tablespoons sugar. Arrange remaining 1 cup strawberries on cheesecake; drizzle with strawberry purée. Chill until serving time. Garnish with mint sprig.

Makes 16 servings

Nabisco Grahams

During the last century, Sylvester Graham, an ordained Presbyterian minister, rose to fame for his touting of unsifted, coarsely ground wheat flour. In 1829, he invented the graham cracker, made from coarsely ground graham flour. It was the National Biscuit Company (forerunner of Nabisco, Inc.) that was able to convert Graham's invention to mass production. Choice winter wheat berries are ground to just the right size to give the cracker its distinctive flavor and texture. Molasses is added for flavor and golden color, creating a perfect snack with wholesome taste made from natural ingredients.

Cookies 'n' Cream Cheesecake

1 cup chocolate sandwich cookie
    crumbs (about 12 cookies)
1 tablespoon margarine, melted
3 (8-ounce) packages PHILADELPHIA
    BRAND® Cream Cheese, softened
1 cup sugar
2 tablespoons all-purpose flour
1 teaspoon vanilla
3 eggs
1 cup coarsely chopped chocolate
    sandwich cookies (about 8 cookies)

• Preheat oven to 325°F.

• Mix together crumbs and margarine in small bowl. Press onto bottom of 9-inch springform pan. Bake 10 minutes.

• Beat cream cheese, sugar, flour and vanilla in large mixing bowl at medium speed with electric mixer until well blended.

• Add eggs, one at a time, mixing well after each addition. Fold in chopped cookies. Pour over crust.

• Bake 1 hour and 5 minutes. Loosen cake from rim of pan; cool before removing rim of pan. Chill. Garnish with thawed COOL WHIP® Whipped Topping, chocolate sandwich cookies, cut in half, and mint leaves, if desired.

Makes 10 to 12 servings

Cream cheese was developed over 100 years ago and was first produced commercially by an ambitious, hard-working farmer in upstate New York. It was primarily used as a flavorful spread for bread, toast or crackers. This fresh, delicate cheese was not used as a recipe ingredient until the mid-1920s. One of the first recipes developed was the "Kraft Philadelphia Cream Cake," which was later retitled "Supreme Cheesecake." This recipe became an instant favorite and what began as a novel idea—cooking with cream cheese—has become a universally accepted concept. Today, Philadelphia Brand Cream Cheese is an indispensable ingredient used by great American cooks like you.

Cookies 'n' Cream Cheesecake

Pumpkin Cheesecake

Crust

1½ cups graham cracker crumbs
¼ cup granulated sugar
⅓ cup butter or margarine, melted

Cheesecake

3 packages (8 ounces each) cream cheese, softened
1 cup granulated sugar
¼ cup packed light brown sugar
1¾ cups (16-ounce can) LIBBY'S® Solid Pack Pumpkin
2 eggs
⅔ cup undiluted CARNATION® Evaporated Milk
2 tablespoons cornstarch
1¼ teaspoons ground cinnamon
½ teaspoon ground nutmeg

Topping

2 cups (16-ounce carton) sour cream, at room temperature
¼ to ⅓ cup granulated sugar
1 teaspoon vanilla extract

For Crust: COMBINE graham cracker crumbs, sugar and butter in medium bowl. Press onto bottom and 1 inch up side of 9-inch springform pan. Bake in preheated 350°F oven 6 to 8 minutes. Do not allow to brown. Remove from oven; cool.

For Cheesecake: BEAT cream cheese, granulated sugar and brown sugar in large mixer bowl until fluffy. Beat in pumpkin, eggs and evaporated milk. Add cornstarch, cinnamon and nutmeg; beat well. Pour into crust.

BAKE in preheated 350°F oven 55 to 60 minutes or until edge is set.

For Topping: COMBINE sour cream, sugar and vanilla in small bowl. Spread over surface of warm cheesecake. Bake at 350°F oven 5 minutes. Cool on wire rack. Remove side of pan; chill for several hours or overnight.   *Makes one 9-inch cheesecake*

Maple Pumpkin Cheesecake

1¼ cups graham cracker crumbs
¼ cup sugar
¼ cup margarine or butter, melted
3 (8-ounce) packages cream cheese, softened
1 (14-ounce) can EAGLE® Brand Sweetened Condensed Milk (NOT evaporated milk)
1 (16-ounce) can pumpkin (about 2 cups)
3 eggs
1 cup CARY'S®, MAPLE ORCHARDS® or MACDONALD'S™ Pure Maple Syrup
1½ teaspoons ground cinnamon
1 teaspoon ground nutmeg
½ teaspoon salt
Maple Pecan Glaze (page 299)

Preheat oven to 300°. Combine crumbs, sugar and margarine; press firmly on bottom of 9-inch springform pan or 13×9-inch baking pan. In large mixer bowl, beat cheese until fluffy. Gradually beat in sweetened condensed milk until smooth. Add pumpkin, eggs, ¼ *cup* pure maple syrup, cinnamon,

Maple Pumpkin Cheesecake

nutmeg and salt; mix well. Pour into prepared pan. Bake 1 hour and 15 minutes or until edge springs back when lightly touched (center will be slightly soft). Cool. Chill. Just before serving, remove side of springform pan. Top with Maple Pecan Glaze. Refrigerate leftovers.

Makes one 9-inch cheesecake

Maple Pecan Glaze: In small saucepan, combine remaining ¾ *cup* pure maple syrup and 1 cup (½ pint) BORDEN® or MEADOW GOLD® Whipping Cream, *unwhipped;* bring to a boil. Boil rapidly 15 to 20 minutes or until thickened; stir occasionally. Add ½ cup chopped pecans. Makes about 1¼ cups.

Chocolate Marble Praline Cheesecake

Crust

- **1 package DUNCAN HINES® Golden Sugar Cookie Mix**
- **1 egg**
- **¼ cup CRISCO® Oil or CRISCO® PURITAN® Oil**
- **1½ tablespoons water**
- **½ cup finely chopped pecans (see Tip)**

Filling

- **1¼ cups packed brown sugar**
- **2 tablespoons all-purpose flour**
- **3 packages (8 ounces each) cream cheese, softened**
- **3 eggs, lightly beaten**
- **1½ teaspoons vanilla extract**
- **1 square (1 ounce) unsweetened chocolate, melted**
- **20 to 25 pecan halves (½ cup)**
- **Caramel flavor topping**

1. Preheat oven to 350°F.

2. **For crust,** combine cookie mix, 1 egg, oil, water and chopped pecans in large bowl. Stir until thoroughly blended. Reserve 1½ cups dough; set aside. Press remaining mixture into bottom of ungreased 9-inch springform pan. Bake at 350°F for 22 to 24 minutes or until edge is light brown and center is set. Remove from oven.

3. **For filling,** combine brown sugar and flour in small bowl; set aside. Place cream cheese in large bowl. Beat at low speed with electric mixer, adding brown sugar mixture gradually. Add beaten eggs and vanilla extract, mixing only until incorporated. Remove 1 cup batter to small bowl; add melted chocolate. Pour remaining plain batter onto warm crust. Drop spoonfuls of chocolate batter over plain batter. Run knife through batters to marbleize. Arrange pecan halves around top edge. Bake at 350°F for 45 to 55 minutes or until set. Loosen cake from side of pan with knife or spatula. Cool completely on rack. Refrigerate 2 hours or until ready to serve.

4. To serve, remove side of pan. Glaze top of cheesecake with caramel flavor topping. Cut into slices and serve with additional caramel flavor topping, if desired.

5. Shape reserved dough into 24 balls. Place 2 inches apart on ungreased baking sheet. Bake at 350°F for 8 to 10 minutes or until set. Cool 1 minute on baking sheet. Remove to cooling rack. Sprinkle with confectioners sugar. Cool completely.

Makes 12 to 16 servings

Tip: For added flavor, toast pecans before chopping. Spread pecans in single layer on baking sheet. Toast in 350°F oven for 3 to 5 minutes or until fragrant. Cool completely.

Chocolate Marble Praline Cheesecake

Cocoa Cheesecake

    2 packages (8 ounces each) cream
        cheese, softened
    ¾ cup plus 2 tablespoons sugar, divided
    ½ cup HERSHEY®S Cocoa
    2 teaspoons vanilla extract, divided
    2 eggs
        Graham Crust (recipe follows)
    1 cup (8 ounces) dairy sour cream
        Fresh fruit, sliced

Heat oven to 375°F. In large mixer bowl, beat cream cheese, ¾ cup sugar, cocoa and 1 teaspoon vanilla until well blended. Add eggs; blend well. Pour batter into prepared Graham Crust. Bake 20 minutes. Remove from oven; cool 15 minutes. *Increase oven temperature to 425°F.* In small bowl, stir together sour cream, remaining 2 tablespoons sugar and remaining 1 teaspoon vanilla until smooth; spread evenly over top of cheesecake. Bake 10 minutes; remove from oven. Loosen cheesecake from side of pan; cool to room temperature. Refrigerate several hours or overnight; remove side of pan. Garnish with fresh fruit. Cover; refrigerate leftover cheesecake.   *Makes 10 to 12 servings*

Graham Crust: In bowl, combine 1½ cups graham cracker crumbs, ⅓ cup sugar and ⅓ cup melted butter or margarine. Press mixture onto bottom and halfway up side of 9-inch springform pan.

Variation:

Chocolate Lover's Cheesecake: Prepare batter as directed above; stir 1 cup Hershey®s Semi-Sweet Chocolate Chips into batter before pouring into crust. Bake and serve as directed.

Philly 3-Step™ Cheesecake

    2 (8-ounce) packages PHILADELPHIA
        BRAND® Cream Cheese or
        PHILADELPHIA BRAND® Neufchâtel
        Cheese, ⅓ Less Fat Than Cream
        Cheese, softened
    ½ cup sugar
    ½ teaspoon vanilla
    2 eggs
    1 prepared graham cracker crumb crust
        (6 ounces or 9 inches)

1. MIX cream cheese, sugar and vanilla with electric mixer on medium speed until well blended. Add eggs; mix until blended.

2. POUR into crust.

3. BAKE at 350°F for 40 minutes or until center is almost set. Cool. Refrigerate 3 hours or overnight.   *Makes 8 servings*

Historical ad promoting Nabisco's® Vanilla Wafers.

Individual Cherry Cheesecakes

12 NILLA® Wafers
2 (8-ounce) packages cream cheese, softened
¾ cup sugar
2 eggs
Cherry pie filling

Place 1 wafer in bottom of each of 12 (2½-inch) paper-lined muffin-pan cups; set aside.

In large bowl, with electric mixer at medium speed, beat cream cheese, sugar and eggs until light and fluffy. Spoon filling into each cup, filling about ⅔ full.

Bake at 350°F for 30 minutes. Turn off oven; open door slightly. Let cool in oven for 30 minutes. Remove from oven; cool completely. Top with pie filling. Chill at least 1 hour.

Makes 12 servings

Marble Cheesecake

Chocolate Crumb Crust (recipe follows)
3 packages (8 ounces each) cream cheese, softened
1 cup sugar, divided
½ cup dairy sour cream
2½ teaspoons vanilla extract, divided
3 tablespoons all-purpose flour
3 eggs
¼ cup HERSHEY¦S Cocoa
1 tablespoon vegetable oil

Prepare Chocolate Crumb Crust. Heat oven to 450°F. In large mixer bowl, beat cream cheese, ¾ cup sugar, sour cream and 2 teaspoons vanilla until smooth. Gradually add flour, blending well. Add eggs, one at a time, beating well after each addition; set aside. Stir together cocoa and remaining ¼ cup sugar. Add oil, remaining ½ teaspoon vanilla and 1½ cups cream cheese mixture; blend well. Spoon plain and chocolate batters alternately over prepared Chocolate Crumb Crust, ending with spoonfuls of chocolate on top; gently swirl with spatula or knife for marbled effect. Bake 10 minutes. *Reduce oven temperature to 250°F;* continue baking 30 minutes. Turn off oven; leave cheesecake in oven 30 minutes without opening door. Remove from oven. Loosen cheesecake from side of pan; cool to room temperature. Refrigerate several hours or overnight; remove side of pan. Cover; refrigerate leftover cheesecake.

Makes 10 to 12 servings

Chocolate Crumb Crust: Heat oven to 350°F. In bowl, stir together 1¼ cups vanilla wafer crumbs, ⅓ cup powdered sugar and ⅓ cup Hershey₀s Cocoa; blend in ¼ cup (½ stick) butter or margarine, melted. Press mixture onto bottom and ½ inch up side of 9-inch springform pan. Bake 8 minutes; cool completely.

Old-Fashioned Pies & Desserts

Create delightful new memories for family and friends by topping off a meal with one of these treasured recipes.

Traditional Cherry Pie

3 cups frozen tart cherries
1 cup granulated sugar
2 tablespoons quick-cooking tapioca
½ teaspoon almond extract
   Pastry for 2-crust, 9-inch pie
2 tablespoons butter or margarine

Preheat oven to 400°F.

In medium bowl, combine cherries, sugar, tapioca and almond extract; mix well. (It is not necessary to thaw cherries before using.) Let cherry mixture stand 15 minutes.

Line 9-inch pie plate with pastry; fill with cherry mixture. Dot with butter. Cover with top crust, cutting slits for steam to escape.

Bake 50 to 55 minutes, or until crust is golden brown and filling is bubbly.
                                    Makes 6 to 8 servings

Favorite recipe from **Cherry Marketing Institute, Inc.**

Traditional Cherry Pie

Elegant and Easy Pear Tart

Elegant and Easy Pear Tart

1 can (29 ounces) Bartlett pears
2 packages (3⅛ to 3½ ounces each)
   vanilla pudding mix
Milk
¼ cup almond-flavor liqueur*
1 (8-inch) pastry shell, baked and
   cooled
Apricot Glaze (recipe follows)

*One-half teaspoon almond extract can be substituted.

Drain pears; reserve 1 cup liquid. Prepare pudding according to package directions substituting reserved pear liquid for part of milk; stir in liqueur. Pour into pastry shell; chill until set. Slice pears and arrange over pudding. Brush with warm Apricot Glaze; refrigerate until cold.

Makes 1 (8-inch) tart

Apricot Glaze: Heat ½ cup apricot or peach preserves and 1 tablespoon almond-flavor liqueur or pear liquid. Press through sieve; discard pulp. Makes about ⅓ cup.

*Favorite recipe from **Pacific Coast Canned Pear Service***

Freestyle Apple Pie

Crumb Topping (recipe follows)
½ cup sugar
1 tablespoon ARGO® or KINGSFORD'S®
  Corn Starch
½ teaspoon cinnamon
4 cups peeled, sliced apples (about
  4 medium)
1 tablespoon lemon juice
1 refrigerated prepared pie crust for
  9-inch pie

Prepare Crumb Topping; set aside. In large bowl combine sugar, corn starch and cinnamon. Add apples and lemon juice; toss to coat. Unfold crust; place on foil-lined cookie sheet. Spoon apples into center of crust, leaving 2-inch edge. Sprinkle Crumb Topping over apples. Fold up edge of crust, pinching at 2-inch intervals. Bake in 400°F oven 15 minutes. *Reduce temperature to 350°F;* bake 35 minutes longer or until apples are tender. *Makes 6 servings*

Crumb Topping: In small bowl combine ½ cup flour and ⅓ cup packed brown sugar. With pastry blender or 2 knives, cut in ½ cup cold MAZOLA® Margarine just until coarse crumbs form.

Fourth of July Cherry Pie

5 cups Northwest fresh sweet cherries,
  pitted
2 tablespoons cornstarch
  Pastry for 2-crust (9-inch) pie
2 tablespoons butter or margarine
⅓ cup sifted powdered sugar
1 tablespoon fresh lemon juice
1 teaspoon grated lemon peel

Preheat oven to 425°F. Sprinkle cornstarch over cherries; toss to coat. Turn into pastry-lined 9-inch pie pan. Dot with butter. Roll remaining pastry into 10-inch circle. Cut into ¾-inch-wide strips. Arrange lattice-fashion over filling; seal and flute edges. Bake 35 to 45 minutes or until filling bubbles. Combine powdered sugar, lemon juice and peel; drizzle over warm pie. *Makes one 9-inch pie*

*Favorite recipe from **Northwest Cherry Growers***

Chilean Raspberry and Blueberry Pie

**Pastry for 2-crust, 9-inch pie
  (homemade or prepared)**
1⅓ cups plus 1 teaspoon sugar
7 tablespoons cornstarch
1 tablespoon grated orange peel
4 cups Chilean raspberries
2 cups Chilean blueberries
1 tablespoon orange liqueur *or*
  ½ teaspoon grated orange peel

Preheat oven to 375°F. Line 9-inch pie pan with pastry. Mix 1⅓ cups sugar, cornstarch and orange peel in bowl; add raspberries, blueberries and orange liqueur. Mix well and pour into pie shell. Cover with top crust. Seal edges and flute or press together with tines of fork. Cut slits for steam to escape. Brush lightly with cold water; sprinkle with remaining 1 teaspoon sugar. Bake until top is golden brown, about 50 minutes. Let cool before serving with slightly sweetened whipped cream. *Makes 8 servings*

*Favorite recipe from **Chilean Fresh Fruit Association***

Apple Brandy Praline Pie

Praline Topping (recipe follows)
¼ cup sugar
3 tablespoons all-purpose flour
¼ teaspoon salt
3 eggs
½ cup **KARO®** Light or Dark Corn Syrup
¼ cup **MAZOLA®** Margarine, melted
2 tablespoons apple or plain brandy
2 medium apples, peeled and thinly sliced
1 unbaked (9-inch) pie crust

Prepare Praline Topping; set aside. In large bowl combine sugar, flour and salt. Beat in eggs, corn syrup, margarine and brandy. Stir in apples. Pour into pie crust. Sprinkle with topping. Bake in 350°F oven 45 to 50 minutes or until puffed and set. Cool completely on wire rack.   *Makes 8 servings*

Praline Topping

1 cup coarsely chopped pecans
¼ cup all-purpose flour
¼ cup packed brown sugar
2 tablespoons MAZOLA® Margarine, softened

In small bowl combine pecans, flour, brown sugar and margarine. Mix with fork until crumbly.

Berry Cheesy Tart

Crust
1 sheet refrigerated pie crust pastry

Filling
2 cups fresh raspberries
1 cup fresh blackberries
1 cup fresh blueberries
¾ cup sugar
¼ cup tapioca
1 tablespoon lemon juice

Streusel Topping
1 cup all-purpose flour
½ cup sugar
1 cup shredded Aged Wisconsin Cheddar cheese
¼ cup butter

Preheat oven to 400°F. Line 9-inch tart pan (removable bottom) with pastry. In large bowl, combine berries, ¾ cup sugar, tapioca and lemon juice; pour into pastry-lined pan. In medium bowl, combine flour, ½ cup sugar and cheese. Cut in butter until crumbs form. Sprinkle over fruit. Bake 50 to 60 minutes or until top is well browned. Cool on wire rack. Remove side of pan and place tart on serving plate.   *Makes 10 servings*

*Favorite recipe from **Wisconsin Milk Marketing Board***

Borden

Elsie, the Borden cow, made her debut in an advertising series for medical journals in 1936. By 1939, Elsie had begun

appearing in national consumer magazines, and later that year, starred in Borden's exhibit at the New York World's Fair. Eventually Elsie replaced the American bald eagle as the logo on Borden's sweetened condensed milk label. By the 1960s, Elsie had become America's best known spokescow—a recognized symbol of wholesomeness and quality.

Impossible Pie

1 (14-ounce) can EAGLE® Brand
    Sweetened Condensed Milk
    (NOT evaporated milk)
1½ cups water
½ cup biscuit baking mix
3 eggs
¼ cup margarine or butter, softened
1½ teaspoons vanilla extract
1 cup flaked coconut

Preheat oven to 350°. In blender container, combine all ingredients except coconut. Blend on low speed 3 minutes. Pour into greased *10-inch* pie plate; let stand 5 minutes. Sprinkle with coconut. Carefully place in oven; bake 35 to 40 minutes or until knife inserted near edge comes out clean. Cool slightly; serve warm or cooled. Refrigerate leftovers.

Makes one 10-inch pie

Traditional Mince Pie

Pastry for 2-crust pie
1 (27-ounce) jar NONE SUCH® Ready-
    to-Use Mincemeat (Regular or
    Brandy & Rum)
1 egg yolk mixed with 2 tablespoons
    water (optional)

Place oven rack in lowest position in oven; preheat oven to 425°. Turn mincemeat into pastry-lined 9-inch pie plate. Cover with top crust; cut slits near center. Seal and flute. Brush egg mixture over crust, if desired. Bake 30 minutes or until golden. Cool. Store covered at room temperature.

Makes one 9-inch pie

Classic Pecan Pie

3 eggs
1 cup sugar
1 cup **KARO®** Light or Dark Corn Syrup
2 tablespoons **MAZOLA®** Margarine, melted
1 teaspoon vanilla
1½ cups pecan halves
1 (9-inch) unbaked or frozen deep dish pie crust*

*If using frozen pie crust, thaw according to package directions before using.

Preheat oven to 350°F. In medium bowl beat eggs slightly. Add sugar, corn syrup, margarine and vanilla; stir until well blended. Stir in pecans. Pour into pie crust. Bake 50 to 55 minutes or until knife inserted halfway between center and edge comes out clean. Cool on wire rack.   *Makes 8 servings*

California Pecan Pie: Stir ¼ cup sour cream into eggs until blended.

Kentucky Bourbon Pecan Pie: Add up to 2 tablespoons bourbon to filling.

Chocolate Pecan Pie: Reduce sugar to ⅓ cup. Melt 4 squares (1 ounce each) semisweet chocolate with margarine.

Almond Amaretto Pie: Substitute 1 cup sliced almonds for pecans. Add 2 tablespoons almond flavored liqueur and ½ teaspoon almond extract to filling.

Pecan Pie

1½ cups **LOG CABIN®** Syrup
3 eggs, slightly beaten
¼ cup sugar
¼ teaspoon salt
1½ cups coarsely chopped pecans or pecan halves
1 unbaked pastry shell (9 inches)

Heat oven to 350°F.

Mix syrup and eggs in medium bowl. Stir in sugar, salt and nuts. Pour into pastry shell.

Bake 1 hour or until knife inserted in center comes out clean. Cool.
Makes 8 to 10 servings

Early packaging for Log Cabin Syrup.

Top to bottom: Almond Amaretto Pie and Classic Pecan Pie

Maple Pecan Pie

Maple Pecan Pie

1 (9-inch) unbaked pastry shell
1 cup CARY'S®, MAPLE ORCHARDS® or
    MACDONALD'S™ Pure Maple Syrup
3 eggs, beaten
½ cup firmly packed light brown sugar
2 tablespoons margarine or butter,
    melted
1 teaspoon vanilla extract
1¼ cups pecan halves or pieces

Place oven rack in lowest position in oven; preheat oven to 350°. In large bowl, combine all ingredients except pastry shell. Pour into pastry shell. Bake 35 to 40 minutes or until golden. Cool. Serve at room temperature or chilled. Refrigerate leftovers.

Makes one 9-inch pie

Libby's® Famous Pumpkin Pie

1 unbaked 9-inch pie crust
2 eggs
1 can (16 ounces) LIBBY'S® Solid Pack
    Pumpkin
1½ cups (12-ounce can) undiluted
    CARNATION® Evaporated Milk
¾ cup granulated sugar
1 teaspoon ground cinnamon
½ teaspoon salt
½ teaspoon ground ginger
¼ teaspoon ground cloves

PREHEAT oven to 425°F.

LINE 9-inch pie plate with crust; decorate edge as desired. Beat eggs lightly in large bowl. Stir in pumpkin, milk, sugar, cinnamon, salt, ginger and cloves; pour into pie crust.

BAKE 15 minutes. *Reduce temperature to 350°F;* bake 40 to 50 minutes or until knife inserted near center comes out clean. Cool on wire rack.   *Makes one 9-inch pie*

Festive Pumpkin Pie

Flaky Pastry Crust (recipe follows)
1 (30-ounce) can pumpkin pie filling
⅔ cup undiluted evaporated milk
½ cup EGG BEATERS® Real Egg
    Product
Nondairy prepared whipped topping,
    for garnish
Orange peel, for garnish

Prepare Flaky Pastry Crust. In large bowl, whisk pie filling, evaporated milk and egg product until well blended. Pour into prepared crust. Bake at 425°F for 15 minutes. *Reduce*

oven temperature to 350°F. Bake 50 to 60 minutes more or until knife inserted 2 inches from center comes out clean. Cool completely. Garnish, if desired.
   Makes 10 servings

Flaky Pastry Crust: Cut ⅓ cup margarine into 1¼ cups all-purpose flour until crumbly. Add 3 to 4 tablespoons ice water, one tablespoon at a time, until moistened. Shape into ball. Roll out to fit 9-inch pie plate. Transfer to plate; trim pastry and pinch to form high fluted edge.

Carnation

In 1899, E. A. Stuart and Thomas E. Yerxa, helped by a Swiss gentleman by the name of Meyerberg, developed a revolutionary method of evaporating milk without the addition of sugar. On the opening day of their factory, 2,744 quarts of fresh milk were condensed to 55 cases of evaporated milk.

ReaLemon® Meringue Pie

1 (9-inch) baked pastry shell
1⅔ cups sugar
6 tablespoons cornstarch
½ cup REALEMON® Lemon Juice from
  Concentrate
4 eggs, separated
1½ cups boiling water
2 tablespoons margarine or butter
¼ teaspoon cream of tartar

Preheat oven to 300°. In heavy saucepan, combine *1⅓ cups* sugar and cornstarch; add ReaLemon® brand. In small bowl, beat egg *yolks;* add to lemon mixture.

Gradually add water, stirring constantly. Over medium heat, cook and stir until mixture boils and thickens, about 8 to 10 minutes. Remove from heat. Add margarine; stir until melted. Pour into prepared pastry shell. In small mixer bowl, beat egg *whites* with cream of tartar until soft peaks form; gradually add remaining *⅓ cup* sugar, beating until stiff but not dry. Spread on top of pie, sealing carefully to edge of shell. Bake 20 to 30 minutes or until golden. Cool. Chill before serving. Refrigerate leftovers.

Makes one 9-inch pie

ReaLime® Meringue Pie: Substitute ReaLime® Lime Juice from Concentrate for ReaLemon® brand. Add green food coloring to filling if desired. Proceed as above.

Creamy Key Lime Tart

Crust

3 cups HONEY ALMOND DELIGHT®
  brand cereal, crushed to 1½ cups
¼ cup packed brown sugar
¼ cup (½ stick) margarine or butter,
  melted

Filling

8 ounces cream cheese, softened
1 can (14 ounces) sweetened
  condensed milk
⅓ cup lime juice
1 teaspoon freshly grated lime peel
2 drops green food coloring (optional)
1 cup nondairy whipped topping

To prepare Crust: Preheat oven to 350°F. In medium bowl combine cereal, sugar and margarine; mix well. Press cereal mixture firmly onto bottom and sides of ungreased 9-inch fluted tart pan or 9-inch pie plate. Bake 8 to 9 minutes or until lightly browned. Cool completely.

To prepare Filling: In large bowl beat cream cheese and milk. Slowly add juice, peel and food coloring, if desired, beating until smooth. Fold in whipped topping. Pour evenly into cooled crust. Chill 1 hour or until set. Garnish with additional lime peel and whipped topping, if desired. *Makes 9 servings*

ReaLemon® Meringue Pie

Key Lime Pie

1 (8- or 9-inch) baked pastry shell or graham cracker crumb crust
3 egg yolks
1 (14-ounce) can EAGLE® Brand Sweetened Condensed Milk (NOT evaporated milk)
½ cup REALIME® Lime Juice from Concentrate
Yellow or green food coloring (optional)
BORDEN® or MEADOW GOLD® Whipping Cream, whipped or whipped topping

Preheat oven to 325°. In large mixer bowl, beat egg *yolks* with sweetened condensed milk, ReaLime® brand and food coloring, if desired. Pour into prepared pastry shell; bake 30 minutes or until set. Cool. Chill. Top with whipped cream. Garnish as desired. Refrigerate leftovers.

Makes one 8- or 9-inch pie

Heavenly Oreo® Angel Pie

3 egg whites
¼ teaspoon salt
⅔ cup sugar
9 Fudge Covered OREO® Chocolate Sandwich Cookies
½ cup PLANTERS® Almonds, finely chopped
1 teaspoon DAVIS® Baking Powder
1 cup heavy cream
1 tablespoon instant coffee granules

In medium bowl, with electric mixer at high speed, beat egg whites and salt until soft peaks form; gradually beat in sugar until stiff and glossy. Coarsely chop 5 cookies. Fold chopped cookies, almonds and baking powder into beaten egg whites. Spread into greased 9-inch pie plate.

Bake at 350°F for 25 to 30 minutes until lightly browned. Cool on wire rack. Beat heavy cream and instant coffee until stiff; spread over pie. Halve remaining cookies; arrange around edge of pie. Chill until serving time. *Makes 8 servings*

No one knows where the name originated, but almost everyone knows the product.

Key Lime Pie

Cherry-Cheese Tart Jubilee

1 container (15 ounces) Wisconsin
    Ricotta cheese
⅓ cup sour cream
⅓ cup sugar
3 tablespoons almond-flavored liqueur
2 tablespoons all-purpose flour
1 teaspoon grated orange peel
¼ teaspoon salt
2 eggs, separated
1 prebaked and cooled 9½-inch
    Tart Shell (recipe follows)
3 cups Northwest frozen pitted dark
    sweet cherries, partially thawed
2 tablespoons red currant jelly, melted
2 to 3 tablespoons toasted sliced
    almonds

Preheat oven to 350°F.

Press cheese through sieve into large bowl. Mix in sour cream, sugar, liqueur, flour, orange peel and salt. Beat in egg yolks. In another bowl beat egg whites to form soft peaks; fold into cheese mixture. Pour into prepared Tart Shell. Bake 50 to 60 minutes until lightly browned, puffy and set. Cool on rack. Just before serving arrange *partially thawed* cherries on tart. Brush cherries with jelly. Garnish with almonds. Serve immediately. *Makes 8 servings*

Tart Shell: Preheat oven to 425°F. In large bowl mix 1 cup flour, 1 tablespoon sugar and ¼ teaspoon salt. Add 6 tablespoons cold butter, cut into chunks. Cut in with pastry blender until mixture resembles coarse meal. Beat 1 egg yolk with 2 tablespoons ice water. Add to flour mixture. Mix with fork and gather into ball. Roll out dough on lightly floured surface into 11-inch circle. Fit into 9½-inch tart pan with removable bottom. Fold pastry overhang back toward inside and press firmly against side of pan, allowing pastry to extend slightly above top. Refrigerate 10 minutes. Prick tart shell all over with fork; line with foil. Fill with pie weights, dried beans or rice. Bake 14 minutes. Remove foil and weights; bake 10 to 15 minutes longer until lightly browned and cooked through. Cool on wire rack.

*Favorite recipe from **Wisconsin Milk Marketing Board***

Mud Pie

1 (14-ounce) can EAGLE® Brand
    Sweetened Condensed Milk
    (NOT evaporated milk)
4 teaspoons vanilla extract
2 cups (1 pint) BORDEN® or MEADOW
    GOLD® Whipping Cream, whipped
    *(do not use nondairy whipped
    topping)*
1 cup coarsely crushed creme-filled
    chocolate sandwich cookies (about
    10 cookies)
1 (9-inch) chocolate crumb crust
    Chocolate fudge ice cream topping or
    chocolate-flavored syrup
    Chopped nuts

In large bowl, combine sweetened condensed milk and vanilla. Fold in whipped cream then cookies. Pour into 9×5-inch loaf pan or other 2-quart container; cover. Freeze 6 hours or until firm. Scoop ice cream into prepared crust. Drizzle with topping. Garnish with nuts. Freeze leftovers. *Makes one 9-inch pie*

Cherry-Cheese Tart Jubilee

Fruit Pizza

1 (20-ounce) package refrigerated
  sliceable sugar cookies
1 (8-ounce) package PHILADELPHIA
  BRAND® Cream Cheese, softened
⅓ cup sugar
½ teaspoon vanilla
  Assorted sliced fruit
½ cup KRAFT® Orange Marmalade,
  Peach or Apricot Preserves
2 tablespoons cold water

• Freeze cookie dough 1 hour.

• Heat oven to 375°F. Slice cookie dough into
⅛-inch slices. Arrange cookie slices, slightly
overlapping, on foil-lined 14-inch pizza pan;
press lightly to form crust.

• Bake 12 minutes or until golden brown.
Cool. Invert onto serving plate; carefully
remove foil. Invert to right side.

• Beat cream cheese, sugar and vanilla in
small bowl with electric mixer on medium
speed until well blended. Spread over crust.

• Arrange fruit over cream cheese layer. Mix
marmalade and water; spoon over fruit.
Refrigerate. Cut into wedges.

Makes 10 to 12 servings

Suggested Fruit Tip: Bananas, kiwi,
strawberries, blueberries, raspberries,
red or green grape halves, pineapple
chunks, maraschino cherry halves, thinly
sliced peaches, pears or apples, or
mandarin orange segments.

Arrange fruit to create a variety of shapes
and designs—try stripes, triangles or circles.

Variation: Substitute Phildelphia Brand® Soft
Cream Cheese for regular Cream Cheese.

Microwave Chocolate Peanut Butter Pie

½ cup sugar
3 tablespoons ARGO® or
  KINGSFORD'S® Corn Starch
2 cups milk
2 egg yolks, slightly beaten
½ cup SKIPPY® Creamy or Super
  Chunk® Peanut Butter
⅓ cup semisweet chocolate chips
1 prepared (9-inch) graham cracker
  crumb crust
1 cup heavy cream
⅓ cup chopped peanuts

In large microwavable bowl combine sugar
and corn starch. Gradually stir in milk, then
egg yolks until smooth. Microwave on HIGH,
stirring 3 times with fork or wire whisk, 7 to 9
minutes or until mixture boils; boil 1 minute.
Stir in peanut butter. In small bowl combine
and stir 1 cup warm peanut butter mixture
and chocolate chips until chocolate melts.
Spread in crust. Cover surface of pie and
remaining peanut butter mixture with plastic
wrap; chill 45 minutes or until cool but not
set. Whip cream until stiff peaks form; gently
fold into remaining peanut butter mixture.
Spoon over chocolate layer in crust.
Refrigerate several hours or overnight. Just
before serving, garnish with peanuts.

Makes 8 servings

Fruit Pizza

Raspberry Razzle Dazzle Tart

1 package DUNCAN HINES® Golden
  Sugar Cookie Mix
1 egg
¼ cup CRISCO® Oil or CRISCO®
  PURITAN® Oil
1½ tablespoons water
½ cup finely chopped almonds
2 packages (8 ounces each) cream
  cheese, softened
2 cups confectioners sugar
½ teaspoon almond extract
1 package (12 ounces) frozen dry pack
  raspberries, thawed
⅓ cup granulated sugar
  Strawberry slices, for garnish
  Kiwifruit slices, for garnish

1. Preheat oven to 350°F. Grease 12-inch
pizza pan.

2. Combine cookie mix, egg, oil, water and
almonds in large bowl. Stir until thoroughly
blended. Spread evenly on pan. Bake at
350°F for 18 to 20 minutes or until edges are
light golden brown. Cool completely.

3. Combine cream cheese, confectioners
sugar and almond extract in medium bowl.
Beat at low speed with electric mixer until
smooth. Spread on cooled crust. Refrigerate
until chilled.

4. Combine raspberries and sugar in small
saucepan. Bring to a boil. Simmer until
berries are soft. Push mixture through sieve
into small bowl. Cool completely. To serve,
cut into wedges. Garnish with strawberry and
kiwifruit slices. Place each wedge on serving
plate with raspberry sauce. Drizzle with
sauce, if desired. Refrigerate leftovers.
Makes 12 to 16 servings

Showboating Margarita Pie

70 Original MR. PHIPPS® Pretzel Chips,
  finely crushed (about 1⅓ cups
  crumbs)
⅓ cup sugar
⅓ cup margarine
1 quart vanilla ice cream, softened
1 (10-ounce) can frozen Margarita
  tropical fruit mixer concentrate,*
  thawed
2 teaspoons grated orange peel
  Few drops green food coloring
  Prepared whipped topping, for
  garnish
  Lime slices, for garnish
  Strawberry halves, for garnish

*One 12-ounce can frozen limeade concentrate
may be substituted.

Combine pretzel chip crumbs, sugar and
margarine. Press onto bottom and side of
9-inch pie plate. Bake at 375°F for 5 to 7
minutes. Cool completely.

Combine ice cream, Margarita concentrate,
orange peel and food coloring until blended.
Spread into prepared crust. Freeze until firm,
about 4 hours.

Let pie stand at room temperature for 10
minutes before serving. Garnish with
whipped topping, lime slices and strawberry
halves.   *Makes 6 to 8 servings*

Raspberry Razzle Dazzle Tart

Cool 'n' Easy Pie

⅔ cup boiling water
1 package (4-serving size) JELL-O
    Brand Gelatin Dessert, any flavor
½ cup cold water
    Ice cubes
1 tub (8 ounces) COOL WHIP Whipped
    Topping, thawed
1 prepared graham cracker crumb crust
    (6 ounces)
    Assorted fruit (optional)

STIR boiling water into gelatin in large bowl 2 minutes or until completely dissolved. Mix cold water and ice to make 1¼ cups. Add to gelatin, stirring until slightly thickened. Remove any remaining ice.

STIR in whipped topping with wire whisk until smooth. Refrigerate 10 to 15 minutes or until mixture is very thick and will mound. Spoon into crust.

REFRIGERATE 4 hours or until firm. Just before serving, garnish with fruit, if desired. Store leftover pie in refrigerator.

Makes 8 servings

Ritz® Mock Apple Pie

Pastry for two-crust 9-inch pie
36 RITZ® Crackers, coarsely broken
    (about 1¾ cups crumbs)
1¾ cups water
2 cups sugar
2 teaspoons cream of tartar
2 tablespoons lemon juice
    Grated rind of 1 lemon
2 tablespoons margarine
½ teaspoon ground cinnamon

Roll out half of pastry and line 9-inch pie plate. Place cracker crumbs in prepared crust. In saucepan, over high heat, heat water, sugar and cream of tartar to a boil; simmer 15 minutes. Add lemon juice and rind; cool. Pour syrup over cracker crumbs. Dot with margarine; sprinkle with cinnamon. Roll out remaining pastry; place over pie. Trim, seal and flute edges. Slit top crust to allow steam to escape.

Bake at 425°F for 30 to 35 minutes or until crust is crisp and golden. Serve warm or let cool completely before serving.

Makes 10 servings

Historical ad for the "dessert that can be made in a minute."

Cool 'n' Easy Pies

Coconut Lime Pie

1 (9-inch) baked pastry shell or graham
    cracker crumb crust
1 cup water
¼ cup cornstarch
3 tablespoons REALIME® Lime Juice
    from Concentrate
4 eggs, separated*
1 (15-ounce) can COCO LOPEZ® Cream
    of Coconut
¼ teaspoon cream of tartar
6 tablespoons sugar
2 tablespoons flaked coconut

*Use only Grade A clean, uncracked eggs.

Preheat oven to 350°. In heavy saucepan,
combine water, cornstarch and ReaLime®
brand; mix well. In small bowl, beat egg
yolks; add to lime mixture. Add cream of
coconut; mix well. Over medium heat, cook
and stir until mixture boils and thickens, about
12 to 15 minutes. Pour into prepared pastry
shell. In small mixer bowl, beat egg whites
with cream of tartar to form soft peaks;
gradually add sugar, beating until stiff but not
dry. Spread on top of pie, sealing carefully to
edge of pastry shell. Top with coconut. Bake
12 to 15 minutes or until golden. Cool. Chill.
Refrigerate leftovers.

Makes one 9-inch pie

Tip: 1 cup (½ pint) BORDEN® or MEADOW
GOLD® Whipping Cream, whipped, *or*
1 (4-ounce) container frozen nondairy
whipped topping (1¾ cups), thawed, can be
substituted for meringue (omit egg whites,
sugar and cream of tartar). Cool pie to room
temperature before topping with whipped
cream. Chill before serving.

Classic Crisco® Crust

8-, 9- or 10-inch Single Crust
1⅓ cups all-purpose flour
 ½ teaspoon salt
 ½ cup CRISCO® Shortening
 3 tablespoons cold water

8- or 9-inch Double Crust
 2 cups all-purpose flour
 1 teaspoon salt
 ¾ cup CRISCO® Shortening
 5 tablespoons cold water

10-inch Double Crust
 2⅔ cups all-purpose flour
 1 teaspoon salt
 1 cup CRISCO® Shortening
 7 to 8 tablespoons cold water

1. Spoon flour into measuring cup and level.
Combine flour and salt in medium bowl.

2. Cut in Crisco® using pastry blender (or
2 knives) until all flour is blended to form
pea-size chunks.

3. Sprinkle with water, 1 tablespoon at a time.
Toss lightly with fork until dough forms a ball.

For Single Crust Pies
1. Press dough between hands to form 5- to
6-inch "pancake." Flour rolling surface and
rolling pin lightly. Roll dough into circle.

2. Trim 1 inch larger than upside-down pie
plate. Loosen dough carefully.

3. Fold dough into quarters. Unfold and press
into pie plate. Fold edge under. Flute.

For Baked Pie Crusts
1. For recipes using baked pie crust, heat
oven to 425°F. Prick bottom and side
thoroughly with fork (50 times) to prevent
shrinkage.

By 1912, Crisco® was being widely advertised as "An absolutely new product—a scientific discovery which will affect every kitchen in America."

2. Bake at 425°F for 10 to 15 minutes or until lightly browned.

For Unbaked Pie Crusts
1. For recipes using unbaked pie crust, follow baking directions given in each recipe.

For Double Crust Pies
1. Divide dough in half. Roll each half separately. Transfer bottom crust to pie plate. Trim edge even with pie plate.

2. Add desired filling to unbaked pie crust. Moisten pastry edge with water. Lift top crust onto filled pie. Trim ½ inch beyond edge of pie plate. Fold top edge under bottom crust. Flute. Cut slits in top crust to allow steam to escape. Bake according to specific recipe directions.

Cherry Danish

2½ to 3 cups all-purpose flour
1 package (¼ ounce) quick-rising yeast
¼ teaspoon salt
¾ cup milk
¼ cup sugar
   Butter or margarine
1 egg
4 ounces almond paste
2 tablespoons light corn syrup
1½ cups pitted and chopped Northwest
   fresh sweet cherries
2 tablespoons sugar
½ teaspoon ground cinnamon

In large bowl, combine 1 cup flour, yeast and salt. In small saucepan, heat milk, sugar and ¼ cup butter to 125° to 130°F. Add warm milk mixture to flour mixture; beat until smooth. Add egg; blend well. Add remaining flour to make soft dough. Knead until smooth and elastic. Cover; let rest 10 minutes.

Roll dough on lightly floured surface to 18×11-inch rectangle; spread with 2 tablespoons softened butter. In small bowl, combine almond paste and corn syrup; spread over butter layer. Combine cherries, sugar and cinnamon; spoon over almond paste. Roll up jelly-roll fashion starting at long edge. Cut into 16 rolls.

Place on greased baking sheet; cover and let rise about 45 minutes or until doubled in bulk. Bake in 375°F oven 15 to 20 minutes or until golden.   *Makes 16 rolls*

*Favorite recipe from **Northwest Cherry Growers***

Mott's® Lots O'Apple Pizza

2 cups MOTT'S® Natural Apple Sauce
1 teaspoon vanilla extract
¾ teaspoon active dry yeast
½ teaspoon granulated sugar
½ cup plus 1 tablespoon warm water
   (105° to 115°F)
1¼ cups all-purpose flour
½ teaspoon salt
⅔ cup raisins
2 cups unpeeled, thinly sliced tart
   apples (about 2 medium)
   Additional raisins (optional)
2 tablespoons powdered sugar

1. In medium saucepan, combine apple sauce and vanilla. Cook over medium heat, stirring occasionally, until reduced by half.

2. In small bowl, sprinkle yeast and granulated sugar over warm water; stir until yeast dissolves. Let stand 5 minutes or until mixture is bubbly.

3. In medium bowl, combine flour and salt. Make well in center of mixture.

4. Pour yeast mixture into flour mixture; stir until soft dough forms. Let rise 5 minutes. Turn out dough onto floured surface; flatten slightly. Knead 5 to 10 minutes or until smooth and elastic. Shape dough into ball; place dough in large bowl sprayed with nonstick cooking spray. Turn dough over so that top is greased. Cover with towel; let rise in warm place 45 minutes to 1 hour or until doubled in bulk.

5. Punch down dough; let rise about 30 minutes in warm place or until doubled in bulk.

Mott's® Lots O'Apple Pizza

6. Preheat oven to 450°F. Spray 12-inch pizza pan with nonstick cooking spray.

7. Spread dough or roll with lightly floured rolling pin into 12-inch circle. Place in prepared pan. Spread half of apple sauce mixture over dough to within ½ inch of edge. Sprinkle with ⅔ cup raisins. Arrange apple slices over pizza, covering raisins. Spread remaining apple sauce mixture over apple slices.

8. Bake 15 to 20 minutes or until edge of crust is lightly browned. Cool completely on wire rack. Garnish with additional raisins, if desired. Sprinkle with powdered sugar. Cut into 12 wedges.   *Makes 12 servings*

Black Forest Parfaits

1 package (8 ounces) PHILADELPHIA BRAND® Cream Cheese, softened
2 cups cold milk
1 package (4-serving size) JELL-O Chocolate Flavor Instant Pudding & Pie Filling
1 can (21 ounces) cherry pie filling
1 tablespoon cherry liqueur
½ cup chocolate wafer cookie crumbs

BEAT cream cheese with ½ cup milk at low speed until smooth. Add pudding mix and remaining milk. Beat until smooth, 1 to 2 minutes.

MIX cherry pie filling and liqueur. Reserve a few cherries for garnish, if desired. Spoon ½ of pudding mixture evenly into individual dessert dishes; sprinkle with cookie crumbs. Top with pie filling, then with remaining pudding mixture. Refrigerate until ready to serve. Garnish with reserved cherries and additional cookie crumbs, if desired.

Makes 4 to 6 servings

Quick Creamy Chocolate Pudding

⅔ cup sugar
¼ cup HERSHEY®S Cocoa
3 tablespoons cornstarch
¼ teaspoon salt
2¼ cups milk
2 tablespoons butter or margarine
1 teaspoon vanilla extract
Whipped topping (optional)
Chopped nuts (optional)

In medium saucepan, stir together sugar, cocoa, cornstarch and salt; gradually stir in milk. Cook over medium heat, stirring constantly, until mixture boils; boil and stir 1 minute. Remove from heat; stir in butter and vanilla. Pour into individual dessert dishes. Press plastic wrap directly onto surface; refrigerate. Remove plastic wrap. Garnish with whipped topping and chopped nuts, if desired.

Makes 4 to 5 servings

Crème Caramel

¾ cup sugar, divided
2 cups 2% milk
1 carton (8 ounces) HEALTHY CHOICE® Cholesterol Free Egg Product
½ teaspoon vanilla extract

Place ½ cup sugar in heavy saucepan. Cook over low heat until sugar melts and turns golden brown. Pour immediately into 6 custard cups; let cool. In medium bowl, combine milk, egg product, remaining ¼ cup sugar and vanilla. Stir until sugar dissolves. Pour into custard cups. Place cups into baking pan; fill pan with 1 inch hot water. Bake in 350°F oven 50 minutes or until custard is soft set in center. Chill in refrigerator. To serve, run knife around edge of cups and unmold onto serving plate.

Makes 6 servings

Black Forest Parfait

Tiramisú

6 egg yolks
½ cup sugar
⅓ cup Cognac or brandy
2 cups (15 ounces) SARGENTO® Old
    Fashioned Ricotta Cheese
1 cup whipping cream, whipped
32 ladyfingers, split in half
3 teaspoons instant coffee dissolved in
    ¾ cup of boiling water
1 tablespoon unsweetened cocoa
    Chocolate curls (optional; see tip
    below)

In top of double boiler, whisk together egg yolks, sugar and Cognac. Place pan over simmering water. Cook, whisking constantly, until mixture is thickened, about 2 to 3 minutes. Cool. In large bowl of electric mixer, beat yolk mixture and ricotta cheese on medium speed until blended. Fold in whipped cream.

Place half of ladyfingers in bottom of 13×9-inch pan, cut side up. Brush with half of coffee; spread with half of ricotta mixture. Repeat layers. Chill 2 hours. Just before serving, dust with cocoa; cut into squares. Garnish with chocolate curls.

Makes 16 servings

Tip: To prepare chocolate curls, combine ½ cup semisweet chocolate chips with 2 teaspoons solid shortening in 2-cup microwavable (or glass) bowl. Microwave at HIGH 1 minute. Stir until chocolate is completely melted. Spread evenly into thin layer on small cookie sheet; cool. Hold small pancake turner upside-down at 45° angle to cookie sheet. Run pancake turner across chocolate, allowing chocolate to curl.

Strawberry Banana Dessert

1 (14-ounce) can EAGLE® Brand
    Sweetened Condensed Milk
    (NOT evaporated milk)
1 cup cold water
1 (4-serving size) package instant
    vanilla flavor pudding mix
2 cups (1 pint) BORDEN® or MEADOW
    GOLD® Whipping Cream, stiffly
    whipped
1 pint fresh strawberries, cleaned,
    hulled and sliced
2 bananas, sliced and dipped in
    REALEMON® Lemon Juice from
    Concentrate
1 (10¾- or 12-ounce) prepared loaf
    pound cake, cut in 12 slices
    Additional strawberries and banana
    slices

In large bowl, combine sweetened condensed milk and water. Add pudding mix; beat well. Chill 5 minutes. Fold in whipped cream, strawberries and bananas. Line side and bottom of 3½-quart glass serving bowl with cake slices. Spoon pudding mixture into prepared bowl. Cover; chill. Garnish with additional strawberries and banana slices. Refrigerate leftovers.

Makes 10 to 12 servings

Tiramisú

From left: Vanilla Rice Pudding and Double Chocolate Rice Pudding (page 335)

Vanilla Rice Pudding

1 package (4-serving size) JELL-O
    Vanilla Flavor Cook & Serve
    Pudding & Pie Filling
4 cups milk
1 egg, well beaten
1 cup MINUTE® Original Rice, uncooked
¼ cup raisins (optional)
    Ground cinnamon (optional)
    Ground nutmeg (optional)

STIR pudding mix into milk and egg in large saucepan. Stir in rice and raisins. Cook and stir on medium heat until mixture just comes to a full boil. Cool 5 minutes, stirring twice.

POUR into individual dessert dishes or serving bowl. Serve warm or refrigerate, if desired. (Place plastic wrap on surface of pudding while cooling.) Sprinkle with cinnamon and nutmeg just before serving.

Makes 10 servings

Double Chocolate Rice Pudding: Prepare as directed above, using Chocolate Flavor Pudding & Pie Filling. Stir in 2 squares BAKER'S® Semi-Sweet Chocolate, chopped, with rice. Omit raisins, cinnamon and nutmeg.

Rainbow Ribbon Dessert

6¼ cups boiling water
5 packages (4-serving size) JELL-O Brand Gelatin Dessert or Sugar Free Gelatin Dessert, any 5 flavors
1 cup (½ pint) BREAKSTONE'S® Sour Cream or plain or vanilla flavored yogurt

STIR 1¼ cups boiling water into 1 flavor of gelatin in small bowl 2 minutes or until completely dissolved. Pour ¾ cup into 9-inch square pan or 6-cup ring mold. Refrigerate about 15 minutes until set but not firm (sticks to finger when touched).

REFRIGERATE remaining gelatin in bowl about 5 minutes until slightly thickened (consistency of unbeaten egg whites); gradually stir in 3 tablespoons sour cream and spoon over gelatin in pan. Refrigerate about 15 minutes until set but not firm (sticks to finger when touched).

REPEAT process with each remaining gelatin flavor, refrigerating dissolved gelatin as directed to create layers.

REFRIGERATE 2 hours or until firm. Cut into squares or unmold. Garnish with whipped topping, if desired. Store leftover dessert in refrigerator.

Makes about 6 cups or 12 servings

JELL-O®
BRAND

It all began with famous inventor Peter Cooper of Tom Thumb Locomotive fame. He was granted the first patent for a gelatin dessert in 1845. Fifty years later, Pearl B. Wait, a cough medicine manufacturer, produced an adaptation of Cooper's idea and his wife coined the name for it— "JELL-O." Unfortunately, people were not interested in the newfangled gelatin dessert, so in 1899 Pearl Wait sold the JELL-O business to his neighbor, Orator F. Woodward, for $450. By 1904, the business was thriving thanks in part to an advertising campaign employing the face of a beautiful little girl named Elizabeth King, who became known as the "JELL-O Girl." The JELL-O Girl helped launch a theme that still holds true today—"You can't be a kid without it."

Bavarian Rice Cloud with Bittersweet Chocolate Sauce

1 envelope unflavored gelatin
1½ cups skim milk
3 tablespoons sugar
2 cups cooked rice
2 cups frozen light whipped topping, thawed
1 tablespoon almond-flavored liqueur
½ teaspoon vanilla extract
  Vegetable cooking spray
  Bittersweet Chocolate Sauce (recipe follows)
2 tablespoons sliced almonds, toasted

Sprinkle gelatin over milk in small saucepan; let stand 1 minute or until gelatin is softened. Cook over low heat, stirring constantly, until gelatin dissolves. Add sugar and stir until dissolved. Add rice; stir until well blended. Cover and chill until the consistency of unbeaten egg whites. Fold in whipped topping, liqueur, and vanilla. Spoon into 4-cup mold coated with cooking spray. Cover and chill until firm. Unmold onto serving platter. Spoon Bittersweet Chocolate Sauce over rice dessert. Sprinkle with almonds.

Makes 10 servings

Bittersweet Chocolate Sauce

3 tablespoons cocoa
3 tablespoons sugar
½ cup low-fat buttermilk
1 tablespoon almond-flavored liqueur

Combine cocoa and sugar in small saucepan. Add buttermilk, mixing well. Place over medium heat; cook until sugar dissolves. Stir in liqueur; remove from heat.

*Favorite recipe from **USA Rice Council***

Original Banana Pudding

½ cup sugar
3 tablespoons all-purpose flour
  Dash salt
4 eggs
2 cups milk
½ teaspoon vanilla extract
43 NILLA® Wafers
5 to 6 ripe bananas, sliced (about 4 cups)

Reserve 2 tablespoons sugar. In top of double boiler, combine remaining sugar, flour and salt. Beat in 1 whole egg and 3 egg yolks; reserve 3 egg whites. Stir in milk. Cook, uncovered, over boiling water, stirring constantly 10 minutes or until thickened. Remove from heat; stir in vanilla.

In bottom of 1½-quart round casserole, spoon ½ cup custard; cover with 8 wafers. Top with generous layer of sliced bananas; pour ⅔ cup custard over bananas. Arrange 10 wafers around outside edge of dish; cover custard with 11 wafers. Top with sliced bananas and ⅔ cup custard. Cover custard with 14 wafers; top with sliced bananas and remaining custard.

In small bowl, with electric mixer at high speed, beat reserved egg whites until soft peaks form. Gradually add reserved 2 tablespoons sugar, beating until mixture forms stiff peaks. Spoon on top of custard, spreading to cover entire surface.

Bake at 425°F for 5 minutes, or until surface is lightly browned. Garnish with additional banana slices if desired. Serve warm or cold.

Makes 8 servings

**Bavarian Rice Cloud with
Bittersweet Chocolate Sauce**

Fudgy Rocky Road Ice Cream

5 (1-ounce) squares unsweetened chocolate, melted
1 (14-ounce) can EAGLE® Brand Sweetened Condensed Milk (NOT evaporated milk)
2 teaspoons vanilla extract
2 cups (1 pint) BORDEN® or MEADOW GOLD® Half-and-Half
2 cups (1 pint) BORDEN® or MEADOW GOLD® Whipping Cream, unwhipped
1½ cups CAMPFIRE® Miniature Marshmallows
¾ cup chopped peanuts

In large mixer bowl, beat chocolate, sweetened condensed milk and vanilla until well blended. Stir in remaining ingredients. Pour into ice cream freezer container. Freeze according to manufacturer's instructions. Freeze leftovers. *Makes about 2 quarts*

Let the Good Times Roll Pinwheels

1 quart softened ice cream, any flavor
1½ cups TEDDY GRAHAMS® Graham Snacks, any flavor, divided
1 quart softened sherbet, any flavor
Chocolate fudge sauce, for garnish
Prepared whipped topping, for garnish
Colored sprinkles, for garnish

Spread ice cream evenly on 15½×10½×1-inch baking pan lined with waxed paper; sprinkle with 1¼ cups graham snacks. Freeze until firm, about 40 minutes. Spread sherbet over graham snack layer. Freeze until firm, about 2 to 3 hours.

Beginning at short end, roll up frozen layers, removing waxed paper; place on serving dish. Cover and freeze at least 1 hour.

To serve, garnish with chocolate fudge sauce, whipped topping, sprinkles and remaining graham snacks. Slice and serve immediately.
Makes 12 servings

Easy Fresh Lemon Ice Cream

2 cups heavy cream or whipping cream or half-and-half
1 cup sugar
Grated peel of 1 SUNKIST® Lemon
⅓ cup fresh squeezed lemon juice

In large bowl, combine cream and sugar; stir to dissolve sugar. Add lemon peel and juice; continue stirring. (Mixture will thicken slightly.) Pour into shallow pan; freeze until firm, about 4 hours. Serve in dessert dishes. Garnish with fresh mint leaves and strawberries, if desired. *Makes 6 to 10 servings*

Lemon and Fruit Variation: Stir ½ cup mashed strawberries, bananas or kiwifruit into slightly thickened lemon mixture before freezing. Makes about 3½ cups.

It was in 1937 in the kitchen of a Massachusett's country inn that the first chocolate chip cookie emerged. This scrumptious concoction was an immediate hit at the inn and wherever else the recipe spread, but the cookies remained a homemade treat. In 1963, Nabisco introduced Chips Ahoy!® Chocolate Chip cookies, the company's first commercially produced chocolate chip cookie with homemade flavor. The product name came about when a simple play on words captured everyone's imagination. The nautical cry "Ships ahoy!" became a descriptive boast of chip-laden cookies, "Chips Ahoy!"

Chipwiches

24 CHIPS AHOY!® Chocolate Chip Cookies
3 cups any flavor ice cream, sherbet, frozen yogurt or whipped topping
Sprinkles, chocolate chips, chopped nuts, toasted or tinted coconut, or other assorted small candies

Spread ice cream about ¾ inch thick on flat side of one cookie. Place another cookie on top. Roll or lightly press edges in sprinkles. Repeat. Freeze until firm, about 4 hours.
Makes 12 servings

Peanut Butter Chipwiches: Spread about 1 tablespoon peanut butter on flat side of each of two Chips Ahoy!® Cookies. Place banana slice in center of peanut butter on one cookie; top with other cookie, peanut butter side down. Continue as above.

Cherry Cheesecake Ice Cream

1 (3-ounce) package cream cheese, softened
1 (14-ounce) can EAGLE® Brand Sweetened Condensed Milk (NOT evaporated milk)
2 cups (1 pint) BORDEN® or MEADOW GOLD® Half-and-Half
2 cups (1 pint) BORDEN® or MEADOW GOLD® Whipping Cream, unwhipped
1 (10-ounce) jar maraschino cherries, well drained and chopped (about 1 cup)
1 tablespoon vanilla extract
½ teaspoon almond extract

In large mixer bowl, beat cheese until fluffy. Gradually beat in sweetened condensed milk until smooth. Add remaining ingredients; mix well. Pour into ice cream freezer container. Freeze according to manufacturer's instructions. Freeze leftovers.
Makes about 1½ quarts

Great-Tasting Cookies & Candies

Everyone loves cookies! Who can resist family favorites like luscious chocolate chip, old-fashioned sugar, fudgy brownie and yummy peanut butter cookies? Discover how these cookies, candies and bars can add a special touch to any get-together.

Chewy Brownie Cookies

1½ cups firmly packed light brown sugar
⅔ CRISCO® Stick (⅔ cup)
1 tablespoon water
1 teaspoon vanilla
2 eggs
1½ cups all-purpose flour
⅓ cup unsweetened baking cocoa
¼ teaspoon baking soda
½ teaspoon salt
2 cups semi-sweet chocolate chips
   (12-ounce package)

1. **Heat** oven to 375°F. **Place** sheets of foil on countertop for cooling cookies.

2. **Combine** brown sugar, shortening, water and vanilla in large bowl. **Beat** at medium speed of electric mixer until well blended. **Beat** eggs into creamed mixture.

3. **Combine** flour, cocoa, baking soda and salt. Mix into creamed mixture at low speed just until blended. **Stir** in chocolate chips.

4. **Drop** rounded measuring tablespoonfuls of dough 2 inches apart onto ungreased baking sheet.

5. **Bake** one baking sheet at a time at 375°F for 7 to 9 minutes, or until cookies are set. DO NOT OVERBAKE. **Cool** 2 minutes on baking sheet. **Remove** cookies to foil to cool completely.

Makes about 3 dozen cookies

Chewy Brownie Cookies

Original Nestlé® Toll House® Chocolate Chip Cookies

2¼ cups all-purpose flour
 1 teaspoon baking soda
 1 teaspoon salt
 1 cup (2 sticks) butter, softened
 ¾ cup granulated sugar
 ¾ cup packed brown sugar
 1 teaspoon vanilla extract
 2 eggs
 2 cups (12-ounce package) NESTLÉ®
   TOLL HOUSE® Semi-Sweet
   Chocolate Morsels
 1 cup chopped nuts

COMBINE flour, baking soda and salt in small bowl. Beat butter, granulated sugar, brown sugar and vanilla in large mixer bowl. Add eggs, one at a time, beating well after each addition; gradually beat in flour mixture. Stir in morsels and nuts. Drop by rounded tablespoons onto ungreased baking sheets.

BAKE in preheated 375°F oven 9 to 11 minutes or until golden brown. Let stand for 2 minutes; remove to wire racks to cool completely.

Makes about 5 dozen cookies

Pan Cookie Variation: Prepare dough as above. Spread into greased 15×10-inch jelly-roll pan. Bake in preheated 375°F oven 20 to 25 minutes or until golden brown. Cool in pan on wire rack. Makes about 4 dozen bars.

Slice and Bake Cookie Variation: Prepare dough as above. Divide in half; wrap in waxed paper. Chill 1 hour or until firm. Shape each half into 15-inch log; wrap in waxed paper. Chill for 30 minutes.* Cut into ½-inch-thick slices; place on ungreased baking sheets. Bake in preheated 375°F oven 8 to 10 minutes or until golden brown. Let stand 2 minutes; remove to wire racks to cool completely. Makes about 5 dozen cookies.

*May be stored in refrigerator for up to 1 week or in freezer for up to 8 weeks.

NestléFoods® *The Nestlé® Toll House®*

Morsels story began in the 1930s when Ruth Wakefield, owner of the Toll House Inn, broke bits of a Nestlé Semi-Sweet chocolate bar into her cookie dough. She expected the chocolate "morsels" to melt, but instead they held their shape, softening slightly to a delicate, creamy texture. Thus the Toll House Cookie was born. The rest is history! Ruth Wakefield's recipe has appeared on more than 2 billion packages of Nestlé Toll House Morsels.

*Original Nestlé® Toll House®
Chocolate Chip Cookies*

Reese's® Chewy Chocolate Cookies

2 cups all-purpose flour
¾ cup HERSHEY®S Cocoa
1 teaspoon baking soda
½ teaspoon salt
1¼ cups (2½ sticks) butter or margarine, softened
2 cups sugar
2 eggs
2 teaspoons vanilla extract
1⅔ cups (10-ounce package) REESE'S® Peanut Butter Chips

Heat oven to 350°F. Stir together flour, cocoa, baking soda and salt. In large mixer bowl, beat butter and sugar until light and fluffy. Add eggs and vanilla; beat well. Gradually add flour mixture, beating well. Stir in peanut butter chips. Drop by rounded teaspoonfuls onto ungreased cookie sheet. Bake 8 to 9 minutes. *(Do not overbake; cookies will be soft. They will puff while baking and flatten while cooling.)* Cool slightly; remove from cookie sheet to wire rack. Cool completely.
Makes about 4½ dozen cookies

Pan Recipe: Spread batter in greased 15½×10½×1-inch jelly-roll pan. Bake at 350°F, 20 minutes or until set. Cool completely in pan on wire rack; cut into bars. Makes about 4 dozen bars.

Ice Cream Sandwiches: Prepare Chewy Chocolate Cookies as directed; cool. Press small scoop of vanilla ice cream between flat sides of cookies. Wrap and freeze.

Located near Chicago, Sokol & Company manufactures and markets Solo and Baker brand retail products as well as ingredients for the baking industry. Solo & Baker fruit and nut cake and pastry fillings can be found in the baking section of the supermarket. The company was established in 1895 by John A. Sokol and has been continuously operated by his family for four generations. Sokol & Company celebrated their centennial year in 1995.

Chocolate-Dipped Almond Horns

1 can SOLO® Almond Paste
3 egg whites
½ cup superfine sugar
½ teaspoon almond extract
¼ cup plus 2 tablespoons all-purpose flour
½ cup sliced almonds
5 squares (1 ounce each) semisweet chocolate, melted and cooled

Preheat oven to 350°F. Grease 2 cookie sheets; set aside. Break almond paste into small pieces and place in medium bowl or food processor container. Add egg whites, sugar and almond extract. Beat with electric mixer or process until mixture is very smooth. Add flour and beat or process until blended.

Spoon almond mixture into pastry bag fitted with ½-inch (#8) plain tip. Pipe mixture into 5- or 6-inch crescent shapes on prepared cookie sheets, about 1½ inches apart. Sprinkle with sliced almonds.

Bake 13 to 15 minutes or until edges are golden brown. Cool on cookie sheets on wire racks 2 minutes. Remove from cookie sheets and cool completely on wire racks. Dip ends of cookies in melted chocolate and place on aluminum foil. Let stand until chocolate is set.

Makes about 16 cookies

Snow-Covered Almond Crescents

1 cup (2 sticks) margarine or butter, softened
¾ cup powdered sugar
½ teaspoon almond extract *or*
 2 teaspoons vanilla
1¾ cups all-purpose flour
¼ teaspoon salt (optional)
1 cup QUAKER® Oats (quick or old fashioned, uncooked)
½ cup finely chopped almonds
 Powdered sugar

Preheat oven to 325°F. Beat margarine, sugar and almond extract until fluffy. Add flour and salt; mix until well blended. Stir in oats and almonds. Using level measuring tablespoonfuls, shape dough into crescents. Bake on ungreased cookie sheet 14 to 17

minutes or until bottoms are light golden brown. Remove to wire rack. Sift additional powdered sugar generously over warm cookies. Cool completely. Store tightly covered.   *Makes about 3 dozen cookies*

Quaker Oats

The Quaker man was America's first registered trademark for a breakfast cereal. The name was chosen when Quaker Mill partner Henry Seymour found an encyclopedia article on Quakers and decided that the qualities described—integrity, honesty and purity—provided an appropriate identity for his company's oat product. In the late 1800s, Seymour joined forces with two other Midwest milling companies to form The Quaker Oats Company. They began to process and sell high-quality oats that were superior in quality to the oats sold in open barrels at general stores.

Peanut Blossoms

1 bag (9 ounces) HERSHEY'S KISSES®
    Milk Chocolates
½ cup shortening
¾ cup REESE'S® Creamy or Crunchy
    Peanut Butter
⅓ cup granulated sugar
⅓ cup packed light brown sugar
1 egg
2 tablespoons milk
1 teaspoon vanilla extract
1½ cups all-purpose flour
1 teaspoon baking soda
½ teaspoon salt
    Granulated sugar

Heat oven to 375°F. Remove wrappers from chocolate pieces. In large mixer bowl, beat shortening and peanut butter until well blended. Add ⅓ cup granulated sugar and brown sugar; beat until light and fluffy. Add egg, milk and vanilla; beat well.

Stir together flour, baking soda and salt; gradually add to peanut butter mixture. Shape dough into 1-inch balls. Roll in granulated sugar; place on ungreased cookie sheet. Bake 10 to 12 minutes or until lightly browned. Immediately place chocolate piece on top of each cookie, pressing down so cookie cracks around edges. Remove from cookie sheet to wire rack. Cool completely.

Makes about 4 dozen cookies

HERSHEY'S

A Century of Excellence

1894   1994

Hershey's 100th anniversary logo.

Irresistible Peanut Butter Cookies

1¼ cups firmly packed light brown sugar
¾ cup creamy peanut butter
½ CRISCO® Stick (½ cup)
3 tablespoons milk
1 tablespoon vanilla
1 egg
1¾ cups all-purpose flour
¾ teaspoon salt
¾ teaspoon baking soda

1. **Heat** oven to 375°F. **Place** sheets of foil on countertop for cooling cookies.

Irresistible Peanut Butter Cookies

2. **Combine** brown sugar, peanut butter, shortening, milk and vanilla in large bowl. **Beat** at medium speed of electric mixer until well blended. **Add** egg. **Beat** just until blended.

3. **Combine** flour, salt and baking soda. **Add** to creamed mixture at low speed. Mix just until blended.

4. **Drop** by heaping teaspoonfuls of dough 2 inches apart onto ungreased baking sheet. **Flatten** slightly in crisscross pattern with tines of fork.

5. **Bake** one baking sheet at a time at 375°F for 7 to 8 minutes, or until set and just beginning to brown. DO NOT OVERBAKE. **Cool** 2 minutes on baking sheet. **Remove** cookies to foil to cool completely.

Makes about 3 dozen cookies

Peanut Butter Bears

1 cup **SKIPPY® Creamy Peanut Butter**
1 cup **MAZOLA® Margarine, softened**
1 cup **packed brown sugar**
⅔ cup **KARO® Light or Dark Corn Syrup**
2 **eggs**
4 cups **flour, divided**
1 tablespoon **baking powder**
1 teaspoon **cinnamon (optional)**
¼ teaspoon **salt**

In large bowl with mixer at medium speed, beat peanut butter, margarine, brown sugar, corn syrup and eggs until smooth. Reduce speed; beat in 2 cups flour, baking powder, cinnamon and salt. With spoon, stir in remaining 2 cups flour. Wrap dough in plastic wrap; refrigerate 2 hours.

Preheat oven to 325°F. Divide dough in half; set aside half. On floured surface, roll out half the dough to ⅛-inch thickness. Cut with floured bear cookie cutter. Repeat with remaining dough. Bake on ungreased cookie sheets 10 minutes or until lightly browned. Remove from cookie sheets; cool completely on wire rack. Decorate as desired.

Makes about 3 dozen bears

Note: Use scraps of dough to make bear faces. Make one small ball of dough for muzzle. Form 3 smaller balls of dough and press gently to create eyes and nose; bake as directed. If desired, use frosting to create paws, ears and bow ties.

Choco-Dipped Peanut Butter Cookies

1 (14-ounce) can **EAGLE® Brand Sweetened Condensed Milk (NOT evaporated milk)**
¾ to 1 cup **peanut butter**
1 **egg**
1 teaspoon **vanilla extract**
2 cups **biscuit baking mix**
1 pound **EAGLE™ Brand Chocolate-Flavored Candy Coating, melted**

Preheat oven to 350°. In large mixer bowl, beat sweetened condensed milk, peanut butter, egg and vanilla until smooth. Add biscuit mix; mix well. Cover; chill at least 1 hour. Shape into 1-inch balls. Place 2 inches apart on ungreased baking sheets. Bake 10 to 12 minutes or until *lightly* browned (*do not overbake*). Cool. Partially dip cookies into warm melted candy coating. Place on waxed paper-lined baking sheets. Let stand until firm. Store tightly covered at room temperature.   *Makes about 5 dozen*

Peanut Butter Bears

Cherry Pinwheel Slices

2 cups all-purpose flour
½ teaspoon salt
1 cup butter or margarine
1 cup dairy sour cream
1 can SOLO® *or* 1 jar BAKER® Cherry, Raspberry or Strawberry Filling, divided
1 cup flaked coconut, divided
1 cup finely chopped pecans, divided
Confectioner's sugar

Place flour and salt in medium bowl. Cut in butter until mixture resembles coarse crumbs. Add sour cream; stir until blended. Divide dough into 4 pieces. Wrap each piece separately in plastic wrap or waxed paper; refrigerate 2 to 4 hours.

Preheat oven to 350°F. Roll out dough, 1 piece at a time, on lightly floured surface into 12×6-inch rectangle. Spread one-fourth of filling over dough and sprinkle with ¼ cup coconut and ¼ cup pecans. Roll up, jelly-roll style, starting from short side. Pinch seam to seal. Place, seam side down, on ungreased cookie sheets. Repeat with remaining dough, filling, coconut and pecans.

Bake 40 to 45 minutes or until rolls are golden brown. Remove from cookie sheets to wire racks. Dust liberally with confectioner's sugar while still warm. Cut into ½-inch slices. Cool completely.

Makes about 4 dozen cookies

Baker's Coconut

In the early days of this country, coconuts were rare, expensive and difficult to convert into a usable form. In 1896, Franklin Baker, a Philadelphia flour miller, changed all that. He devised an easier way to use coconut. His solution, a method of packing the pre-grated coconut while still retaining that tree-fresh goodness, is still practiced today by Baker's Coconut, now part of Kraft Foods, Inc.

Marvelous Macaroons

1 can (8 ounces) DOLE® Crushed Pineapple in Juice
1 can (14 ounces) sweetened condensed milk
1 package (7 ounces) flaked coconut
½ cup margarine, melted
½ cup DOLE® Chopped Almonds, toasted
1 teaspoon grated lemon peel
¼ teaspoon almond extract
1 cup all-purpose flour
1 teaspoon baking powder

Preheat oven to 350°F. Drain pineapple well, pressing out excess juice with back of spoon. In large bowl, combine drained pineapple, milk, coconut, margarine, almonds, lemon peel and almond extract.

In small bowl, combine flour and baking powder. Beat into pineapple mixture until blended. Drop heaping tablespoonfuls of dough 1 inch apart onto greased cookie sheets.

Bake 13 to 15 minutes or until lightly browned. Garnish with whole almonds, if desired. Cool on wire racks. Store in covered container in refrigerator.

Makes about 3½ dozen cookies

Coconut Macaroons

1⅓ cups (3½ ounces) BAKER'S® ANGEL
    FLAKE® Coconut
½ cup chopped almonds
⅓ cup sugar
2 tablespoons flour
⅛ teaspoon salt
2 egg whites
½ teaspoon almond extract

HEAT oven to 325°F.

MIX coconut, almonds, sugar, flour and salt in large bowl. Stir in egg whites and almond extract until well blended. Drop by teaspoonfuls onto lightly greased cookie sheets.

BAKE 20 minutes or until edges of cookies are golden brown. Immediately remove from cookie sheets. Cool on wire racks.

Makes about 1½ dozen

Note: Recipe can be doubled.

Traditional Oat 'n' Raisin Cookies

1 cup vegetable shortening
1 cup granulated sugar
1 cup packed brown sugar
2 eggs
1 teaspoon vanilla extract
1½ cups all-purpose flour
1 teaspoon baking soda
1 teaspoon ground cinnamon
¼ teaspoon ground nutmeg
3 cups 3-MINUTES BRAND® Quick or
    Old Fashioned Oats
1 cup raisins

Preheat oven to 350°F. Lightly grease cookie sheet. Beat shortening and sugars until creamy. Add eggs and vanilla; beat well. Combine flour, baking soda, cinnamon, nutmeg and 1 teaspoon salt, if desired; mix well. Add to shortening mixture; mix well. Stir in oats and raisins; mix well.

Drop by rounded teaspoons onto prepared cookie sheet. Bake 10 to 12 minutes or until light golden brown. Let stand 1 minute before removing to racks to cool. *Makes 5 dozen*

Chewy Oatmeal Cookies

¾ **BUTTER FLAVOR* CRISCO® Stick
    (¾ cup)**
1¼ **cups firmly packed light brown sugar**
 1 **egg**
⅓ **cup milk**
1½ **teaspoons vanilla**
 3 **cups quick cooking oats, uncooked**
 1 **cup all-purpose flour**
½ **teaspoon baking soda**
½ **teaspoon salt**
¼ **teaspoon ground cinnamon**
 1 **cup raisins**
 1 **cup coarsely chopped walnuts**

*Butter Flavor Crisco® is artificially flavored.

1. **Heat** oven to 375°F. **Grease** baking sheets with shortening. **Place** sheets of foil on countertop for cooling cookies.

2. **Combine** shortening, brown sugar, egg, milk and vanilla in large bowl. **Beat** at medium speed of electric mixer until well blended.

3. **Combine** oats, flour, baking soda, salt and cinnamon. **Mix** into creamed mixture at low speed just until blended. **Stir** in raisins and nuts.

4. **Drop** rounded tablespoonfuls of dough 2 inches apart onto baking sheet.

5. **Bake** one baking sheet at a time at 375°F for 10 to 12 minutes, or until lightly browned. DO NOT OVERBAKE. **Cool** 2 minutes on baking sheet. **Remove** cookies to foil to cool completely.

Makes about 2½ dozen cookies

Cherry Cashew Cookies

 1 **cup butter or margarine, softened**
¾ **cup granulated sugar**
¾ **cup packed brown sugar**
 1 **teaspoon vanilla extract**
 2 **eggs**
2¼ **cups all-purpose flour**
 1 **teaspoon baking soda**
 1 **package (10 ounces) vanilla milk
    chips (about 1⅔ cups)**
 1 **cup broken, salted cashews**
1½ **cups dried tart cherries**

Preheat oven to 375°F.

In large mixer bowl, combine butter, granulated sugar, brown sugar, vanilla and eggs. Mix with electric mixer on medium speed until thoroughly combined. Combine flour and baking soda; gradually add flour mixture to butter mixture. Stir in vanilla milk chips, cashews and dried cherries. Drop by rounded tablespoonfuls onto ungreased baking sheets.

Bake 12 to 15 minutes or until light golden brown. Cool on wire racks and store in airtight container.

Makes 4½ dozen cookies

*Favorite recipe from **Cherry Marketing Institute, Inc.***

Chewy Oatmeal Cookies

Aunt Jemima ®

The Aunt Jemima trademark was inspired by a popular vaudeville routine of the late 1800s. The performers wore aprons and red bandannas and danced to a tune called "Aunt Jemima." The inventor of the first ready-mix, a packaged pancake mix, chose this trademark for his new convenience product and registered it in 1890. The Quaker Oats Company acquired the rights to the Aunt Jemima trademark in 1925. Today, the trademark represents a line of more than 40 convenience products from original pancake mix to microwavable breakfast entrées.

Mini Mince Lemon Tarts

1⅓ cups (one-half 27-ounce jar) NONE
    SUCH® Ready-to-Use Mincemeat
    (Regular or Brandy & Rum)
1½ teaspoons grated lemon peel
1 (15-ounce) package refrigerated pie
    crusts

Preheat oven to 375°. In small bowl, combine mincemeat and peel; mix well. Cut pastry into 24 (2¼-inch) circles; press each circle into

1¾-inch muffin cup. Fill with mincemeat mixture. From pastry scraps, cut out small designs; top tarts with cutouts. Bake 20 to 25 minutes or until lightly browned. Cool. Remove from pans. Store loosely covered at room temperature.   *Makes 2 dozen tarts*

Lemon Wafers

¾ cup (1½ sticks) margarine, softened
½ cup sugar
1 egg
1 tablespoon grated lemon peel (about
    1 medium lemon)
2 cups QUAKER® or AUNT JEMIMA®
    Enriched Corn Meal
1½ cups all-purpose flour
½ teaspoon salt (optional)
¼ cup milk

Preheat oven to 375°F. Beat margarine and sugar until fluffy. Blend in egg and lemon peel. Add combined dry ingredients alternately with milk, mixing well after each addition. Shape dough into 1-inch balls. Place on ungreased cookie sheet. Using bottom of glass dipped in sugar, press into ⅛-inch-thick circles. Bake 13 to 15 minutes or until bottoms are lightly browned. Cool 2 minutes on cookie sheet; remove to wire rack. Cool completely. Store tightly covered.
          Makes about 3 dozen cookies

Date-Nut Macaroons

1 (8-ounce) package pitted dates, chopped
1½ cups flaked coconut
1 cup PLANTERS® Pecan Halves, chopped
¾ cup sweetened condensed milk (not evaporated milk)
½ teaspoon vanilla extract

Preheat oven to 350°F.

In medium bowl, combine dates, coconut and nuts; blend in sweetened condensed milk and vanilla. Drop by rounded tablespoonfuls onto greased and floured cookie sheets. Bake 10 to 12 minutes or until light golden brown. Carefully remove from cookie sheets; cool completely on wire racks. Store in airtight container. *Makes about 2 dozen cookies*

Pecan Drops

¾ cup sugar
½ cup FLEISCHMANN'S® Margarine, softened
¼ cup EGG BEATERS® Egg Product
1 teaspoon vanilla extract
2 cups all-purpose flour
⅔ cup PLANTERS® Pecans, finely chopped
3 tablespoons jam, jelly or preserves, any flavor

In small bowl, with electric mixer at medium speed, cream sugar and margarine. Add egg product and vanilla; beat 1 minute. Stir in flour until blended. Chill dough 1 hour.

Preheat oven to 350°F. Form dough into 36 (1¼-inch) balls; roll in pecans, pressing into dough. Place, 2 inches apart, on greased cookie sheets. Indent center of each ball with thumb or back of wooden spoon. Bake 10 minutes; remove from oven. Spoon ¼ teaspoon jam into each cookie indentation. Bake 2 to 5 more minutes or until lightly browned. Remove from sheets; cool on wire racks. *Makes about 3 dozen cookies*

Walnut-Granola Clusters

¼ cup butter
1 (10½-ounce) package miniature marshmallows
½ teaspoon ground cinnamon
2 cups chopped California walnuts
3 cups rolled oats
1 cup flaked coconut
2 (1-ounce) squares semi-sweet chocolate

Microwave Directions: Microwave butter in large mixing bowl 40 seconds or until melted. Stir in marshmallows and cinnamon. Microwave 1½ minutes until melted, stirring halfway through. Quickly stir in walnuts, oats and coconut. With wet hands, form small balls and place on wax paper-lined baking sheets. Microwave chocolate in glass measuring cup until melted, about 2½ minutes. Stir and lightly drizzle over clusters. (May be stored at room temperature, uncovered, 4 to 5 days.) *Makes 5 dozen*

*Favorite recipe from **Walnut Marketing Board***

Versatile Cut-Out Cookies

3½ cups unsifted all-purpose flour
1 tablespoon baking powder
½ teaspoon salt
1 (14-ounce) can EAGLE® Brand
Sweetened Condensed Milk
(NOT evaporated milk)
¾ cup margarine or butter, softened
2 eggs
1 tablespoon vanilla extract *or*
2 teaspoons almond or lemon
extract

Combine flour, baking powder and salt. In large mixer bowl, beat sweetened condensed milk, margarine, eggs and vanilla until well blended. Add dry ingredients; mix well. Cover; chill 2 hours. Preheat oven to 350°. On floured surface, knead dough to form a smooth ball. Divide into thirds. On well-floured surface, roll out each portion to ⅛-inch thickness. Cut with floured cookie cutter. Place 1 inch apart on greased baking sheets. Reroll as necessary to use all dough. Bake 7 to 9 minutes or until lightly browned around edges *(do not overbake).* Cool. Frost and decorate as desired. Store loosely covered at room temperature.

Makes about 6½ dozen 3-inch cookies

Chocolate Cookies: Decrease flour to 3 cups. Add ½ cup unsweetened cocoa to dry ingredients. Chill and proceed as directed. Makes about 6½ dozen cookies.

Sandwich Cookies: Prepare, chill and roll dough as directed. Use 2½-inch floured cookie cutter. Bake as directed. Sandwich 2 cookies together with ready-to-spread frosting. Sprinkle tops with confectioners' sugar if desired. Makes about 3 dozen cookies.

Stained Glass Cookies: Prepare, chill and roll dough as directed. Use 3-inch floured cookie cutters. Cut out holes for "stained glass" in each cookie with small cutters or knife. Place on aluminum foil-lined baking sheets. Fill holes with crushed hard candies. (If planning to hang cookies, make hole in each cookie near edge with straw.) Bake 6 to 8 minutes or until candy has melted. Cool 10 minutes; remove from foil. Makes about 8 dozen cookies.

Cookie Pecan Critters: Prepare and chill dough as directed. For each critter, arrange 3 pecan halves together on ungreased baking sheets. Shape 1 teaspoonful dough into 1-inch ball. Press firmly onto center of arranged pecans. Repeat until all dough is used. Bake 12 to 14 minutes. Spread tops with Chocolate Frosting.* Makes about 6½ dozen cookies.

*Chocolate Frosting: In small saucepan, melt ¼ cup margarine or butter with ¼ cup water. Stir in ½ cup unsweetened cocoa. Remove saucepan from heat; beat in 2 cups confectioners' sugar and 1 teaspoon vanilla until smooth. Stir in additional water for thinner consistency if desired. Makes about 1 cup.

Mincemeat Peek-A-Boo Cookies: Prepare, chill and roll dough as directed. Use 3-inch round floured cookie cutter. Using sharp knife, cut "X" in center of half the rounds. Place 1 teaspoon NONE SUCH® Ready-to-Use Mincemeat in center of remaining rounds. Top with cut rounds. Bake 8 to 10 minutes. Cool. Sprinkle tops with confectioners' sugar if desired. Makes about 4 dozen cookies.

Cinnamon Pinwheel Cookies: Decrease baking powder to 2 teaspoons. Prepare and chill dough as directed. Divide into quarters.

Versatile Cut-Out Cookies

On well-floured surface, roll out each quarter into 16×8-inch rectangle. Brush with melted margarine or butter. Top each with 2 tablespoons sugar combined with ½ teaspoon ground cinnamon. Roll up tightly beginning at 8-inch side. Wrap tightly; freeze until firm, about 20 minutes. Cut into ¼-inch slices. Place on ungreased baking sheets. Bake 12 to 14 minutes or until lightly browned. Makes about 6½ dozen cookies.

Chocolate Snow Balls: Prepared dough as directed for Chocolate Cookies, increasing eggs to 3; add 1 cup finely chopped nuts. Cover; chill 2 hours. Shape into 1-inch balls. Roll in confectioners' sugar. Bake 8 to 10 minutes. Cool. Roll again in confectioners' sugar. Makes about 6½ dozen cookies.

Valentine Stained Glass Hearts

½ cup butter or margarine, softened
¾ cup granulated sugar
2 eggs
1 teaspoon vanilla extract
2⅓ cups all-purpose flour
1 teaspoon baking powder
  Red hard candies, crushed (about ⅓ cup)
  Frosting (optional)

Cream butter and sugar in mixing bowl. Beat in eggs and vanilla. Sift flour and baking powder together. Gradually stir in flour mixture until dough is very stiff. Cover and chill. *Dough needs to chill 3 hours to overnight.*

Preheat oven to 375°F. Roll out dough to ⅛-inch thickness on lightly floured surface. To prevent cookies from becoming tough and brittle, do not incorporate too much flour. Cut out cookies using large heart-shaped cookie cutter or use sharp knife and cut heart design. Transfer cookies to foil-lined baking sheet. Using small heart-shaped cookie cutter, cut out and remove heart design from center of each cookie. Fill cutout sections with crushed candy. Bake 7 to 9 minutes or until cookies are lightly browned and candy has melted. *Do not overcook.*

Remove from oven; immediately slide foil off baking sheet. Cool completely; carefully loosen cookies from foil. If desired, pipe decorative borders with frosting around edges.

Makes about 2½ dozen medium cookies

Favorite recipe from **The Sugar Association, Inc.**

Crispy Nut Shortbread

6 tablespoons margarine, softened
⅓ cup sugar
1 egg
1 teaspoon vanilla
½ cup QUAKER® or AUNT JEMIMA® Enriched Corn Meal
½ cup all-purpose flour
½ cup finely chopped, husked, toasted hazelnuts or walnuts
½ cup semi-sweet chocolate pieces
1 tablespoon vegetable shortening
  Coarsely chopped nuts (optional)

Preheat oven to 300°F. Grease 13×9-inch baking pan. Beat margarine and sugar until fluffy. Blend in egg and vanilla. Add combined corn meal, flour and nuts; mix well. Spread onto bottom of prepared pan. Bake 40 to 45 minutes or until edges are golden brown.

In saucepan over low heat, melt chocolate pieces and shortening, stirring until smooth.* Spread over shortbread. Sprinkle with coarsely chopped nuts, if desired. Cool completely. Cut into 48 squares; cut diagonally into triangles. Store tightly covered.   *Makes 8 dozen cookies*

*Microwave Directions: Place chocolate pieces and shortening in microwavable bowl. Microwave at HIGH 1 to 2 minutes, stirring after 1 minute and then every 30 seconds until smooth.

Valentine Stained Glass Hearts

Ultimate Sugar Cookies

1¼ cups granulated sugar
 1 BUTTER FLAVOR* CRISCO® Stick
 (1 cup)
 2 eggs
 ¼ cup light corn syrup or regular
 pancake syrup
 1 tablespoon vanilla
 3 cups all-purpose flour plus
 4 tablespoons, divided
 ¾ teaspoon baking powder
 ½ teaspoon baking soda
 ½ teaspoon salt
 Decorations of your choice:
 granulated sugar, colored sugar
 crystals, frosting, decors, candies,
 chips, nuts, raisins, decorating gel

*Butter Flavor Crisco® is artificially flavored.

1. **Combine** sugar and shortening in large bowl. **Beat** at medium speed of electric mixer until well blended. **Add** eggs, syrup and vanilla. **Beat** until well blended and fluffy.

2. **Combine** 3 cups flour, baking powder, baking soda and salt. **Add** gradually to creamed mixture at low speed. **Mix** until well blended. **Divide** dough into 4 quarters.

3. **Heat** oven to 375°F. **Place** sheets of foil on countertop for cooling cookies.

4. **Spread** 1 tablespoon flour on large sheet of waxed paper. **Place** one-fourth of dough on floured paper. **Flatten** slightly with hands. **Turn** dough over and **cover** with another large sheet of waxed paper. **Roll** dough to ¼-inch thickness. **Remove** top sheet of waxed paper.

5. **Cut** out cookies with floured cutter. **Transfer** to ungreased baking sheet with large pancake turner. **Place** 2 inches apart. **Roll** out remaining dough. **Sprinkle** with granulated sugar, colored sugar crystals, decors or leave plain to frost or decorate when cooled.

6. **Bake** one baking sheet at a time at 375°F for 5 to 9 minutes, depending on the size of your cookies (bake smaller, thinner cookies closer to 5 minutes; larger cookies closer to 9 minutes). DO NOT OVERBAKE. **Cool** 2 minutes on baking sheet. **Remove** cookies to foil to cool completely, then **frost** if desired.
Makes about 3 to 4 dozen cookies

Tip: For well-defined cookie edges, or if dough is too sticky or too soft to roll, do the following. **Wrap** each quarter of dough with plastic wrap. **Refrigerate** 1 hour. **Keep** dough balls refrigerated until ready to roll.

Ultimate Sugar Cookies

Watermelon Slices

Watermelon Slices

1 package **DUNCAN HINES® Golden Sugar Cookie Mix**
1 **egg**
¼ cup **CRISCO® Oil or CRISCO® PURITAN® Oil**
4½ teaspoons **water**
12 drops **red food coloring**
5 drops **green food coloring**
Chocolate sprinkles

1. Combine cookie mix, egg, oil and water in large bowl. Stir until thoroughly blended; reserve ⅓ cup dough.

2. For red cookie dough, combine remaining dough with red food coloring. Stir until evenly tinted. On waxed paper, shape dough into 12-inch-long roll with one side flattened. Cover; refrigerate with flat side down until firm.

3. For green cookie dough, combine reserved ⅓ cup dough with green food coloring in

small bowl. Stir until evenly tinted. Place between 2 layers of waxed paper. Roll dough into 12×4-inch rectangle. Refrigerate 15 minutes.

4. Preheat oven to 375°F.

5. To assemble, remove green dough rectangle from refrigerator. Remove top layer of waxed paper. Trim edges along both 12-inch sides. Remove red dough log from refrigerator. Place red dough log, flattened side up, along center of green dough. Mold green dough up to edge of flattened side of red dough. Remove bottom layer of waxed paper. Trim excess green dough, if necessary.

6. Cut chilled roll with flat side down into ¼-inch-thick slices with sharp knife.* Place 2 inches apart on ungreased baking sheets. Sprinkle chocolate sprinkles on red dough for seeds. Bake at 375°F for 7 minutes or until set. Cool 1 minute on baking sheets. Remove to cooling racks. Cool completely. Store between layers of waxed paper in airtight container.   *Makes 3 to 4 dozen cookies*

*To make neat, clean slices, use unwaxed dental floss.

Roman Meal® Granola Bars

    ½ cup shortening
    ¾ cup packed brown sugar
     1 egg
    ½ teaspoon vanilla
     1 cup all-purpose flour
    ½ teaspoon salt
     2 cups ROMAN MEAL® Granola
     1 cup raisins
    ⅓ cup flaked coconut

Cream shortening and sugar. Add egg and vanilla; beat well. Stir together flour and salt; add to shortening mixture. Add granola, raisins and coconut; mix thoroughly. Press into greased and floured 9×9×2-inch baking pan. Bake at 350°F about 30 minutes or until nicely browned and springs back when touched lightly. Cool 20 minutes; cut into bars.   *Makes 30 to 36 bars*

Apple Crumb Squares

     2 cups QUAKER® Oats (quick or old fashioned, uncooked)
    1½ cups all-purpose flour
     1 cup packed brown sugar
    ¾ cup butter or margarine, melted
     1 teaspoon ground cinnamon
    ½ teaspoon baking soda
    ½ teaspoon salt (optional)
    ¼ teaspoon ground nutmeg
     1 cup applesauce
    ½ cup chopped nuts

Preheat oven to 350°F. In large bowl, combine all ingredients except applesauce and nuts; mix until crumbly. Reserve 1 cup oats mixture. Press remaining mixture on bottom of greased 13×9-inch pan. Bake 13 to 15 minutes; cool. Spread applesauce over partially baked crust; sprinkle with nuts. Sprinkle reserved 1 cup oats mixture over top. Bake 13 to 15 minutes or until golden brown. Cool in pan on wire rack; cut into 2-inch squares.   *Makes about 24 squares*

The Original Rice Krispies Treats® Recipe

3 tablespoons margarine
1 package (10 ounces, about 40)
    regular marshmallows *or* 4 cups
    miniature marshmallows
6 cups KELLOGG'S® RICE KRISPIES®
    cereal
Vegetable cooking spray

1. Melt margarine in large saucepan over low heat. Add marshmallows and stir until completely melted. Remove from heat.

2. Add Kellogg's® Rice Krispies® cereal. Stir until well coated.

3. Using buttered spatula or waxed paper, press mixture evenly into 13×9×2-inch pan coated with cooking spray. Cut into squares when cool.

Makes 24 (2-inch-square) treats

Tony's Tiger Bites®

1 package (10 ounces, about 40)
    regular marshmallows *or* 4 cups
    miniature marshmallows
¼ cup margarine
⅓ cup peanut butter
7½ cups (10-ounce package)
    KELLOGG'S® FROSTED FLAKES®
    cereal
Vegetable cooking spray

Microwave Directions:

1. In 4-quart microwave-safe bowl, melt marshmallows and margarine at HIGH 3 minutes, stirring after 1½ minutes.

2. Stir in peanut butter until mixture is smooth. Add Kellogg's® Frosted Flakes® cereal, stirring until well coated.

3. Using buttered spatula or waxed paper, press mixture into 13×9×2-inch pan coated with cooking spray. Cut into 1½×2-inch bars when cool. *Makes 32 bars*

Rich Lemon Bars

1½ cups plus 3 tablespoons unsifted
    flour
½ cup confectioners' sugar
¾ cup cold margarine or butter
1½ cups granulated sugar
4 eggs, slightly beaten
½ cup REALEMON® Lemon Juice from
    Concentrate
1 teaspoon baking powder
Additional confectioners' sugar

Preheat oven to 350°. In medium bowl, combine *1½ cups* flour and *½ cup* confectioners' sugar; cut in margarine until crumbly. Press firmly on bottom of lightly greased 13×9-inch baking pan. Bake 15 minutes or until lightly browned. Meanwhile, in large bowl, combine granulated sugar, eggs, ReaLemon® brand, baking powder and remaining *3 tablespoons* flour; mix well. Pour over hot baked crust; bake 20 to 25 minutes or until lightly browned. Cool. Cut into bars. Sprinkle with additional confectioners' sugar. Store covered in refrigerator.

Makes 24 to 36 bars

Lemon Pecan Bars: Omit 3 tablespoons flour in lemon mixture. Sprinkle ¾ cup finely chopped pecans over top of lemon mixture. Bake and store as above.

Crimson Ribbon Bars

**6 tablespoons butter or margarine,
  softened**
½ cup firmly packed brown sugar
1 teaspoon vanilla
½ cup all-purpose flour
¼ teaspoon baking soda
1½ cups rolled oats
1 cup chopped walnuts
**½ cup chopped BLUE RIBBON®
  Calimyrna or Mission Figs**
**⅓ cup SMUCKER'S® Red Raspberry
  Preserves**

Heat oven to 375°F. Combine butter, brown sugar and vanilla; beat until well blended. Add flour and baking soda; mix well. Stir in oats and walnuts. Reserve ¾ cup mixture for topping. Press remaining oat mixture in 8-inch square baking pan. Combine figs and preserves; spread mixture to within ½ inch of edges. Sprinkle with reserved oat mixture; press lightly.

Bake for 25 to 30 minutes or until golden brown. Cool in pan; cut into bars.

Makes 20 bars

Oreo® Shazam Bars

28 OREO® Chocolate Sandwich Cookies
¼ cup margarine, melted
1 cup shredded coconut
1 cup white chocolate chips
½ cup chopped nuts
**1 (14-ounce) can sweetened condensed
  milk**

Finely roll 20 cookies. Mix cookie crumbs and margarine; spread over bottom of 9×9×2-inch baking pan, pressing lightly. Chop remaining cookies. Layer coconut, chips, nuts and chopped cookies in prepared pan; drizzle evenly with condensed milk. Bake at 350°F for 25 to 30 minutes or until golden and set. Cool completely. Cut into bars.

Makes 24 bars

In 1897, Jerome M. Smucker opened a small custom apple cider mill in Orrville, Ohio. As word of his cider spread, he expanded his operation and began making apple butter using a family recipe passed on from his Pennsylvania Dutch grandfather. The apple butter sold well, and in the 1920s, a full line of preserves and jellies was added. Today, the J.M. Smucker Company is the number one producer of jellies, jams, preserves and ice cream toppings in the United States. The company is managed by the third and fourth generations of the Smucker family and the headquarters is still located on the site of the original cider mill.

Marshmallow Krispie Bars

1 package DUNCAN HINES® Chocolate
   Lovers' Fudge Brownie Mix, Family
   Size
1 package (10½ ounces) miniature
   marshmallows
1½ cups semi-sweet chocolate chips
1 cup JIF® Creamy Peanut Butter
1 tablespoon butter or margarine
1½ cups crisp rice cereal

1. Preheat oven to 350°F. Grease bottom of
13×9×2-inch pan.

2. Prepare and bake brownies following
package directions for original recipe.
Remove from oven. Sprinkle marshmallows
on hot brownies. Return to oven. Bake 3
minutes longer.

3. Place chocolate chips, peanut butter and
butter in medium saucepan. Cook on low
heat, stirring constantly, until chips are
melted. Add rice cereal; mix well. Spread
mixture over marshmallow layer. Refrigerate
until chilled. Cut into bars.

Makes 24 bars

*Carnation's Holstein herds grazing in pastures
helped coin the slogan "Milk From Contented
Cows."*

Raspberry Coconut Layer Bars

1⅔ cups graham cracker crumbs
 ½ cup butter or margarine, melted
2⅔ cups (7-ounce package) flaked
   coconut
1¼ cups (14-ounce can) CARNATION®
   Sweetened Condensed Milk
 1 cup red raspberry jam or preserves
 ⅓ cup finely chopped walnuts, toasted
 ½ cup NESTLÉ® TOLL HOUSE® Semi-
   Sweet Chocolate Morsels, melted
 ¼ cup (1½ ounces) chopped NESTLÉ®
   Premier White Baking Bar, melted

COMBINE graham cracker crumbs and
butter in medium bowl. Spread evenly over
bottom of 13×9-inch baking pan, pressing to
make compact crust. Sprinkle with coconut;
pour sweetened condensed milk evenly over
coconut.

BAKE in preheated 350°F oven 20 to 25
minutes or until lightly browned; cool.

SPREAD jam over coconut layer; chill for 3 to
4 hours. Sprinkle with walnuts. Drizzle semi-
sweet chocolate then white chocolate over
top layer to make lacy effect; chill. Cut into
3×1½-inch bars.   *Makes 24 bar cookies*

From left: Magic Cookie Bars and Choco-Dipped Peanut Butter Cookies (page 348)

Magic Cookie Bars

½ **cup margarine or butter**
1½ **cups graham cracker crumbs**
  1 **(14-ounce) can EAGLE® Brand**
    Sweetened Condensed Milk
    (NOT evaporated milk)
  1 **cup (6 ounces) semi-sweet chocolate**
    chips
  1 **(3½-ounce) can flaked coconut**
    (1⅓ cups)
  1 **cup chopped walnuts**

Preheat oven to 350° (325° for glass dish). In 13×9-inch baking pan, melt margarine in oven. Sprinkle crumbs evenly over margarine; pour sweetened condensed milk evenly over crumbs. Top with all remaining ingredients; press down firmly. Bake 25 to 30 minutes or until lightly browned. Cool. Chill if desired. Cut into bars. Store loosely covered at room temperature. *Makes 24 to 36 bars*

Chocolate Caramel Bars

Crust

MAZOLA® No Stick Corn Oil Cooking
    Spray
2 cups flour
¾ cup (1½ sticks) MAZOLA® Margarine
    or butter, slightly softened
½ cup packed brown sugar
¼ teaspoon salt
1 cup (6 ounces) semisweet or milk
    chocolate chips

Caramel

¾ cup (1½ sticks) MAZOLA® Margarine
    or butter
1 cup packed brown sugar
⅓ cup KARO® Light or Dark Corn Syrup
1 teaspoon vanilla
½ cup chopped walnuts

For Crust: Preheat oven to 350°F. Spray
13×9×2-inch baking pan with cooking spray.
In large bowl with mixer at medium speed,
beat flour, margarine, brown sugar and salt
until mixture resembles coarse crumbs; press
firmly into prepared pan. Bake 15 minutes or
until golden brown. Sprinkle chocolate chips
over hot crust; let stand 5 minutes or until
shiny and soft. Spread chocolate evenly; set
aside.

For Caramel: In heavy 2-quart saucepan,
combine margarine, brown sugar, corn syrup
and vanilla. Stirring frequently, bring to a boil
over medium heat. Without stirring, boil 4
minutes. Pour over chocolate; spread evenly.
Sprinkle with walnuts. Cool completely.
Refrigerate 1 hour to set chocolate; let stand
at room temperature until softened. Cut into
2×1-inch bars. Store in tightly covered
container at room temperature.

Makes about 4 dozen bars

Planters® Nut Bark

6 ounces semisweet chocolate or white
    chocolate
1 cup PLANTERS® Almonds,
    PLANTERS® Salted Peanuts or
    PLANTERS® Cashew Halves

In top of double boiler, over hot *(not boiling)*,
water, melt chocolate.

Spread Planters® nuts in lightly greased
9-inch square baking pan. Pour melted
chocolate over nuts, spreading lightly with
spatula. Cool. Break into pieces. Store in
airtight container.   *Makes ½ pound*

White Chocolate Pecan Corn

1 pop & serve bag (3.5 ounces) JOLLY
    TIME® 100% All Natural Microwave
    Pop Corn, Butter Flavored or
    Natural Flavor, popped
8 ounces vanilla flavored candy coating
    (white chocolate) *or* 1 package
    (10 ounces) large vanilla flavored
    baking chips
½ cup pecan halves

Place popped pop corn in large bowl. Put
candy coating in 1-quart glass measuring
cup. Microwave on HIGH 1 to 1½ minutes, or
until candy coating is shiny; stir to melt
completely. Stir in pecans. Add mixture to pop
corn and mix well. Spread on cookie sheet;
allow to cool completely.

Makes about 2 quarts

Baked Caramel Corn

Baked Caramel Corn

Nonstick cooking spray
6 quarts popped JOLLY TIME® Pop
   Corn
1 cup butter or margarine
2 cups firmly packed brown sugar
½ cup light or dark corn syrup
1 teaspoon salt
½ teaspoon baking soda
1 teaspoon vanilla

Preheat oven to 250°F. Coat bottom and sides of large roasting pan with nonstick cooking spray. Place popped pop corn in roasting pan. In heavy saucepan, slowly melt butter; stir in brown sugar, corn syrup and salt. Bring to a boil, stirring constantly; boil without stirring 5 minutes. Remove from heat; stir in baking soda and vanilla. Gradually pour over popped pop corn, mixing well. Bake 1 hour, stirring every 15 minutes. Remove from oven; cool completely. Break apart and store in tightly covered container.

Makes about 6 quarts

From left: Candied Orange Peel, Chocolate Dipped Candied Orange Peel and Chocolate Dipped Fresh Peeled Orange Segments

Chocolate Dipped Fresh Peeled Orange Segments

5 to 6 SUNKIST® Oranges, hand-peeled
4 ounces sweet, bittersweet or white
** sweet chocolate**

Separate oranges into double segments and place on paper towel. Melt chocolate in small metal bowl over hot, not boiling, water; stir occasionally. Dip one end of each double segment in melted chocolate to cover ⅓ of segment. Shake off excess chocolate. Side of segment to be laid flat should not have excess covering of chocolate. Lay on parchment paper or aluminum foil-lined baking sheets. Chill until chocolate is set; loosely cover with plastic wrap.

Makes about 25 to 30 pieces

Chocolate Dipped Candied Orange Peel

**6 ounces sweet, bittersweet or white
  sweet chocolate
1 pound Candied Orange Peel
  (recipe below)**

Melt chocolate in small metal bowl over hot, not boiling water; stir occasionally. Individually dip each piece of Candied Orange Peel in chocolate (covering only ½ to ⅔ of each piece). Shake off excess chocolate. Cool on waxed paper until chocolate is set.

Variation: Substitute semi-sweet chocolate pieces and 2 teaspoons shortening for sweet chocolate. Melt chocolate pieces with shortening; proceed as above.

Candied Orange Peel

**4 to 5 SUNKIST® Oranges*
12 cups cold water, divided
2 cups sugar, divided
½ cup honey
1¾ cups boiling water**

*Six Sunkist® Lemons or Sunkist® Grapefruit may be substituted.

Wash fruit; score peel into lengthwise quarters. Remove sections of peel; cut into ⅜-inch-wide strips to measure 3 cups peel. Bring 6 cups cold water and peel to a boil; boil 10 minutes. Drain and rinse. Repeat process with 6 cups fresh water.

In large saucepan, bring 1½ cups sugar, honey and water to a boil; boil 1 minute. Add peel and briskly simmer 40 to 45 minutes; stir frequently to avoid sticking. Drain well. In large bowl, toss drained peel with remaining ½ cup sugar to coat well. Spread on wire racks over waxed paper to dry. (Peel may need to be redipped in sugar as it dries.) Store in tightly covered container.

Makes about 1 pound

Chocolate Peanut Butter Cups

**¾ cup sifted confectioners sugar
¼ cup KARO® Light or Dark Corn Syrup
¼ teaspoon salt
¼ cup SKIPPY® Super Chunk or Creamy
  Peanut Butter
1 package (11½ ounces) milk chocolate
  chips, melted**

Place 36 (1×¾-inch) foil or paper petit four cups on tray. In small bowl with mixer at medium speed, beat confectioners sugar, corn syrup and salt until smooth. Stir in peanut butter; if necessary, knead until blended.

Shape scant teaspoonfuls of peanut butter mixture into 36 balls; place on waxed paper. Spoon 1 rounded teaspoonful melted chocolate into each cup. Place peanut butter ball in each cup; gently push down. Chill until firm. *Makes 36 candies*

Teddy Grahams®, a line of bear-shaped snack cookies, captured the popularity of teddy bears in a bite-size form. This fun-to-eat, wholesome snack for kids comes in three whimsical teddy bear shapes and three flavors—honey, cinnamon and chocolate. Teddy Grahams were the first major line of miniature cookies. Although small in size, they are big in taste!

Barking Bears

7 ounces white confectionary coating
1 cup Chocolate TEDDY GRAHAMS®
   Graham Snacks, divided
7 ounces milk chocolate or light cocoa
   confectionary coating
1 cup Cinnamon TEDDY GRAHAMS®
   Graham Snacks, divided

In small saucepan, over very low heat, melt white confectionary coating. Remove from heat and stir in ½ cup chocolate graham snacks; set aside.

In another small saucepan, over very low heat, melt milk chocolate confectionary coating. Remove from heat; stir in ½ cup cinnamon graham snacks. On lightly

greased, waxed paper-lined 13×9×2-inch baking pan, alternately spoon both mixtures. With fork, gently swirl together to marble and spread mixture into thin layer. Sprinkle with remaining graham snacks. Let stand until firm. Break into pieces. Store in airtight container. *Makes about 1 pound*

Chex® Muddy Buddies® Brand Snack

9 cups of your favorite CHEX® brand
   cereals (Corn, Rice, Wheat, Double,
   Multi-Bran and/or Graham)
1 cup semi-sweet chocolate chips
½ cup peanut butter
¼ cup margarine or butter
1 teaspoon vanilla extract
1½ cups powdered sugar

1. Pour cereals into large bowl; set aside.

2. In small saucepan over low heat, melt chocolate chips, peanut butter and margarine until smooth, stirring often. Remove from heat; stir in vanilla.

3. Pour chocolate mixture over cereal, stirring until all pieces are evenly coated. Pour cereal mixture into large resealable plastic food storage bag with powdered sugar. Seal securely and shake until all pieces are well coated. Spread on waxed paper to cool.
Makes 9 cups

Note: Do not use reduced-fat margarine or butter; it may cause chocolate mixture to clump and will not coat cereal mixture evenly.

The Ultimate Caramel Apple

1 cup water
1 cup sugar
½ cup heavy cream
6 Red Delicious or Golden Delicious apples
3 ounces white chocolate, finely chopped
3 ounces semi-sweet chocolate, finely chopped
¼ cup coarsely chopped natural pistachios
Red hot cinnamon candies or other small candy
Edible gold dragées

1. In medium, heavy saucepan, combine water and sugar. Over low heat, stir mixture gently until sugar is completely dissolved. Increase heat to medium-low; cook, without stirring, until mixture is dark amber. Remove from heat; slowly stir in heavy cream (mixture will bubble up and spatter a bit). Set aside until barely warm and thickened.

2. Insert popsicle sticks or small wooden dowels into bottom center of apples. Use 10-inch-square piece styrofoam as a stand for apples; cover top of styrofoam with waxed paper to catch caramel drippings.

3. Dip top half of each apple into thickened caramel; stand caramel-topped apples on styrofoam, allowing caramel to run down sides; refrigerate to harden. Meanwhile, melt white chocolate in top of double boiler of gently simmering water; stir until smooth. Transfer melted chocolate to pastry bag fitted with small writing tip. Drizzle thin, random lines of melted chocolate over each apple. Repeat melting and drizzling with semi-sweet chocolate. Decorate each apple with pistachios, candies and gold dragées, if desired. Serve or refrigerate to serve later.

Makes 6 caramel apples

*Favorite recipe from **Washington Apple Commission***

The Washington Apple Commission

People around the world who have only a vague idea where Washington state is, know that it's the place where they grow those apples. The image of Washington as one of the top apple-growing regions of the world, and of Washington apples as an international standard of excellence is due to the Washington Apple Commission. Founded in 1937 and headquartered in Wenatchee, Washington, the Commission promotes Washington apples through marketing, public relations and health and food communications.

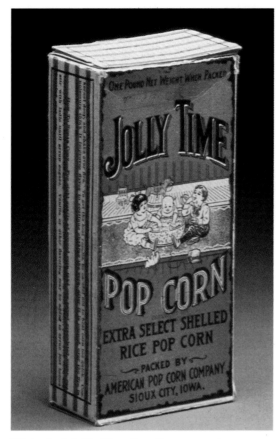

Historical Jolly Time Pop Corn container.

In 4-quart microwave-safe glass bowl, microwave butter on HIGH until melted, about 45 seconds. Stir in brown sugar and corn syrup. Microwave on HIGH until mixture boils, 1 to 3 minutes, stirring once. Microwave on HIGH 3 minutes without stirring. Stir in baking soda and vanilla. Stir in popped pop corn, mixing well. Microwave on 70% POWER 1 minute. Remove and stir. Microwave on 70% POWER another 1 minute. Remove from oven; stir again to coat pop corn evenly. Cool completely on cookie sheet. Break apart and store in tightly covered container.

Makes about 2½ quarts

Coconut Honey Pop Corn Balls

3 quarts popped JOLLY TIME® Pop Corn
¾ cup coconut
⅓ cup honey
½ teaspoon ground cinnamon
Dash of salt
3 tablespoons butter or margarine

Line shallow pan with aluminum foil. Place popped pop corn in pan. Keep pop corn warm in 250°F oven. Spread coconut in shallow baking pan; toast coconut, stirring once, about 8 to 10 minutes. Combine honey, cinnamon and salt in small saucepan. Heat to boiling; boil 1½ minutes, stirring constantly. Add butter; stir until melted. Pour honey mixture over pop corn. Add coconut. Toss well. Cool just enough to handle. With Jolly Time® Pop Corn Ball Maker or buttered hands, shape into balls.

Makes about 10 pop corn balls

Microwave Caramel Corn

10 cups popped JOLLY TIME® 100% All Natural Microwave Pop Corn
⅓ cup butter or margarine
⅔ cup firmly packed brown sugar
⅓ cup light corn syrup
¼ teaspoon baking soda
½ teaspoon vanilla

Acknowledgments

The publisher would like to thank the companies and organizations listed below for the use of their recipes and photographs in this publication.

American Dairy Association

American Egg Board

American Lamb Council

American Spice Trade Association

Best Foods, a Division of CPC International Inc.

Black-Eyed Pea Jamboree—Athens, Texas

Blue Diamond Growers

Borden Kitchens, Borden, Inc.

California Apricot Advisory Board

California Kiwifruit Commission

California Table Grape Commission

California Tree Fruit Agreement

Canned Food Information Council

Canned Fruit Promotion Service, Inc.

Chef Paul Prudhomme's Magic Seasoning Blends®

Cherry Marketing Institute, Inc.

Chilean Fresh Fruit Association

Colorado Potato Administrative Committee

ConAgra Frozen Foods

Cookin' Good

Corte & Co.

The Creamette Company

Cucina Classica Italiana, Inc.

Dean Foods Vegetable Company

Delmarva Poultry Industry, Inc.

Del Monte Corporation

Dole Food Company, Inc.

Filippo Berio Olive Oil

Florida Department of Agriculture and Consumer Services, Bureau of Seafood and Aquaculture

Florida Tomato Committee

The Fremont Company, Makers of Frank's & SnowFloss Kraut

Golden Grain/Mission Pasta

Grandma's Molasses, a division of Cadbury Beverages Inc.

Healthy Choice®

Heinz U.S.A.

Hershey Foods Corporation

Hunt Food Co.

The HVR Company

Idaho Potato Commission

Jolly Time® Pop Corn

Kellogg Company

Kikkoman International Inc.

The Kingsford Products Company

Kraft Foods, Inc.

Lawry's® Foods, Inc.

Thomas J. Lipton Co.

Louis Rich Company

McIlhenny Company

Minnesota Cultivated Wild Rice Council

MOTT'S® U.S.A., a division of Cadbury Beverages Inc.

Nabisco, Inc.

National Broiler Council

National Honey Board

National Live Stock & Meat Board

National Pasta Association

National Pork Producers Council

National Sunflower Association

Nestlé Food Company

Newman's Own, Inc.

Norseland, Inc.

Northwest Cherry Growers

Pacific Coast Canned Pear Service

The Procter & Gamble Company

The Quaker Oats Company

Ralston Foods, Inc.

RED STAR® Yeast & Products, A Division of Universal Foods Corporation

Refined Sugars Inc.

Roman Meal Company

Sargento Foods Inc.®

The J.M. Smucker Company

Sokol & Company

StarKist Seafood Company

The Sugar Association, Inc.

Sunkist Growers

USA Rice Council

Walnut Marketing Board

Washington Apple Commission

Wisconsin Milk Marketing Board

Index

Index

Metric Chart

VOLUME MEASUREMENTS (dry)

$\frac{1}{8}$ teaspoon = 0.5 mL
$\frac{1}{4}$ teaspoon = 1 mL
$\frac{1}{2}$ teaspoon = 2 mL
$\frac{3}{4}$ teaspoon = 4 mL
1 teaspoon = 5 mL
1 tablespoon = 15 mL
2 tablespoons = 30 mL
$\frac{1}{4}$ cup = 60 mL
$\frac{1}{3}$ cup = 75 mL
$\frac{1}{2}$ cup = 125 mL
$\frac{2}{3}$ cup = 150 mL
$\frac{3}{4}$ cup = 175 mL
1 cup = 250 mL
2 cups = 1 pint = 500 mL
3 cups = 750 mL
4 cups = 1 quart = 1 L

VOLUME MEASUREMENTS (fluid)

1 fluid ounce (2 tablespoons) = 30 mL
4 fluid ounces ($\frac{1}{2}$ cup) = 125 mL
8 fluid ounces (1 cup) = 250 mL
12 fluid ounces (1$\frac{1}{2}$ cups) = 375 mL
16 fluid ounces (2 cups) = 500 mL

WEIGHTS (mass)

$\frac{1}{2}$ ounce = 15 g
1 ounce = 30 g
3 ounces = 90 g
4 ounces = 120 g
8 ounces = 225 g
10 ounces = 285 g
12 ounces = 360 g
16 ounces = 1 pound = 450 g

DIMENSIONS

$\frac{1}{16}$ inch = 2 mm
$\frac{1}{8}$ inch = 3 mm
$\frac{1}{4}$ inch = 6 mm
$\frac{1}{2}$ inch = 1.5 cm
$\frac{3}{4}$ inch = 2 cm
1 inch = 2.5 cm

OVEN TEMPERATURES

250°F = 120°C
275°F = 140°C
300°F = 150°C
325°F = 160°C
350°F = 180°C
375°F = 190°C
400°F = 200°C
425°F = 220°C
450°F = 230°C

BAKING PAN SIZES

Utensil	Size in Inches/Quarts	Metric Volume	Size in Centimeters
Baking or Cake Pan (square or rectangular)	8×8×2	2 L	20×20×5
	9×9×2	2.5 L	22×22×5
	12×8×2	3 L	30×20×5
	13×9×2	3.5 L	33×23×5
Loaf Pan	8×4×3	1.5 L	20×10×7
	9×5×3	2 L	23×13×7
Round Layer Cake Pan	8×1½	1.2 L	20×4
	9×1½	1.5 L	23×4
Pie Plate	8×1¼	750 mL	20×3
	9×1¼	1 L	23×3
Baking Dish or Casserole	1 quart	1 L	—
	1½ quart	1.5 L	—
	2 quart	2 L	—